David Gawrock | Helmut Reimer |
Ahmad-Reza Sadeghi | Claire Vishik (Eds.)

Future of Trust in Computing

T0208237

Microsoft Dynamics NAV
by P. M. Diffenderfer and S. El-Assal

From Enterprise Architecture to IT Governance
by K. D. Niemann

Trusted Computing
by N. Pohlmann and H. Reimer (Eds.)

ISSE 2008 Securing Electronic Business Processes
by N. Pohlmann, H. Reimer and W. Schneider (Eds.)

Understanding MP3
by M. Ruckert

Process Modeling with ARIS
by H. Seidlmeier

The New PL/I
by E. Sturm

www.viewegteubner.de

David Gawrock | Helmut Reimer |
Ahmad-Reza Sadeghi | Claire Vishik (Eds.)

Future of Trust in Computing

Proceedings of the First International Conference
Future of Trust in Computing 2008

With 58 illustrations

VIEWEG+
TEUBNER

Bibliographic information published by the Deutsche Nationalbibliothek
The Deutsche Nationalbibliothek lists this publication in the Deutsche Nationalbibliografie;
detailed bibliographic data are available in the Internet at http://dnb.d-nb.de.

1st Edition 2009

Editorial Office: Sybille Thelen | Andrea Brossler

Vieweg+Teubner is part of the specialist publishing group Springer Science+Business Media.
www.viewegteubner.de

Cover design: KünkelLopka Medienentwicklung, Heidelberg
Typesetting: Oliver Reimer, Jena
Printing company: Krips b.v., Meppel
Printed on acid-free paper
Printed in the Netherlands

ISBN 978-3-8348-0794-6

Contents

Foreword

Several constituencies are working on building and preserving users' trust in the digital economy through advances in technology, mature regulations, education and influencing of user behavior in various computing environments. Trusted Computing technology lies at the intersection of many disciplines, and its success depends on the efforts of many stakeholders. Cryptographers are working on new approaches and techniques suitable for today's dynamic computing. Security researchers in other areas are developing technologies for the new generation of network, computer, and data security tools. Social scientists are examining new behaviors associated with ubiquitous connectivity and mobile computing as well as the trust necessary for these models to operate. Privacy professionals are working on means to enhance privacy using new technologies and processes in order to ensure that concerns about privacy do not negatively affect the users' trust in the technology. Regulators are defining regulatory frameworks where users' rights are protected and technology is designed in a way to make sure it can be trusted. Consumer advocates are ensuring that users' requirements and concerns are understood and recognized. Economists are defining business models and economic conditions for the optimal implementations of trusted systems. And technologists and architects in industry are designing products and technologies that are ready for adoption in various markets.

All these stakeholders use the term "trust" in different contexts. Each of these contexts is essential to form a coherent view of trust that is necessary for the progress of computing and technology in general. However, the multi-disciplinary work in this area is just the beginning; views of different constituencies are only now starting to be exchanged.

This book contains papers that were presented at the conference "Future of Trust in Computing" in Berlin (June 30th-July 2nd 2008). One of the goals of the event was to bring academics, regulators, technologists, and practitioners (working in diverse areas of trust) from various parts of the world together to discuss issues they are facing and begin to form a common framework. The area is large, and papers in this book reflect the breadth of the subject: You will read about security and privacy threats and remedies, core trust technologies, innovative applications, regulatory frameworks, privacy and usability, economics and provable security and assurance. Many papers touch upon innovative topics and technologies and begin to define new fields of research, new types of technologies.

Although the book cannot include debates that took place during lively panel discussions, it reflects the challenges a large field like "trust in computing" inevitably faces and outlines a vision for the future that, while still not complete, reflects very impressive progress that Trusted Computing and adjacent areas have achieved during the last decade.

Ahmad-Reza Sadeghi   *Claire Vishik*

Session 1:
Security Environment and Threats

Study on Information Security and e-Trust in Spanish households

Instituto Nacional de Tecnologías de la Comunicación (INTECO)

Avd. José Aguado 41. Edificio INTECO
León, Spain
observatorio@inteco.es

Abstract

The study on Information Security and e-Trust in Spanish households has been conducted by **INTECO** (The National Institute of Communication Technologies) through the **Information Security Observatory**. It is a study on the incidence and trust of users in the Internet by means of measuring the frequency of the episodes of individual risk in a wide sample of users that are monitored online on a monthly basis, combining quantitative data of incidences (monthly scans of home computers) and qualitative perception data (quarterly surveys). The study is supplied with data from more than 3,000 households with Internet connection, spread across the whole country.

For the first time, it allows an evolutionary comparison of the situation regarding security, trust and the level of security incidents in the households of Spanish Internet users. In addition, it shows the habits that affect security on the Internet: security equipment at the households, the measures users take before and after incidents and the perception regarding security on the Internet in Spanish households. It also shows the increasing need of users to force Public Administrations "to make the Internet a safe place".

1 Objectives

The general objective of this Study is to assess the security, trust and security level incidents in Spanish Internet user households. All this with the aim of promoting the knowledge and monitoring the main indicators and public policies related to Information Security and e-Trust.

This assessment will be carried out with a temporal perspective, with the aim of supporting and generating proposals with the aim of the Government making decisions to reduce the possible limitations and obstacles related to the security and trust of the users of the Net that affect the development of the Information Society in Spain.

Security Habits

- Know the intentions for adopting the progresses regarding security in Internet in the near future.
- Study the general demands of Internet users, households and citizens, for the better development of a secure and trustworthy Information Society.
- To find out how habits of Internet use are developing and their possible influence on security risks.

Security and Vulnerability Incidents:

- Determine the level of the general impact of the risks of malware: computer viruses, Trojan horses, worms, spyware, etc.

D. Gawrock, H. Reimer, A.-R. Sadeghi, C. Vishik (Editors): Future of Trust in Computing, Vieweg+Teubner (2009), 3-14

- Catalogue the most frequent types of malware, their capacity for spreading and their seriousness.
- Itemize the differential exposure to risks per age group, level of training, experience as an Internet user, income, and other sociologically relevant variables.

Perception of Security

- Obtain the general perception of the risk in view of computer viruses, threats to privacy and the security of payments, amongst others, as well as their evolution in time.
- Determine the level of electronic trust from the users' point of view.
- Detect the groups with a high risk perception that may be limiting their adoption of solutions related to the Information Society and promoting specific policies for improving the security and trust of these groups of citizens.
- Detect groups with a low risk perception that are risking their security and that of other users on being involuntary spreaders of the threats.

System of Indicators:

- To establish a complete and consistent system of indicators to enable monitoring of the evolution of security on the Internet in access from households.
- To understand the situation regarding Incidents and e-Trust of various groups and social strata, as well as the temporal trends of this situation.

2 Methodological design

With a view to reach the objectives explained, strict incidence measures have been combined with subjective ones of security perception and trust in the Net.

The aim is to establish a solid base on which information about the changes in the level of security and trust in Spanish homes can be gathered. This requires obtaining solid data about a sample that will provide longitudinal information, i.e., it is necessary to collect data about the homes and users at different moments of time. The methodology that best fulfills these criteria is the Dedicated online panel.

INTECO has developed an innovative methodology for its household Panel. It is made up of 3,000 households from around the country that have an Internet connection from which information is extracted from two sources:

- On the one hand, the real level of security is analyzed with software that analyses the security incidents in home computers. This computer program – developed by INTECO – is given to the panelists for them to install it on their computers. This software monthly scans the panelists' computers, detecting all malware present in them and also gathers data on the operating system and the state of its up-to-dateness. The software sends this information to INTECO, who treats it completely anonymously and as a whole. The panelists are informed that they will not receive any information on their security incidents, even though the incidents may be dangerous for their computers, as the interest for knowing the general situation as reliably as possible prevails over warnings for solving individual problems. The panelists are duly informed of this situation and accept to participate under these conditions.
- On the other hand, the perception and level of trust of domestic users will be analyzed by means of personal surveys. The panelists will answer a quarterly survey on their perception of security and their practices and behavior on the Net.

This will allow analyzing and contrasting two parallel sources of information in the computer security area, which provides a great comparative advantage: it is possible to know the differences existing between the perception of security and the real situation of the panelists.

In addition, this methodology also allows monitoring the following aspects through time:
- The real security level.
- The changes in perspective, opinions and habits, regarding security, undergone by users.

In general, the gathering of information will be carried out according to the following plan:
- Recruitment of the dedicated panel, by means of e-mail invitations.
- Information on the type of collaboration required, incentive system and confidentiality conditions.
- Invitation to scan the panelist's computer that has access to the analysis program by a personalized identifier, in order to control participation and merge the data from the survey.
- Quota control according to the sample design indicated in the "Sample size and distribution".
- The second wave of the Study represents a complete quarterly scanning and survey cycle. It allows for a first evolutive comparison of the situation of Security and e-Trust.

2.1 Data sheet

2.1.1 Scope

Spanish Internet users that have frequent access to the Internet from their homes and that are older than 15 years. To delimit the concept of user with more precision, we limit ourselves to users that connect to the Internet at least once a month from their homes.

2.1.2 Sample size and distribution

A representative sample of more than 3,000 Internet users, with a stable participation in the Panel has been extracted. This participation has been considered valid only in the cases in which the panelist had correctly completed the quarterly survey and correctly carried out a scan of her/his computer in, at least, two of the three months of each wave.

The sample has been fixed according to a multistage model:
- Stratification by regions, in order to guarantee a minimum set of subjects in each of these entities.
- Sampling by quotas of home size, age, gender, work activity and size of habitat.

Although the differences between the obtained sample and the theoretical one have been small, the sample has been adjusted to the scope, based on the data of the population by region, for the previously described scope and the quota variables, in order to reach a more perfect adjustment. In Table 1, we can see the sample distribution, according to demographical variables used to establish the said quotas.

Given the fact that the final data of the survey has been adjusted to the same scope of the study, they are perfectly homogeneous when it comes to the geographical distribution, gender, size of the household and other relevant sociodemographic variables, that is to say, they do not show variations in those aspects for the purposes of the analysis.

Table 1: Sample distribution by sociodemographic categories

Concept	Sample Obtained	Theoretical Sample
Activity		
Employed	68.9	69.2
Unemployed	4.6	5.0
Studying	19.7	19.0
Retired	2.7	2.2
Other non-workers	4.1	4.6
Size of the household		
1	7.1	7.6
2	25.5	25.7
3	27.3	27.4
4 and more	40.1	39.3
Gender		
Male	51.7	47.3
Female	48.3	52.7
Habitat		
Up to 20.000	23.2	23.1
From 20.001 to 100.000	19.4	22.8
More than 100.000 and capital cities	57.4	54.1
Age		
Up to 24	25.4	25.5
25-35	39.2	40.0
35-49	27.6	27.2
50 and more	7.8	7.3

2.1.3 Sampling error

In accordance with the criteria of simple random sampling for dichotomic variables in which $p=q=0.5$ and for a confidence level of 95.5%, the following calculations of the sampling error are established.

Sampling error $\pm 1.80\%$.

2.2 Consistency and robustness of the sample

The consistency of the sample, in terms of a possible self-selection bias because of accepting panelists scanning their computer, has been analyzed in detail. It has been concluded that the sample does not show significant bias in this aspect.

In order to check the robustness of the analysis, the results of the scans and surveys are monitored throughout the life of the panel.

- The results regarding the habits, opinions and attitudes and the Security indicators panel show a considerable consistency, which corresponds to variables, which change rather slowly under stable conditions.
- The data of the scanning, expressed as a percentage of malware detections in the months of the life of the panel since January 2007, also show that the variations of the sample are included in the normal variation, established by the sampling error and by the logical and normal development of security habits of Spanish users.

The obtained results can be considered suitable and it is possible to establish them as a basis for a future analysis of temporal series, which will allow to measure the past development and predict possible future situations.

The sample is, therefore, exempt from bias and structural problems. The variations produced in the sample over time are the result of the panel's dynamism, which reflects how the incidents detected in the users are evolving.

2.3 Technical design of the system of statistical indicators

Every analysis and all the information about security incidents and e-trust, shown in the final report can be simplified in the calculation of a series of indicators that systematically customize the information of the Study in a segmented way.

The system consists of seven indicators and includes, for example, usage habits, such as the equipment in security or real malware incidents. It is segmented into sociodemographic variables, such as age, education, etc.

2.3.1 Objectives and Advantages

The system of indicators is expected to serve as a means to monitor the evolution and trends of security on the Internet, as well as the trust of households.

The system of indicators, designed by INTECO, has the following benefits:

- It is integral, as it encompasses both usage habits and equipment in security, or the real malware incidents.
- It is synthetic, as it summarizes all relevant aspects of security into a set of seven indicators.
- It is sensitive, as it has detected small variations of security and has shown to be relevant to detect risk situations in specific segments of the population.
- It is stable, as it permits to have a general vision of the situation of security of any market, segment or sub-segment, related to the scores, whose reference is always 100 on the scale. Even if the number of questions that form the indicator varies, the system would maintain its stability and historical comparability.
- It is operative, as it permits to easily detect the system's vulnerabilities and to instigate measures to reduce them.
- It is strategic, as it helps to understand the consequences of the individual situations regarding the lack of protection for the system and it permits to introduce the connection between the Administration's security policy and users´ individual behavior.

2.3.2 Status and values of the indicators

The value of the seven indicators ranges from 0 to 100 points. It is given in points, except for the indicator IS.5: computers with some malware incident, which shows the percentage of computers with at least one incident of malware, coming from the data of the scanning, and which is included within the system of Indicators, due to the relevance of the data. That is to say, even though the indicator IS.7, Indicator of computers with potentially high dissemination risk, has a value of, for example, 27.3, it does not mean that 27.3% of computers have a high dissemination risk, but that the result of the combined calculations used to obtain the result shows a value of 27.3 points.

They show a combined calculation of different items and parameters that form each indicator. For example, IS.2) analyzes, among other things, the following behaviors:

- I report those pages I know that use users´ data for fraudulent purposes.
- When I receive a notification about the existence of a new virus, I report this to the people I know.
- When I see that somebody has not updated his/her security programs, I recommend him/her to review them and install the latest version.

This system facilitates temporary analysis and comparisons between the different waves.

2.3.3 Structure of the System of Indicators

The seven indicators are classified into two groups:

- Indicators related to protection: IS.1 and IS.2
- Indicators related to risk: IS.4, IS.5, IS.6 and IS.7

IS.3, which completes the list, presents users´ perception, i.e. the indicator of personal security perception represents the balance variable, which evaluates the protection against risks.

The first group includes the factors that increase protection, while the second group includes those factors that measure the risks. The system modifies the parameters of the indicators of both groups, in order to keep the perception of users high. In this way, changes in the habits and behavior of Spanish households may be analyzed. The system of the set of indicators is balanced: an increase in the incidents tends to be compensated by more security equipment and prudent habits, in order to restore the balance, marked by high e-Trust (Figure 2).

IS.1 Indicator of equipment in security

It measures the equipment and the adoption of security measures.

It is calculated according to certain measures of the available security equipment by comparing the data with an optimal security situation, which is reached with full equipment. The equipment for the calculation of the indicator includes the security measures that are most used: antivirus programs, firewalls, pop-up blockers, deletion of temporary files and cookies, antispam programs, antispyware, passwords (equipment and documents), security updates of the operating system, backups of important files and document encryption. The calculation of the indicator does not only focus on the security of the system, but also includes measures that favor the security of information.

IS.2 Indicator of solidarity behavior

It measures the intensity of the solidarity behavior to other users regarding security on the Internet.

It is established as the score obtained in the defining behaviors of the solidarity component, regarding the maximum possible score, as defined in the Study: I report those pages I know that use user's data for fraudulent purposes, when I receive a notification about the existence of a new virus, I report this to the people I know, when I see that somebody has not updated his/her security programs, I recommend him/her to review them and install the latest version, If I sent an attached file through e-mail, I check that it does not contain any virus, when I receive an e-mail from an unknown person containing an infected file, I report this to the sender.

IS.3 Indicator of personal security perception

It measures the subjective perception of security when the Internet is used.

Score obtained in the following criteria of security perception (regarding the maximum possible mark): the connection I use is fairly secure against intruders who want to access my equipment; my computer is reasonably protected; the devices and protection systems I use are up-to-date and efficient.

IS.4 Indicator of reckless behavior

It measures the intensity of the risk habits in the use of the Internet.

Score obtained in the following reckless behaviors (regarding the maximum possible score): I open e-mails from unknown senders if they appear interesting; I give my e-mail address when people ask for it, even if I do not know them; I add contacts to Messenger, even if I do not know who the person is; I click on the links that appear in conversations on Messenger, without asking what they are about; if necessary, I modify the security measures of the computer in order to access the services or games I am interested in; I share Software without checking if it is infected or not (P2P networks).

IS.5 Indicator of computers with some malware incident

Indicates the percentage of computers with some malware incident, detected with the scans.

IS.6 Indicator of computers with potentially high risk

Indicates the percentage of computers with some malware incident, detected with the scans.

The malware that is considered to be high risk consists of the following families: Trojans, viruses, worms, dialers, keyloggers, exploits, rootkit.

IS.7 Indicator of computers with potentially high dissemination risk

The calculation of this indicator includes concepts, which involve, to a greater or lesser extent, a potential risk of dissemination between the rest of the users: the real state of security updates of the operating system, computers with some malware incident, like a worm or script, the use of instant messaging, files downloading, frequency and intensity of Web-surfing, software sharing without checking whether it is infected or not and sending e-mails without checking if they contain any virus.

3 Main results

The main question mark which has motivated this Study is determining the security level in Spanish Internet households/users and the trust they generally have in the Information Society, and particularly regarding Internet. The way to reach this objective has been twofold: on the one hand assessing the trust and perception of security of the users, and on the other, carrying out an analysis on the real security level incidents in the computers in Spanish Internet user households. The result of contrasting the two variables is a series of user segments and profiles according to information security.

Three navigation styles have been detected regarding security habits which define three user segments:

1. **Sensible and inconsiderate use**. Characterized by an individualist approach focusing on private defense and forgetting to share experiences for considerate defense. 58% of the users belong to this type.

2. **Sensible and considerate use**. They add individual protection, concerned about sharing and mutual help in security aspects. They are 33% of the users.

3. **Reckless use**. 9% of the users. They do not respect the basic rules and habits of caution. They suffer many serious incidents, but even so do not change their reckless habits.

Seen as a whole (socially and technologically), the Internet security system is empirically defined by the following characteristics:

Firstly, the majority of the users use basic protection equipment for connecting to Internet. Antivirus and firewalls are used by more than 75% of the users. Other protections such as antispam, antispyware, passwords and operating system security updates are used by around 50% of the users.

Other security measures requiring a more active behavior from the user, such as backups, hard disk partition or encrypting, are fairly minority. However, these same measures included in a concept of "proactive security of the user" are those with the highest forecast for growth in the months to come according the opinions of the users themselves.

In general, users seem to look for security methods that do not require constant attention, nor interfere in the feeling of the free use of Internet.

The level of incidents declared by the users is considerable, although the frequency of serious incidents is lower. Amongst the most frequent consequences declared by the users, we can highlight 40.4% of the households who had to format their hard disk and 23.6% who lost files, at least once, since they have been connected to Internet from home due to security incidents.

Amongst security incidents, the most frequent is receiving spam. Only in the last week 66.1% of households have suffered this type of incident. In the last year 52.8% declare to have suffered computer viruses, but other serious threats such as fraud or theft in bank accounts or credit cards, do not reach 5%.

In general, an attitude of following the basic security recommendations is observed in the users' behavior, although serious incidents are still occurring.

For its part, computer scanning has revealed that three out of four users have some type of malicious code in their computer (, although the majority of these codes have a moderate or low level of danger. 51.8% of the computers scanned have some type of high risk code. Incidents with Trojan horse or adware malicious code incidents are currently more frequent, the objectives of which are mainly to go unnoticed in the infected system. This is possible given the increase in concealing techniques such as rootkits. That is why the infections are more unnoticed by the users. The change in the production trend from worms and virus malicious codes, which caused big epidemics, to Trojan horses and adware, is an accurate reflection that malware production is focused on fraud and the economic benefit of the creators of these codes. The big variety of existing malicious codes and the daily appearance of a multitude of variants is added to this situation.

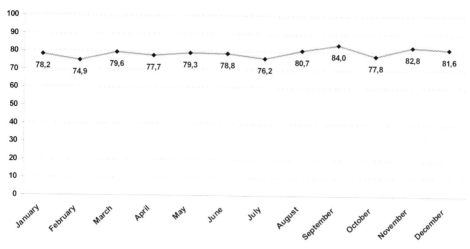

Figure 1: Malware incidence evolution 2007 (%)

The effect of the incidents on user behavior is developed in two aspects:

1. **Updating, renewing and installing new protection barriers**. The measure most frequently acted on is the antivirus program, both by updating and changing the supplier or installing it for the first time.

2. **Changing their opinions and habits in the Net**. In this case the raising awareness of being more informed is appreciated, as well as maximizing precautions, increasing consideration with other users and demanding greater action from the Government.

The analysis generally indicates that the incidents are not driving the users to abandon services or stop using Internet. The user has a high perception of security, with the majority of users, 86%, indicating that their computer is reasonably protected. Only faced with a considerable increase in the number of incidents in the household's computer, are behavior and security measures modified to keep the perception of security high. However, amongst the users who have not suffered serious security incidents, the reaction to an incident is to continue using the same Internet services as before. Although almost half of the households indicated that they would use more services if they knew how to reduce the risk. There is a delay effect on the development of the Information Society, and this effect must be looked for amongst the non-users, those who do not feel sufficiently protected to fully develop in Internet.

In general, regular Internet users have included online services in their lifestyle to such an extent that is very difficult for them to do without them. The reason may be operational, given that unique service conditions govern them. It can also concern a series of conditions which make it compulsory for the user to only carry out their activity in this way. In this context, the incidents suffered are interpreted as warnings for increasing their protection equipment and/or being more sensible in their habits, but they are not interpreted as reasons for abandoning or reducing the use of Internet. Simply, for many users, the second alternative does not seem possible.

In these cases, more attention to what is happening in Internet is demanded, complemented with greater diligence in pursuing the offenders and using more force against them.

In spite of the incidents declared, and the quite realistic knowledge of the risk declared by the users, the general feeling is a comfortable security in Internet use. The vast majority considers that their connection and computer guarantee them safe navigation. This is why the users, even for the services they perceive as dangerous, consider that their level of risk is moderate. Users perceive that security in Internet has evolved positively in the last year. Likewise, users think that their computers are better protected now than a year ago, which can make them act less sensibly.

The analysis carried out highlight that e-trust stands at an average of 75.2 points in a scale from 0 to 100 (Figure 2). This e-trust is high in all the user groups, with no differences in their risk habits or the level of their security equipment. It is only below 70 points in those who have repeatedly suffered important security incidents (more than 3 serious consequences).

The conclusion that can be drawn is that high trust is a prerequisite for a rewarding Internet use. The users tend to keep this e-trust above 75 points.

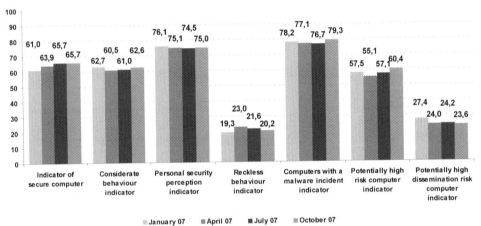

Figure 2: System of Statistical Indicators

When the sensation of security is broken by an unexpected incident, the user tries to repair the balance increasing their security equipment, increasing their caution or both at the same time.

Generally, these changes help to return to a comfortable level of e-trust. But if things are not as expected (repeated incidents), the need for support from a third party starts to become necessary. This third party for support is the Government.

Specifically, the role the users give the Government in security matters seems to consist of being a last resort. The result must be to guarantee security when the measures within the reach of the user and sensible navigation habits are revealed to be insufficient. In general, this intervention is accepted and demanded by more than 70% of the users.

The overall result of this restabilisation process in time is that users think that both the amount and seriousness of the incidents suffered in their computers has been reduced in the last year. This reinforces their idea that restabilisation the suitable strategy.

Given that the level of basic equipment is similar in the majority of users, caution in usage habits has been revealed to be an important additional protection factor. In fact, the results of the computer scanning show how the security habits generally mark the differences in incidents amongst the users with antivirus and updated operating systems.

In security maters, we can talk about an e-paradox: some users feel safe with their updated protection systems. But their actual number of incidents is greater because their practices become reckless. The users with sensible habits and updated protection systems are those who have the lowest amount of actual incidents. As has been indicated, protection systems, on their own, are insufficient to guarantee system security.

The Government has a key role: information must be channeled both regarding protection systems and safe practices.

It has been possible to empirically prove, thanks to computer scanning, the impact of "healthy habits" in Internet security (caution and consideration for other users). For example, it is noteworthy that most Internet users, 70%, get in touch with the senders of electronic mails when they contain infected files. This type of practice contributes to controlling infections and limits damages caused by the malware. These habits are related to a reduction in Trojan horses of 31.0% and almost 21.0% in the case of virus.

If these results are compared with the isolated impact of antivirus programs in reducing malicious codes, the difference between having an antivirus or not is only two per cent in the percentage of infected computers. These figures are explained by the special situation the sector is presently undergoing. On the other hand, it has been shown that updating the operating system is important for improving the state of the infections, but, given that vulnerabilities exist that affect programs which are not the operating system itself, just updating the operating system is not sufficient by itself. That is why both updating all the computer's software, and the sociological factor are very important for improving security.

The data indicates that the actual security incidents detected in the scanning seem to have their solution in two relatively independent factors: the real presence of security devices and the preventative and considerate usage habits. Both factors constitute the pillars of the system security and its complementary nature must be strengthened as far as possible: there is no security without the simultaneous presence of both of them.

Three **weaknesses in the System** have been identified with the study:

- Possibly the main empirical vulnerability, **reckless behavior**, strongly increases as age is lowered. It is a behavior typical in the young, mainly males who live at home or who do not share their computer with anybody else. This behavior will end up affecting other parts of the general system due to the interactive and social nature of the Internet phenomenon and the communication services and media between users: electronic mail, file and programme exchange, etc. It has also been detected that the shared use of the terminal is a positive factor in reducing incidents, given that users who share the same computer are more cautious when navigating.
- A second fragile point in the System, which is less intense, comes from **users with less experience and a shortage of security equipment**, who do not manage to reduce their real risk in spite of showing sensible navigation habits.
- The System's third weakness, which affects the majority of users, consists of them **tending to place e-trust in the computer and in individual solutions**, perhaps influenced by the communication and marketing of these products, not worrying about security habits, which have been shown to be essential for maintaining the computer's security. The significance of "invisible" threats for the user must be added to this, such as those detected by the scanning programme installed in the households. These threats are not detected by the users at any moment and are they are therefore not aware of their consequences.

It is therefore necessary to make an effort on two fronts: on the one hand, fostering the use of security devices and on the other, stressing the need for the responsible use of the computers, for these devices to be effective. This would enable the prevention of the paradoxical effect commented above that the security equipment entails too reckless behavior which promotes system vulnerability.

That is why we must stress a culture of security. It is necessary for the users to be aware of the utility of the solutions such as the antivirus, firewalls, antispam, security updates, etc., but they must also know their limits, the real threats, and the additional recommendations, so that a false sense of security is not created. To increase security it is vital to provide users with greater information with a view to using the new technologies responsibly and safely, with usage habits based on caution and protection.

4 Conclusion

Even though both security measures and users' behavior reduce the number of detected incidents, it is noteworthy the fact that **computers' behavior is the reason for a greater decrease in the amount of malware found on the machines**.

Given that the basic level of equipment is similar for most users, prudence in usage habits has become an important additional factor for protection. In fact, computer scan results show how security habits differentiate incidents between users with antivirus software and up-to-date operating systems and those without.

It exists a **false feeling of security**, i.e. users have the perception that incidents do not reach the level that in fact exists and that they are less and less serious. Moreover, it has been detected that many users neglect their security habits after installing protection measures on their computers, which means that the risks to their systems will increase instead of decreasing, as it should be.

Thus, it is confirmed that the installation of security tools is necessary but not enough. It is also important to take other complementary actions, such as good practices and proper security habits. **Security on the Internet is not a question of machines and technology, but of people!**

Therefore, the use of security measures and devices - e.g. anti-virus software, firewall, anti-spam software or security updates - **must be encouraged** and **users must be trained in security habits** at a technical level, so that technical measures, whether active and passive, can be really efficient.

References

[BrWM06] Braverman, Matthew; Williams Jeff; Mador, Ziv: Security Intelligence Report. Microsoft, 2006.

[Rede07]   Red.es: Panel de Hogares:. Red.es, 2007.

Session 2:
Technical Issues with Trust in Computing and Proposed Solutions

Implementing a Portable Trusted Environment

John Zic · Surya Nepal

CSIRO ICT Centre PO Box 76, Epping NSW 1710
Australia

{john.zic | surya.nepal}@csiro.au

Abstract

The development of trusted systems, as envisaged by the Trusted Computing Group, assumed that the computing environments are uniform in terms of their operational environment, including hardware configuration, execution of a standard set of applications, operating system and facilities and procedures that allow the issue, revocation and maintenance of critical encryption keys and authorization certificates. These assumptions may be applicable to a single managed enterprise infrastructure. However, in situations where the users are mobile, or the computing environment is heterogeneous and the Internet provides the connectivity, the management of trust between enterprises becomes overwhelmingly difficult, if not impossible. As a result, deployment and uptake of trusted secure systems based on Trusted Platform Module have not been as successful as first envisaged. In this paper, we report on our experiences in designing and implementing a prototype personal trusted device called the *Trust Extension Device*, or TED, that provides users with a portable trustworthy environment for conducting transactions on any Internet connected computer.

1 Introduction

The problem of assuring trust in any transactions dealing with sensitive medical, financial or personal information motivates significant research and development activities in academia, industry and government. CSIRO was involved in one of such activities commissioned by the Australian Department of Health and Aging [OKGG05] towards developing prototype systems for patient-centric control of medical information. An eConsent system was developed and demonstrated to its stakeholders in 2003. The system supports transfer of medical records among collaborating healthcare facilities. We observed that assuring trust among collaborating facilities relies heavily on the administrative users (e.g., clerks, system administrators, etc) who need to interpret and transform policies from one administrative domain to another. Some of these policy statements are themselves sensitive and should not be revealed to other than the intended users. Automatic way of assuring trust alleviates this problem. This led us to the investigation of the use of technologies provided by the Trusted Computing Group (TCG).

An investigation of augmenting trust in the eConsent system with hardware support through the Trusted Platform Module (TPM) was commenced in early 2004. We successfully developed a prototype system that demonstrated the use of the TPM controllers in an extended eConsent model [NZKJ07] and showed that trust can be established among collaborating facilities without the intervention of administrative users. During the development of the system, it was noted that there were some issues faced by any implementation that relied on the attestation protocols that underpinned the TPM system of ensuring

D. Gawrock, H. Reimer, A.-R. Sadeghi, C. Vishik (Editors): Future of Trust in Computing, Vieweg+Teubner (2009), 17-29

trust. Probably the most significant issue was a *philosophical* issue rather than a technical issue. The attestation protocols rely on the exchange of a summary of the entire state of each machine between each of the trusted machines. This state information is calculated by performing a set of mathematical operations on the entire machine, from the applications that are running, to the libraries loaded, to the operating system and onto the hardware of the machine (including the TPM microcontroller). *Any* change in *any* of these components will result, as expected, in the attestation failing for that machine, and so, transactions cannot proceed.

This prototype system was demonstrated to an expert group from government and several banks, and supported out conclusions that this system would be very difficult to implement and maintain even in a well-managed enterprise environment, and would be totally inappropriate to release to the general public who are accessing their information from a heterogeneous environment of machines and configurations. Further discussions with this group lead us to turning the basic idea around so that an issuing authority such as a bank or government agency could issue a small device with its own "locked down" environment (operating system and applications) with the added feature of being able to utilise the attestation protocols and TPM to assure the device's integrity. The small portable personal device we called the *Trust Extension Device* or *TED*.

This paper presents a brief overview of our experiences in developing different trusted systems leading to TED as follows. Section 2 reviews the Trusted Medical Application that extended the earlier eConsent work. Section 3 presents a summary of the architecture of TED and its associated system components. Section 4 describes our trusted e-mail system (again, motivated by medical specialists requiring to exchange confidential information in a trusted manner). Section 5 concludes our work and summarises the future directions.

2 A Trusted Medical Application

Healthcare providers are responsible for the creation, storage and management of their client patients' medical records. The privacy and security of the patient records is assured if the healthcare providers and their facilities are self-contained. However, healthcare providers are also charged with ensuring the best possible outcomes for their patients, and this may require coordinated treatment between different healthcare facilities, possibly owned by other providers. This implies that the facilities need to securely share their patient records while maintaining the individual's privacy and confidentiality. In order to address the issue of control of private medical information, the CSIRO ICT Centre was involved in the development of an eConsent model [OKGG05] within the Electronic Consent Project[1]. The term "eConsent" was coined to refer to a mechanism through which patients can express their consent policies on their electronic records being accessed and shared between healthcare facilities.

In our eConsent model, the sender facility has to trust the receiver facilities (and vice versa). That is, the sender, as well as authenticating the identity of the receiver, has to rely on the receiver having the right software and hardware system components and configuration to enforce the sender's policies on privacy and confidentiality at all times. Similarly, the receiver also must ensure that it is always in the correct state and configuration for accepting any incoming record. Both facilities need to ensure and enforce the patients' consent policies for their electronic records when these records are accessed and transferred. This eConsent model relies upon a person at the receiver facilities entering a patient's consent requirements in the receiver facility's system.

---

1 The Electronic Consent Project was commissioned by the Australian Government Department of Health and Aging (DoHA)

These limitations on trust led to the development of an electronic consent application using trusted computing technologies as part of the CeNTIE project[2]. The implemented system consisted of six software components as shown in Figure 1.

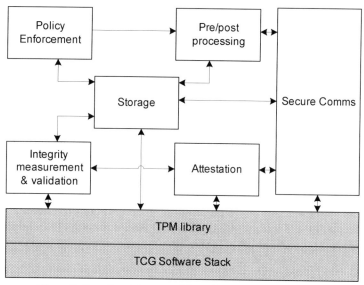

Figure 1: Overall architecture of Trusted MedicClient Application

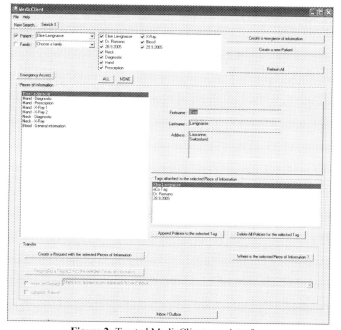

Figure 2: Trusted MedicClient user interface

2   The Centre for Networking Technologies for the Information Economy Project supported by the Australian Government through the Advanced Networks Program of the Department of Communications, Information Technology and the Arts.

- **Policy enforcement engine:** responsible for enforcing policies and resolving conflicts while accessing and transferring medical records. It is also responsible for generation and maintenance of transaction logs (required for auditing).
- **Integrity measurement/validation:** responsible for measuring the current environment of the host computer and verifying that the measurements sent by remote facility are as expected, and so can be trusted.
- **Secure communication:** encrypts the outgoing information and decrypts incoming information.
- **Attestation:** responsible for authenticating and determining the identity of the remote facility.
- **Pre/post processing:** responsible for processing records for transfer.
- **Storage and Retrieval:** responsible for storing and retrieving records from a set of SQL databases.

In our system, doctors access, create and share medical information by use of the Trusted MedicClient software. Figure 2 shows a screenshot of the main interface for the system. Once a doctor is authorized to use the system and selects a patient, MedicClient displays the health information view for the patient. We omit the details of operation of the system here due to the limitation of the space and refer the reader to [NZKJ07] for a more comprehensive explanation of the system. Needless to say, it was duly noted when the system was demonstrated that establishing trust would be difficult to maintain because of the precision of the attestation protocols in relying on the operational environments to be exactly as expected on all machines involved in the transactions.

3 The Trust Extension Device

The mechanisms for establishing trust between two parties and their host computers in current state of the art is that they are tightly coupled to both the hardware of a specific machine and its associated software environment and that there exist suitable attestation protocols between the parties. This (by definition) hinders the portability and mobility of trust. The tight coupling also presents a non-trivial system management problem each time a new piece of software or hardware is introduced into the host computer. For example, if an enterprise's agent needs to visit a customer's office to work on their files, then the agent must only use the issued "trusted" computer to work at the customer's office. Ideally, the agent would like to use any computer, including an untrusted customer's machine, and yet still be able to establish the strong trust relationship with the enterprise. Establishing strong trust relationships requires that user's machines, the enterprises and the users at both ends are known to each other with a great deal of certainty. Providing portability and mobility of trust and being able to use any machine anywhere in the world is not possible with existing approaches. Our solution to these issues was our *Trust Extension Device* (TED) [NZHD07]. The TED uses three basic technologies to provide mobility and portability of trust in hostile, open and untrusted environments.

1. It is implemented on a small portable device, such as flash memory, allowing device mobility and portability to any platform environment.
2. Trusted Platform Module (TPM) cryptographic microcontroller is used to provide hardware-based keys for trust establishment as well as the associated cryptographic functions and protocols for attestation.
3. Virtual machine technology is used for two reasons. First, it provides an environment within an untrusted host machine to create a trusted environment running under a variety of platforms. Second, it provides a degree of isolation of the operational environment of the TED from the host machine environment.

Figure 7 presents the TED abstract architecture. It includes the Trusted Platform Module (TPM), virtualization software including Virtual Machine Operating System, and a secure application within a portable device (e.g., flash memory).

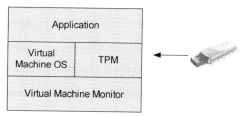

Figure 3: TED Abstract Architecture

TED is central to providing trust mobility, while not relying on having direct access to a secure, trusted, and managed infrastructure. A user can, for example, plug a portable device into any untrusted networked host machine to create his/her own trusted working environment, which is isolated from the host machine's environment. The created client environment appears as a virtual machine to the agent, on which they can do their work and through which they can communicate with the remote (home) server. A key part of this work is that trust mechanisms are utilised to provide attestation for all transactions between the created mobile client environment on the host machine and the remote server. The novelty in this work is that it combines trusted hardware and virtual machine mechanisms within a portable device. When an agent terminates a working session, on the untrusted machine, no remnant of client data or transactions will be traceable on the host, i.e. when the created virtual environment is terminated all data associated with it disappears.

Figure 4 presents a typical scenario of use of the proposed trust extension device. As can be seen, it involves four components: an enterprise including remote application server, trust extension device, untrusted local machine, and untrusted network connection between the local machine and remote server.

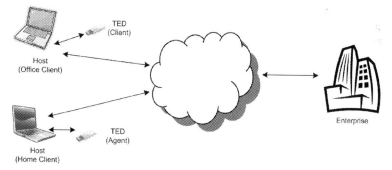

Figure 4: A Typical TED Use-Case Scenario

We next describe a typical scenario of use for the TED in a financial application. Consider an agent, working on behalf of a bank, who needs to visit a client's premises in order to clarify some financial issues. On arrival, the agent plugs the TED into the client's host machine that is running an unknown and untrusted software configuration and operating system. The TED is preconfigured so that when it is plugged into the client's machine, it automatically creates a trusted environment to deal in a predictable manner with the bank. In an ideal scenario, the trusted environment acquires control of the host machine's resources (memory, storage, I/O, and networking) for its own use in such a way that these resources, when used by the trusted environment, are isolated from the host machine's operational environment[3].

To perform tasks on behalf of a client, the agent invokes a secure (customized) application that is embedded on the TED. However, before the secure application is used, the TED is attested as being trustworthy. This is achieved by a mechanism that operates between an embedded trust entity on the TED and a trust verification entity running on a remote host or server. This mechanism establishes a relationship that may be understood in general terms as, verify that you are who you say you are and that you aren't going to do bad things to my information, before we start our exchange. Once the trust relationship is established, each subsequent application-related transactions may also be attested by this mechanism. Within this trusted context, an agent may download confidential client data, from say the bank database, operate on the data using the secure application, and then upload the modified client data back to the database. To terminate the working session, the agent may either remove the TED from the client's machine, or quit the secure application and then shutdown the TED's virtual machine, and then remove the TED from the host machine. In either case, when a session is terminated, all information exchanged between the agent and the bank is destroyed, and all the acquired resources on the untrusted host are released back to the host. It is important to note here that all information exchanged are stored in TED that expires with the particular session.

Our current TED prototype was implemented as a Type II Virtual Machine (VM), shown in the TED Implementation Architecture, Figure 5. The VM executes entirely within the application space of an untrusted host machine. Fundamental to our design was that the use of the TED required no specialised drivers or any changes to be performed on the host machine, and the host machine does not require rebooting. This was motivated by the requirement to be able to use TED on any networked computer, anywhere and anytime so as to maximise mobility for the user.

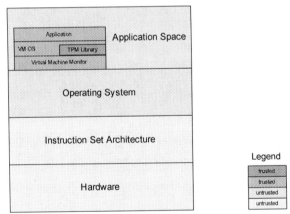

Figure 5: The TED Implementation Architecture

We chose the Type II VM because it virtualises the entire host platform, and allows us to accommodate the situation where the guest and host machines do not have a common Instruction Set Architecture (ISA), as the (now superseded) PowerPC based Apple machines and those of the more "generic" PC platforms based on Intel or similar chipsets. It is important to note that there are well understood, inherent limitations with respect to isolation while using Type II VM which have been discussed elsewhere.

---

3 The shortcomings of currently available type II virtual machine technologies in achieving a completely isolated virtual environment are beyond the scope of the paper. Our concept of TED assumes that virtualization technology provides complete isolation of the guest environment.

We utilised QEMU version 8.2.0 for Microsoft's Windows XP [QemuVM] as TED's virtual machine. QEMU executed in full system mode, allowing complete emulation of a CPU and peripherals required launch a guest operating system. As a full system emulator, QEMU can run an unmodified guest operating system, such as GNU/ Linux or Windows, and all its applications in a virtual machine.

The TED prototype used a customised Ubuntu 6.06 i386 GNU/Linux distribution as its guest operating system. This was stored as a disk image file on the TED's storage area. This customised operating system is presented to the user after the QEMU has successfully acquired and isolated the resources from the host machine.

In order to support the attestation protocols and certificate management required within the device, it was decided very early in the prototype development to utilise a TPM library consisting of an emulator, device drivers and associated APIs. To that effect, we adopted the "berlios" TPM emulator [TPMe], while the device drivers and APIs from IBM's TrouSers TSS project (version 0.2.7) [TrouSF] and jTss-Wrapper (version 0.2.1) [JTSSdo] respectively.

Besides these components within the TED, successful operation of the TED requires the adoption of a suitable enterprise architecture to support the applications and transactions that are to be executed within a trustworthy environment. There are three components to the TED enterprise architecture:

1. TED *Issuer and Manager* that is responsible for generating digital keys, issuing and revoking the TED as well as possibly responsible for the device's manufacture.

2. A *Privacy Certifying Authority*, that is responsible for verifying that the TED is valid and authentic.

3. An *Application Server*, deployed within the enterprise, to perform the basic transactions required from the customer.

3.1 TED Issuer and Manager

It is envisaged that the manufacture of the TED will be authorized by an enterprise (such as department of health or bank). The role of the enterprise in the manufacture of the TED is to supply the necessary credentials as shown in Figure 6 that include cryptographic keys for each TED, and in particular, the Endorsement Key pair for the Endorsement Credential where the Endorsement Credential is embedded into the TPM component of the TED. In our current architecture, we assume that the TED issuer and manager within the enterprise will assume this role. That is, a single enterprise can authorise many TEDs through the TED issuer and manager. The TED manager will sign the credentials using its cryptographic private key. The TED manager, therefore, will generate, for a single TED, the following data:

- *TED Credential* containing data that identifies the person/client to whom the TED is issued by the enterprise. The details of the client are signed by the enterprise; in our enterprise architecture, this is done by the TED manager.

- *Endorsement Credential* includes the public part of the endorsement key that is unique to each TED. The TPM manufacturer signs the endorsement key. This is done by the TED manager in our enterprise architecture.

- *Platform Credential* includes the TED's operating environment consisting of VM software and VM OS. In our architecture, the TED manager signs the details of the platform. It is possible to have an independent third party supplying the platform description.

- *Validation Credential* includes service component descriptions consisting of their digests that are loaded into the TED. One could have an independent validation manager. In our simple enterprise architecture this is also achieved by the TED manager.

The TED Manager or issuer manufactures the TED with the credential details explained above so that it can be used to establish the trust relationship as described in a later section.

3.2 Privacy CA

The TCG uses a trusted third party, the privacy certification authority (Privacy CA), to verify and authenticate the TPM. The same concept is used in TED. Each TED is issued with the credentials, including an RSA key pair called the Endorsement Key (EK). The Privacy CA is assumed to know the credential details along with the public parts of the Endorsement Keys of all TEDs. That is, the TED manager supplies the credential details to the Privacy CA. Whenever a TED needs to communicate with the enterprise, it generates a second RSA key pair, called an Attestation Identity Key (AIK), sends an identity key certification request to the Privacy CA, which contains, (a) an identity public key, (b) a proof of possession of identity for the private key, and (c) the endorsement certificate containing the TED's endorsement public key. The privacy CA checks whether a TED issuer has signed the endorsement certificate. If the check is successful, the privacy CA returns an identity certificate encrypted with the TED's endorsement public key. The TED can then provide this certificate to the application server to verify and authenticate itself with respect to the AIK. If the TED is reported as stolen or lost, the Privacy CA can compute the corresponding public key and tag it as a rogue TED.

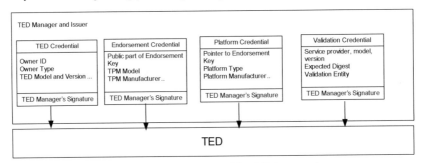

Figure 6: TED's Credentials managed by TED issuer and manager

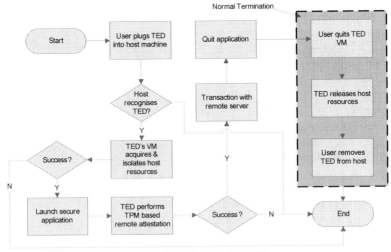

Figure 7: The TED Runtime Flow Diagram

In summary, an enterprise can issue one or many TEDs. Since the enterprise is involved in the manufacturer of the TEDs, it has all the issued credential information of the TED. In addition, the enterprise has two additional components, the Enterprise's Application Server and the Enterprise's Privacy Certificate Authority as discussed above. The Enterprise's Server is used when a TED's application requires a service from the enterprise. The Enterprise's Privacy Certificate Authority is used to perform remote attestation whenever a TED connects to the enterprise's network.

It is important to note that there is no requirement for the components' functions to be performed by three different entities. For example, a bank could provide all three components: its own enterprise applications, be responsible for the issuing and management of the TED, as well as act as a Privacy Certifying Authority. In other situations the enterprise may opt to take on the responsibility of being the application server only, and use trusted third parties to provide the Privacy Certifying Authority and TED Issuer and Manager. The decision as to ownership and responsibility of these components is a entirely a business decision.

The TED can be used in a variety of applications. We have demonstrated its use in three applications: one for simple banking [NZHD07], another as a distributed real-time collaboration environment for medical specialists [CeNTIE] and finally for synchronous trusted mail exchange [JaNZ08]. We present a summary of the trusted mail exchange application in the following section.

4 TED Application: Trusted Email Client

The TED was invented to address the problem of mobility and portability of trust offered by trusted computing technologies. To demonstrate this, we by developed a prototype system for trusted email exchange within the eConsent scenario.

During a specific component of this scenario, a patient's medical record may be transferred for referral to a specialist from a different healthcare facility, with the medical record is available to only the specific specialist and for the short duration of time. We implemented this functionality by combining the mobility of trust offered by TED and the Ephemerizer key management service service [JaNZ08]. The high level components of the implemented system architecture and protocol are shown in Figure 8. We implemented the system such that only the receiving TED can be used in conjunction with Ephemerizer and storage services to decrypt the data. We refer readers to [JaNZ08] for details and next describe our implementation briefly.

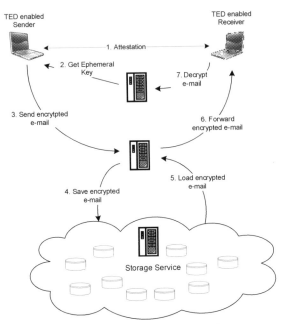

Figure 8: Components and protocol

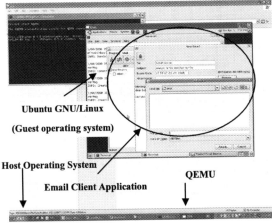

Figure 9: A snapshot of different components in operation at the sender's Trusted mail
client application

4.1 Privacy Certifying Authority Service

As explained earlier, it is envisaged that the manufacture of the TED will be authorised by an enterprise. The role of the enterprise in the manufacture of the TED is to supply the necessary credentials,
in particular, the Endorsement Key (EK) pair for the Endorsement Credential, where the Endorsement
Credential is embedded into the TPM component of the TED. In our current architecture, the TED issuer
within the enterprise will assume this role. As a concept demonstrator, we emulated this manufacturing

process by: packing QEMU in the 2GB flash disk; installing a customised Ubuntu Linux on top of the QEMU; installing a device driver and an emulator for TPM; deploying the IBM TPM API to create a Endorsement Key and its certificate for each TED, and finally deploy the Email Client Application.

The Privacy CA maintains all known Endorsement credentials of TED as a TreeMap. Whenever a TED needs to communicate with the enterprise, it generates a second RSA key pair, called an Attestation Identity Key (AIK), sends an identity key certification request to the Privacy CA along with the Endorsement Certificate. The privacy CA only returns the Identity Credential when it finds a matching Endorsement Certificate from the Endorsement Certificate TreeMap.

4.2 Ephemerizer Service

As indicated, we have developed a prototype implementation of an Ephemerizer service similar to [TrouSF]. The Ephemerizer is responsible for two functions: first, the issuing of ephemeral keys is based on a user-defined expiry time as an input, and returns an ephemeral key, where as the checking function accepts an input parameter that is typically an encrypted secret that is encrypted by the public part of the ephemeral key. If the expiry times has not elapsed, the Ephemerizer server decrypts the received input blob and returns encrypted secret to the requestor.

It should be noted that the keys that are issued and used to encrypt the data are such that the email contents cannot be decrypted without the explicit use of the Ephemerizer service.

4.3 Storage Service Operator SSO

A simple user API (read and write bytes into the storage fabric) is provided by the SSO to access the underlying storage fabric. Refer to [NeJZ07, CNC+07] for details. For this service, there are two operations. The first is used to store encrypted email data into the storage fabric managed by SSO. This function returns an identifier that uniquely identifies the stored (encryped) email data inside the SSO. The second function is used to retrieve the encrypted data stored inside SSO. It takes an identifier as an input parameter and returns the encrypted content when there is a match and successful retrieval, and null if there is no match.

4.4 Putting it all together

For our developed Mail Service it was decided to routes emails between mail senders and mail recipients. Rather than saving emails on its own file system, our Mail Server contacts a specialised Storage Service Operator (SSO) to store encrypted emails.

A hospital (or department of health) issues TED for its healthcare workers such as doctors and nurses. Each healthcare worker plugs a TED to one of their office PCs. As seen in the Figure 5, regardless of the underlying host operating environment, the TED creates its own trusted environment using a virtual machine (in our case, Qemu) and runs a guest operating system (such as Ubuntu GNU/Linux). The guest operating system launches a secure application (such as Email Client Application and Trusted MediClient). As the Email Client Application is launched, it uses the embedded TPM emulator to collect credentials (such as Endorsement Certificate and Attestation Identity Key) and runs an attestation protocol with the Privacy CA – a role enterprise headquarter plays to ensure that the credential requests are from genuine TED(s) issued by it. Once the attestation protocol is successfully run, the integrity of TED's running environment is in a known state, and the email transactions may commence. The doctor composes an email containing private, encrypted medical records that expires as specified within the encryption key. The email itself is encrypted using the keys issued by the embedded TPM emulator on the TED and then sent to another doctor (specialist).

As the email arrives, the Mail Server (that runs typically at the enterprise headquarters, along with Privacy CA and Ephemerizer, as shown in Figure 8) first authenticates the email sender. If verified successfully, the Mail Server saves the encrypted email to one of the specialized storage fabric managed by the Storage Service Operator (SSO).

Once email is saved by the SSO, the Mail Server sends a notification to the recipient. The recipient uses the TPM emulator embedded in its TED device to collect its credentials and send them to the Mail Server. As done it similarly for the email sender, the Mail Server then verifies the recipient's credentials and authorisation and indentity, the Mail Server retrieves the encrypted mail from the SSO and sends it to the recipient.

In our current implementation, the email is sent in such a way that it can only be viewed by the receiver, but can not be saved. This enables the application to enforce the sender's expiration policy.

5 Conclusions

With TED, we have provided mechanisms for users to create and use a trusted environment on any untrusted host machine. Additionally, these mechanisms provide both mobility and portability of trust. Our approach used TPM to provide the necessary certificates and attestation protocols, and virtual machine technologies for providing an isolated environment, and the adoption of a suitable enterprise architecture to support the required transactions and applications.

A key learning for us during the project has been that developing trustworthy platforms must be motivated by the ability for the issuing enterprise to completely control and attest the operational environment of the devices used between the client and the issuing enterprise. A general computing platform such as a commodity PC, with its high degree of heterogeneity, by definition is extremely difficult to implement uniform management of all client PCs. The attestation protocols and calculations required as part of the trust establishment are also difficult to implement in this environment in any practical sense. By allowing the enterprise to issue a small, controlled environment, carrying the appropriate digital certificates, associated cryptographic and attestation protocols and their own dedicated applications, the problems of establishing trust are no longer applicable. It was this learning that led us to develop our prototype Trust Extension Device (TED) that offers the ability to be "plugged into" any PC and utilise its connectivity back to the issuing enterprise and associated Privacy Certifying Authority.

Though the concept of TED as a personal trust device to provide portability and mobility of trust is valid for many enterprise applications, the current implementation described in this paper has some notable problems which are discussed as follows.

Isolation – it is difficult to achieve a complete isolation of the trusted applications from the untrusted applications running in the host machines due to the use of type II virtual machine. We have conducted a series of experiments and tested possible attacks. We found that it is possible to do keyboard loggers, screen scrapers and memory attacks in its current implementation. We also observed that we can overcome some of these attacks by deploying a simple mechanism such as virtual keyboard for keyboard loggers. Further research in the area will examine methods for obtaining complete isolation of the guest environment from the host environment without compromising its portability or mobility, as well as incorporating mechanisms to counteract standard attacks on Type II virtual machines such as keyboard loggers, screen scrapers and memory attacks.

Root of trust – it is difficult to establish a root of trust in our current implementation as it uses the software emulator and type II virtual machines. The root of trust can be established by using hardware implementation of TED and running all core applications within it. Further research in this area will examine the hardware implementation of TED and running trusted applications within TED.

Trusted I/O - the current implementation of TED relies on the devices on the untrusted host machine for input and output. These input and output devices are not isolated and hence subjected to attacks from other malicious codes. Further research in this area will examine providing a minimum level of input and output capability with TED. Towards this, we have already extended the TED and introduced a bio-metric TED (Bio-TED) with the ability of biometric input and digital display for out-of-band validation of transactional data. We are further investigating the use of the input and output device in Bio-TED for general purpose.

References

[NZKJ07] S. Nepal, J. Zic, G. Kraehenbuehl, and F. Jaccard. *A trusted system for sharing patient electronic records in autonomous distributed healthcare systems.* International Journal of Healthcare Information Systems and Informatics: 2(1):14-34, January-March, 2007

[NZJK06] S. Nepal, J. Zic, F. Jaccard and G. Krachenbuehl. *A Tag-based Data model for privacy-preserving medical applications.* In Proceedings of EDBT IIHA Workshop, Munich, Germany, 2006, pp. 77-88.

[NZKJ06] S. Nepal, J. Zic, G. Krachenbuehl and F. Jaccard. *Secure Sharing of Electronic Patient Records,* 1st European Conference on eHealth, 2006, Fribourg, Switzerland, October 12 – 13, 2006, pp. 47-58.

[JaNZ06] J. Jang, S. Nepal and J. Zic. *Establishing a Trust Relationship in Cooperative Information Systems.* Proceedings of Cooperative Information Systems (CoopIS), 2006, LNCS 4275, pp. 426-443

[NZHD07] S. Nepal, J. Zic, H. Hwang, D. Moreland. *Trust Extension Device: providing mobility and portability of trust in cooperative information systems.* Proceedings of Cooperative Information Systems (CoopIS), 2007, LNCS 4803. Vilamoura, Algarve, Portugal. 28-30 November 2007. Pp. 253-271.

[OKGG05] O'Keefe, C.M., Greenfield, P., and Goodchild, A. (2005) *A Decentralised Approach to Electronic Consent and Health Information Access Control.* Journal of Research and Practice in Information Technology, Vol. 37(2):161-178, May 2005.

[JaNZ08] J. Jang, S. Nepal, J. Zic. *Trusted Email Protocol: Dealing with Privacy Concerns from Malicious Email Intermediaries.* IEEE 8th International Conference on Computer and Information Technology CIT'2008: July 8-11, 2008, Sydney, Australia, to appear

[Perl05] Radia Perlman. The Ephemerizer: *Making Data Disappear.* Sun Microsystems Technical Report SMLI TR-2005-140 February 2005.

[TrouSF] TrouSerS FAQ http://trousers.sourceforge.net/faq.html

[TPMe] http://developer.berlios.de/projects/tpm-emulator/

[TrouSS] http://trousers.sourceforge.net/

[JTSSdo] http://trustedjava.sourceforge.net/jtss/javadoc/

[CeNTIE] www.centie.net/

[NeJZ07] S. Nepal, J. Jang and J. Zic. *Anitya: An Ephemeral Data Management Service and Secure Data Access Protocols for Dynamic Coalitions,* PDCAT 2007, pp. 219-226, 3-6 Dec 2007, Adelaide, Australia

[CNC+07] Shiping Chen, Surya Nepal, Jonathan Chan, David Moreland, John Zic: *Virtual Storage Services for Dynamic Collaborations.* WETICE 2007: 186-191

[QemuVM] http://bellard.org/qemu/ The QEMU Open Source Processor Emulator

New Directions for Hardware-assisted Trusted Computing Policies (Position Paper)

Sergey Bratus · Michael E. Locasto · Ashwin Ramaswamy
Sean W. Smith

Dartmouth College Hanover, New Hampshire, USA
sergey.bratus@dartmouth.edu, {locasto | sws}@cs.dartmouth.edu

Abstract

The basic technological building blocks of the TCG architecture seem to be stabilizing. As a result, we believe that the focus of the Trusted Computing (TC) discipline must naturally shift from the design and implementation of the hardware root of trust (and the subsequent trust chain) to the higher-level application policies. Such policies must build on these primitives to express new sets of security goals. We highlight the relationship between enforcing these types of policies and debugging, since both activities establish the link between expected and actual application behavior. We argue that this new class of policies better fits developers' mental models of expected application behaviors, and we suggest a hardware design direction for enabling the efficient interpretation of such policies.

1 Introduction

There exists an important design specification and engineering gap to fill before researchers and practitioners can flesh out and experiment with actual policies. Arguably, this gap represents the greatest current challenge facing TC as a discipline. The gap exists between the hardware elements of the TCG architecture and meaningful policy specifications (specifically, the type and structure of the event stream that such policies operate on). The engineering uncertainly created by this gap has served, in our opinion, as one of the factors that has stymied the development and acceptance[1] of TC platforms. The gap results from an under-specification; the presence of this uncertainty discourages development of higher layer solutions precisely because such solutions have nothing on which to rely.

We claim that the essence of this gap is expressed in the lack of a common specification for both the system of events that TC-based policies need to monitor as well as how the event handlers for such policy systems would cooperate with the basic TCG architecture elements (which are, by definition, passive, and should remain so[2]). To close or reduce this gap, we believe it might be advisable to revisit and enhance the parts of the TC hardware specification that deal with the post-boot life of TC applications.

The ultimate goal of Trusted Computing is to produce development platforms and environments for more trustworthy software. Notably, Trusted Computing promises to offer new kinds of security primi-

---

1 We refer to developer acceptance of TCG as a useful engineering platform rather than acceptance of TCG as a technology by the broader public. In the latter case, concerns over draconian DRM schemes and Big Brother present obstacles beyond the technical ones we address in this paper.
2 For the discussion of this requirement see [Pro05].

D. Gawrock, H. Reimer, A.-R. Sadeghi, C. Vishik (Editors): Future of Trust in Computing, Vieweg+Teubner (2009), 30-37

tives and trust policies. In contrast, other existing protection initiatives aim to harden software against known classes of exploits and thus to restore trust into existing development models and security primitives[3]. Consequently, an implicit requirement for TC's success is that the policies we discuss must be flexible and easy to write, adapt, and maintain. Indeed, the transition from the TCG architecture fundamentals to high-level policy primitives usable by programmers and administrators proves to be the core significant challenge we highlight.

This challenge has not gone unaddressed. For example, a substantial amount of effort has gone into making TC-based architectures more flexible and expressive, through use of virtualization, on-demand creation of trusted compartments, etc. [BCG+06, HCF04, SPvD05, SZJvD04]. The gist of this research is to transform the rather inflexible (but the only known effective) way of measuring software by hash digest into more flexible security policy primitives and frameworks. However, we recognize the fundamental problem as a much broader one, to which virtualization and compartmentalization are only partial solutions.

We point to [AAH+07] as an excellent example illustrating the problem of bridging the gap between low-level security primitives as provided by hardware and the OS and the desired application-level security properties such as decision continuity and attribute mutability. In this example, taken from the healthcare domain, Agreiter et al. highlight the importance of enforcing an access control policy throughout the lifetime of an application process and the ability to change its access privileges based on its observed behavior to date. Their policy implementation mechanism leverages the SELinux MAC to restrict privileged information access to the single process that interprets a dynamic model-based policy and grants or denies access to all other processes, acting, in effect, as a userland "reference monitor", and holding all the logic and state information needed to enforce a dynamic policy. We note the two general design aspects that will be highlighted in our later discussion: (1) reliance on an OS mediation mechanism[4] for the applications' trustworthiness-related access operations and (2) the placement of the policy logic and the corresponding applications state data.

Another example of dynamic runtime enforcement can be found in [BS05]. Again, the policy mechanism's design is driven by the analysis of system events that have the potential of changing the system's trustworthiness.

In this position paper we consider the problem of engineering security primitives and enforcement mechanisms from several unusual angles, and attempt to distill the qualities that are shared by primitives and mechanisms that proved successful and attracted a substantial following among developers.

In particular, we relate the well-known definition of trust in a computing system as relying on the system to behave as expected to the common and familiar developer experience of debugging software to link its expected behavior to its actual behavior.

We argue that developers' knowledge of their program's expected behaviors, and, more importantly, of behaviors that they trust to never occur while the system remains trustworthy, is a great and mostly untapped source of meaningful application policies. We believe that allowing developers to express this knowledge in policies will help close the above mentioned engineering gap.

We suggest that in order to tap into this resource, future additions to the TCG architecture should provide developers with ways to express policy conditions similar to those used by advanced debug-

---

3 For example, address space randomization and stack integrity protections do not prevent developers from accidentally creating buffer and heap overrun conditions. Instead, they just make these vulnerabilities much lower exploitation risks. Thus, the applications' own security checks (rendered useless by these classes of exploits) once again become relevant.
4 The Linux Security Modules (LSM) system that underlies SELinux's syscall hooks.

ging tools, such as DTrace and its extensions. These conditions, of course, will need to be efficiently monitored and enforced without ruining performance; we speculate on how an appropriate enforcement mechanism can be achieved with some extra hardware's help.

2 Policy Engineering

This issue of policy engineering presents a clear and non-trivial challenge to systems designers who aim to produce strong and usable security primitives for the use of application developers.

The discipline of software engineering has developed arguments explaining why some design and programming practices endure better than others. More importantly, software engineering has developed practices and tools to make it easier for programmers to produce, debug, analyze, and modify software aimed at non-trivial objectives.

By contrast, there is yet hardly any comparable analysis to explain why some proposed security primitives have much better adoption records than others, let alone tools capable of handling comparably complex behaviors. We attempted to present an instance of such analysis comparing SELinux and virtualization-based policy solutions [BFMS07]. We apply similar analysis [BDSS08] to address the TOCTOU problem in the TCG architecture.

We note that the challenge faced by proponents of novel software engineering primitives is the same as that facing designers of new security primitives: both require adoption by a wider community of developers who must find the proposed semantics natural and only a minor burden compared to developers' current practices.

In particular, we make the following historical observations with regard to security policy mechanisms. We regard them as fundamental to policy engineering, in much the same way as desirability of code reuse, encapsulation, polymorphism, etc., are fundamental observations that lead to maturation of the object-oriented programming paradigm in software engineering.

1. **Policy design is event-centric.** Defining a manageable set of events for the policy mechanism to monitor and control is crucial to engineering usable and effective policies, because it ultimately determines which security goals can and cannot be easily expressed in the policies.

2. **Context precision is critical to the processing of event streams.** The common trait of successful policy mechanisms is to limit the amount of information that needs to be processed at its event-based decision points to just that relevant to the security goal, and no other. Having to deal with too many pieces of information weighs heavily on developers, because, instead of additional flexibility, it likely translates to having to classify all the combinations of their values as either conforming to or contravening the policy goals, which is serves as a deterrent to adopting the policy mechanism in question.[5]

3. **A little semantic annotation goes a long way when supported by OS and hardware.** Significant practical advances in improving trustworthiness of software followed from a combination of a new lowerlevel security primitive (e.g., a new OS kernel system call or hardware trapping capability) and a small additional amount of code annotation by programmers. This annotation expressed some semantic securityrelated properties of resulting binary code or data objects (e.g., "after this point the process no longer needs these elevated privileges", or "this data is not supposed to change within the lifetime of this process" or even – on the ABI level – "this

---

5 SELinux's strict policies that require the system administrator to classify an ever-increasing amount of program's file accesses are an example of such quandary.

area of memory does not contain any executable code"), and was automatically translated to binary code or data representation by the compiler toolchain.

4. **Strength through cross-layer amalgamation.** The actual machine execution of the program's logical flow becomes a combination of hardcoded fast immutable logic performing the bulk of the necessary eventhandling tasks and of program code modified to seamlessly integrate with it. For example, with the introduction of virtual address translation this flow includes a sizeable component of logic performed inside the MMU. The use of x86 segmentation in the Linux kernel strengthening patches such as OpenWall and PaX provides another example. A novel, effective event system usually introduces an extra computational load on the system; however, most of it can be offset by conceptually simple hardware changes of manageable complexity.

We note that the TCG specification concentrates primarily on load-time static software measurements as a means of ensuring the trustworthiness of a process. Consequently, it needs to be complemented by a mechanism that intercepts and mediates such transitions in the running program's state that can render it untrustworthy.

We call such transitions trust events and note that, rather than being arbitrary asynchronous OS-level events or system calls, they should be defined for each application as changes in its state that the developer "trusts will not happen" when designing the logic that protects the applications most valuable and sensitive information, its "crown jewels". Such assumptions about the application's and environment's behavior may include pure userland events not mediated by the syscall mechanism, such as writes to or even reads from certain data objects.

It should also be noted that not all OS-level events necessarily have the same impact on the application's trustworthiness, and thus mediating them is not equally important for ensuring it. In other words, the concept of sensitive and trusted data for an application need not necessarily coincide with being accessed through the OS kernel. SELinux implicitly assumes the latter, and this implicit assumption (and the resulting need to describe all allowed accesses by an application in order to get any degree of protection), in our opinion, leads to severe usability issues.

Once the developer has formulated what constitutes trust events for his application, these events must be monitored and mediated cheaply and "inline". This brings us to the next crucial component of a policy mechanism: system traps.

3 Traps and Security

We next highlight the relationship between event trap semantics, the implementation of a trap system, and policy goal formulation and enforcement. At first glance, the connection between a trap system for a particular platform and the security properties of that platform may not seem obvious. They are, however, directly and intimately related.

We believe that it is natural to formulate security properties as those preserved across normal transitions in the system's state space, given that the system starts in a trustworthy state. Abnormal transitions should cause traps, after which the system's state may no longer be considered trustworthy or "secure." Accordingly, trap handlers contain much of a security system's functionality.

For security policies, events that correspond to the system's transitions between trusted states play a similar central role in the design and implementation of the policy mechanism. Namely, the policy mechanism is charged with allowing only "safe" transitions that preserve the desired security properties. While such mechanisms can be implemented purely in software, in practice they rely on hardware-supported traps whenever possible, to let application code execute at full speed between mediated events, and as to provide additional assurance of separation between the more and less trusted parts of the system. In practice, therefore, traps form a core mechanism upon which to implement security policy interpreters. As such, they directly or indirectly affect all aspects of the latter. The details of the trap system shapes, de facto, the capabilities and performance of the policy system.

3.1 Traps and Debugging

Informally speaking, the process of debugging an application has much in common with the process of enforcing a policy. Instead of "trustworthiness", a bug-hunter tries to ensure that the system behaves according to her mental model of what the code is supposed to do and catch the moment when it begins to deviate[6] from that model. That moment – more precisely, that event – is assumed to be the manifestation of the hunted bug.

Simply put, debugging is the activity that establishes the link between the expected application behavior and its actual behavior. But so is the enforcement of a security policy!

We believe that this connection has deep implications for future policy design. In our experience, many developers, despite having a reasonably good idea of what constitutes the "crown jewels" and the "worst nightmare" of their applications, and indeed expressing it in various ways throughout the debugging and testing process, cannot easily impart such knowledge to runtime environments. Yet, this knowledge would be eminently useful for a security policy intended to preserve the process' trustworthiness, even as an "80/20 percent solution" that counters only the more frequent threats.

Of course, the programmer's mental model of a program's intended behavior can be more complicated than that of its security properties. As a result, the set of events that the developer needs to monitor to debug the program can be harder to describe than the set of security-related events that require mediation. As a result, debugging likely needs much more flexible support than security policy enforcement. Yet, the available hardware support on commodity platforms remains in its infancy (to put it somewhat bluntly, in an equivalent of the Stone Age).

We believe that the continued lack of a flexible means to describe events relevant to debugging is caused by the absence of a more comprehensive set of hardware primitives. Although software systems can provide this rich set of primitives (Pin [LCM+05] is a good example), real production software constantly pushes the limits of computing speed, making the use of software– level debugging unattractive for such systems. Therefore, we believe that a flexible hardware trap system (one that allows execution to proceed at the highest possible CPU speeds until an event of interest occurs) is a necessary condition of increasing trustworthiness – and, therefore, security, of software.

3.2 Tracing and policy

We point to an interesting use of the OS's tracing functionality, meant primarily for debugging, to monitor security-related properties of an application process. Beauchamp et al. demonstrated[7] RE:Trace and RE:Dbg, extensions of DTrace, that allowed the user to express complex application logic conditions involving both user-level and kernel objects. Among other trustworthiness-related conditions, they were

---

6 We note that behaving as expected is one of the definitions of "trust." Thus a "bug" in the program, from the programmer's point of view, is exactly what breaks the trust.
7 See [BW08], also http://blog.poppopret.org/?m=200806 for the updated version of their results and presentation.

able to catch exploitation of vulnerabilities via stack and head overflows and suspend the compromised processes.

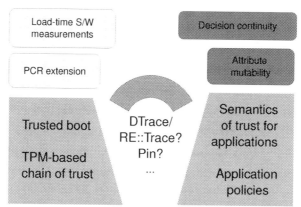

Figure 1: Bridging the Trust Policy Engineering Gap.
Since the requirements for dynamic, application-level trust assessments outstrip the available capabilities of standard TCG hardware, we propose debugging-like primitives to help reason about trust and store related state.

We note that DTrace itself can be a powerful tool for expressing auditing policies that enforce application logic-level conditions. In particular, a developer can use it to specify conditions that are trusted to never happen in the application's trustworthy state, and register the loss of trustworthiness should the respective probe "fire".

Of course, due to the fundamental architectural properties of DTrace, this approach would work only for auditing, since the probes are processed asynchronously, and cannot be used to mediate the respective trust events that triggered them (moreover, there are no specific guarantees as to how soon after the event a specific probe would fire). These properties of the DTrace architecture are quite deliberate and are due to performance considerations – they recognize the fact that full debugger-style mediation of a process, even in the OS kernel, cannot currently be fast enough to be compatible with acceptable performance expectations.

Still, we recognize the great potential of specifying policies on such higher level, which is also a much better match for developers' mental models of their applications' expected (and explicitly not expected) behaviors. Thus we propose to turn to hardware for help in enforcing such policies.

4 Proposed Hardware Features

Changing the way systems trap and service memory events requires both programmability and speed. In essence, we need an architecture that simultaneously allows more complex analysis and a faster overall (amortized) trap service speed. We propose an architecture that contains two primary components. First, an FPGA configured to act as a memory event stream parser interacts with the CPU and MMU to obtain a stream of memory events and a series of interrupts. Second, a memory event analysis policy is loaded into the memory of the FPGA to direct the actions of the FPGA. With the architecture in Figure 2, we hope to satisfy the twin demands of flexible analysis and better trap performance. We point to successful uses of FPGA implementations of application-aware policies to improve trustworthiness of special purpose applications [IKP+07].

The capabilities of FPGA logic enables the TC community to define a richer set of events and their contexts – contexts that previously could only be defined and handled by debuggers (e.g., watchpoints that "fire" only under particular circumstances or that depend on the state of the process context). While policy designers could express many security goals quite naturally as conditions for a tracing debugger to check, the overhead of doing so makes efficient policy enforcement entirely infeasible. The introduction of the FPGA, however, makes it possible to trace a limited set of such conditions efficiently, since the FPGA provides both the place to store necessary state information and fast logic to update and check such information.

5 Self-healing Perspective

We believe that one of the important considerations in designing the TCGcompatible event systems and policy mechanisms should be leaving room for self-healing. In production environments, security goals tend to compete with availability requirements in that security mechanisms can represent a negative impact on performance. Availability, however, is itself a cornerstone security requirement. In our opinion, it would be disadvantageous for TC to settle on policy mechanisms that exclude self-healing as a way of providing availability.

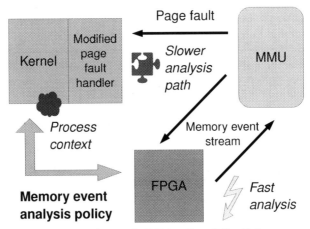

Figure 2: An Architecture for Efficient Trust Policy Enforcement.
We propose an architecture aimed at servicing most basic policy events at machine speed (rather than serviced by a software interrupt) by trapping and interpreting policy events within an FPGA.

6 Conclusion

We believe that the current capabilities of TCG infrastructure exhibits a gap between the needs of security policy writers and the existing TC hardware specification. We argue that specifying a system of events, trapped and monitored by a mechanism compatible with the fundamental passive elements of the TCG architecture is necessary for development of flexible and usable Trusted Computing policies.

Further, we point to the basic similarities between debugging, trust and policy enforcement. We argue that allowing developers to express their applications' trustworthiness assumptions in forms such as might be used for debugging with DTrace or Pin could become a useful source of dynamic policies, connecting expected behavior of a running applications and its trustworthiness. We note that the role and knowledge of a developer in achieving the latter is crucial, but to date has received little attention in the design of policy mechanisms.

Finally, we propose the use of FPGAs as a basic primitive to efficiently handle memory and process-related trust events that would play a central role in the proposed class of policies.

7 Acknowledgements

This work was supported in part by the National Science Foundation, under grant CNS-0524695, the U.S. Department of Homeland Security under Grant Award Number 2006-CS-001-000001, and the Institute for Security Technology Studies, under Grant number 2005-DD-BX-1091 awarded by the Bureau of Justice Assistance. The views and conclusions do not necessarily represent those of the sponsors.

References

[AAH+07] B. Agreiter, M. Alam, M. Hafner, J.-P. Seifert, and X. Zhang. Model Driven Configuration of Secure Operating Systems for Mobile Applications in Healthcare. In In Proceedings of the 1st International Workshop on Model-Based Trustworthy Health Information Systems, 2007.

[BCG+06] Stefan Berger, Ramon Caceres, Kenneth Goldman, Ronald Perez, Reiner Sailer, and Leendert van Doorn. vTPM – Virtualizing the Trusted Platform Module. In 15th Usenix Security Symposium, pages 305–320, 2006.

[BDSS08] Sergey Bratus, Nihal D'Cunha, Evan Sparks, and Sean Smith. TOCTOU, Traps, and Trusted Computing. In Proceedings of the TRUST 2008 Conference, March 2008. Villach, Austria.

[BFMS07] Sergey Bratus, Alex Ferguson, Doug McIlroy, and Sean Smith. Pastures: Towards Usable Security Policy Engineering. In ARES '07: Proceedings of the The Second International Conference on Availability, Reliability and Security, pages 1052–1059, Washington, DC, USA, 2007. IEEE Computer Society.

[BS05] Kwang-Hyun Baek and Sean W. Smith. Preventing theft of quality of service on open platforms. Technical Report TR2005-539, Dartmouth College, Computer Science, Hanover, NH, May 2005.

[BW08] Tiller Beauchamp and David Weston. DTrace: The Reverse Engineer's Unexpected Swiss Army Knife. Blackhat Europe, 2008.

[HCF04] V. Haldar, D. Chandra, and M. Franz. Semantic Remote Attestation: A Virtual Machine Directed Approach to Trusted Computing. In USENIX Virtual Machine Research and Technology Symposium, 2004.

[IKP+07] Ravishankar K. Iyer, Zbigniew Kalbarczyk, Karthik Pattabiraman, William Healey, Wen-Mei W. Hwu, Peter Klemperer, and Reza Farivar. Toward Application-Aware Security and Reliability. IEEE Security and Privacy, 5(1):57–62, 2007.

[LCM+05] Chi-Keung Luk, Robert Cohn, Robert Muth, Harish Patil, Artur Klauser, Geoff Lowney, Steven Wallace, Vijay Janapa Reddi, and Kim Hazelwood. Pin: Building Customized Program Analysis Tools with Dynamic Instrumentation. In Proceedings of Programming Language Design and Implementation (PLDI), June 2005.

[Pro05] G.J. Proudler. Concepts of Trusted Computing. In Chris Mitchell, editor, Trusted Computing, pages 11–27. IET, 2005.

[SPvD05] Elaine Shi, Adrian Perrig, and Leendert van Doorn. BIND: A Fine-Grained Attestation Service for Secure Distributed Systems. In IEEE Symposium on Security and Privacy, pages 154–168, 2005.

[SZJvD04] Reiner Sailer, Xiaolan Zhang, Trent Jaeger, and Leendert van Doorn. Design and Implementation of a TCG-based Integrity Measurement Architecture. In USENIX Security Symposium, pages 223–238, 2004.

Smart Cards and remote entrusting

Jean-Daniel Aussel · Jerome d'Annoville · Laurent Castillo
Stephane Durand · Thierry Fabre · Karen Lu · Asad Ali

Gemalto
Technology & Innovation
{jean-daniel.aussel | jerome.d-annoville | laurent.castillo}@gemalto.com

Abstract

Smart cards are widely used to provide security in end-to-end communication involving servers and a variety of terminals, including mobile handsets or payment terminals. Sometime, end-to-end server to smart card security is not applicable, and smart cards must communicate directly with an application executing on a terminal, like a personal computer, without communicating with a server. In this case, the smart card must somehow trust the terminal application before performing some secure operation it was designed for. This paper presents a novel method to remotely trust a terminal application from the smart card. For terminals such as personal computers, this method is based on an advanced secure device connected through the USB and consisting of a smart card bundled with flash memory. This device, or USB dongle, can be used in the context of remote untrusting to secure portable applications conveyed in the dongle flash memory. White-box cryptography is used to set the secure channel and a mechanism based on thumbprint is described to provide external authentication when session keys need to be renewed. Although not as secure as end-to-end server to smart card security, remote entrusting with smart cards is easy to deploy for mass-market applications and can provide a reasonable level of security.[1]

1 Introduction

Smart cards are tamper resistant devices conventionally used for securely storing keys and credentials and performing cryptographic operations. In a wide range of applications, smart cards are used to implement secure protocols with remote servers, in which secrets are shared between a remote server and the smart card. This is the case for example for mobile phone authentication, in which the smart card and server both share a set of secret keys for authenticating the user to the network.

In such end-to-end protocols, the server and smart cards are considered as trusted systems, whereas the host on which the card is connected is considered as un-trusted and acts merely as a gateway to the network. The host on which the smart card is inserted is generally referred as the terminal, and can be a personal computer, mobile phone, or point-of-sale terminal.

End-to-end protocols are used successfully for a wide range of applications such as end-user authentication or remote management of the content of the smart card. However, some classes of applications require that the smart card communicates with an application on the terminal without communicating with a server. Examples of such applications are a Voice-over-IP (VoIP) software client on the terminal that uses the smart card for user authentication, or digital signature software on the terminal that uses the smart card for signing documents. In this case, it is important that the smart card can trust the terminal application, to prevent malware to perform VoIP calls or digitally sign documents without the user consent and knowledge.

---

1 This work was supported in part by the European Commission (contract N° 021186-2 for the RE-TRUST project)

D. Gawrock, H. Reimer, A.-R. Sadeghi, C. Vishik (Editors): Future of Trust in Computing, Vieweg+Teubner (2009), 38-45

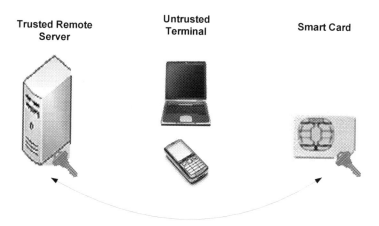

Trusted Remote Server **Untrusted Terminal** **Smart Card**

Figure 1: End-to-end security with smart cards and servers –
A secret is shared between the server and the smart card, and used to establish a secure channel. The terminal is un-trusted and is only a gateway for passing secure channel messages back and forth; the terminal does not share the secret and messages are opaque to the terminal.

The trusted platform module (TPM) is an attempt at solving the issue of trusting terminal applications. TPM typically manage keys and verify operating system components during startup to ensure that the terminal has not been tampered with. However, user credentials such as VoIP keys or public key infrastructure (PKI) keys are generally used by non-operating system components, and linked to the user identity rather than the terminal and operating system. TrustZone is an alternative technology, in which a security module is installed in the terminal to provide a security framework for applications. Both TrustZone and TPM require specific hardware and operating system support.

In this paper, we present how USB smart cards can be used to remotely entrust applications running on the terminal using white-box cryptography [WyseurB] and application monitoring, without requiring any specific security hardware, nor operating system modifications.

2 Remote Entrusting

In remote entrusting, an application is running on an un-trusted platform and sends requests to a trusted remote platform, typically a server [NagraJ,ScandariatoR]. The application execution is trusted with the collaboration of a local monitor embedded in the terminal, and of the trusted remote platform. The monitor logs local properties, such as tag sequences, memory thumbprints or execution time [CeccatoM]. The monitor logs are sent periodically to the remote trusted platform using a secure transmission protocol. The remote trusted platform analyzes the monitor logs, and track deviations from the expected logs. In case of tampering, the communication channel is closed and the service is stopped for the untrusted application.

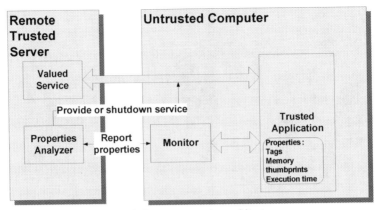

Figure 2: Remote entrusting architecture –

A remote trusted server is providing a valued service, such as an online game, to a trusted client application executing on an un-trusted terminal. In parallel, a monitor executing on the client is monitoring the client application and sending some properties to a remote control service, or properties analyzer. Upon tampering detection in the properties, the properties analyzer instructs the trusted server to stop the valued service operation.

The monitor is a critical component in the architecture because like the client application, the monitor is exposed to attacks. The monitor is typically protected against tampering using code replacement techniques. Generally, the monitor is merged with the client application, which implies that the security provided by remote entrusting requires application providers to modify the client application.

Remote entrusting assumes that the client application is a remote client of an application service executing remotely on the network, otherwise no coercive control can done remotely by the trusted platform. In some variations of remote entrusting, such as in Figure 3, the control service can be delegated locally to a local control service executing on the terminal on trusted hardware, such as a smart card.

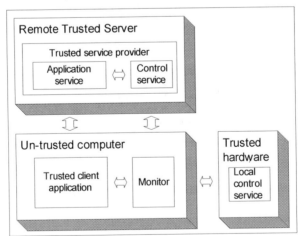

Figure 3: Remote entrusting using a local control service executing on a local trusted hardware, such as a smart card.

The monitor is sending monitored properties both to the remote control service, and to a local control service, which can disrupt the client application execution upon tampering detection.

The remote entrusting principle has been extended to trust terminal applications from a smart card, which acts as the remote trusting platform. Remote entrusting has been made possible by the recent evolutions of the smart cards.

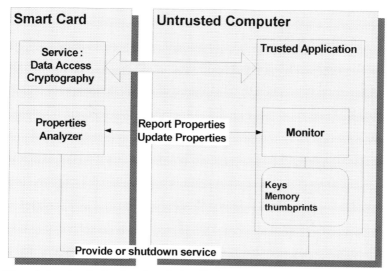

Figure 4: Smart card entrusting of terminal applications executing on an un-trusted terminal.

The smart card is providing some remote service to the terminal, such as cryptography (e.g. signing or ciphering) or data access (e.g. phonebook storage). The terminal trusted application embeds a monitor which reports execution properties to the properties analyzer executing on the smart card. Upon tampering detection from the properties, the properties analyzer executing on the smart card closes down the smart card services.

3 The USB Smart Card

Until recently, smart cards were devices communicating with the terminal thru a smart card reader using a half-duplex serial interface. The latest generation of smart cards communicates with the terminal using a high speed USB interface, which was developed to avoid the deployment of smart card readers, to improve the data transfer rate, and to provide new operating system interfaces in addition to the conventional smart card interfaces [AusselJD].

Because this new device is an extension of the classical smart card it is more appropriate to use another term like dongle or USB smart card to designate it.

Smart cards do not require any smart card readers on the PC terminal if they implement the Integrated Circuits Card Devices (ICCD) USB class standard, supported by most operating systems.

About the data transfer rates, the memory size of the smart cards increased of several orders of magnitude, from a few kilobytes to a few gigabytes, and high-speed USB allow fast data transfer that were not possible using the serial port communication.

Finally, the smart cards can now appear to the operating system as a mass-storage device (using the same interface as a memory stick, and appearing as a removable drive to the operating system), or as a network interface card using the USB Communication Device Class Ethernet Emulation Model (CDC-

EEM). With CDC-EEM, smart cards can be accessed by terminal application using TCP/IP protocols. Typically, a USB smart card can appear to the operating system as a mass-storage device (read/write memory stick or read-only CDROM or both), a smart card reader for legacy cryptographic applications, and remote TCP/IP system.

In the remote entrusting model the trusted platform both provides an application service and controls the integrity of the application. By taking advantage from the evolution of the smart card this integrity role is delegated to the card. With this design a monitor sends application properties to the local control service located on the smartcard that is able to check for the integrity of the code.

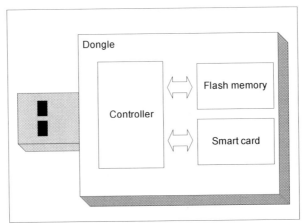

Figure 5: USB Dongle: an advanced smartcard

The dongle includes flash memory that will appear as removable drives to the operating system, and a conventional smart card. A controller is providing a mass-storage USB interface to the terminal, and managing communication between the terminal and the smart card and mass-storage

4 Levels of Trust

A first basic level of trust is implemented with the read-only mass-storage partition of the dongle, which acts as a protected storage, and appears as a CDROM to the operating system. Since all applications located on the CDROM partition of the dongle are read-only, it is not possible for malware to tamper with these applications persistently. However, malware can still modify these applications on the fly, e.g. at load time or at run time.

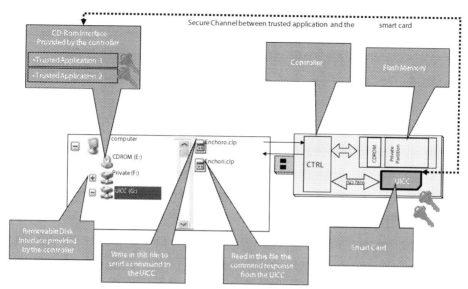

Figure 6: USB smart card dongle

The flash memory on the dongle is partitioned as a CDROM partition and a private removable drive partition. The smart card is a conventional smart card communicating with the controller using an ISO7816 serial port interface. The dongle is viewed as three partitions by the operating system: a CDROM partition E:, a private partition F: which is only visible when a personal identification number (PIN) is correctly entered on the smart card, and finally a communication drive G:. Applications are communicating with the smart card using two files, an input file enchori.clp and an output file enchoro.clp. Trusted applications are stored on the CDROM partition and embed a set of keys shared with the smart card.

4.1 White Box Cryptography

In addition, white-box cryptography is used to establish a secure channel between the trusted terminal application and the smart card, and exchanging application runtime data measured by the monitor.

Each trusted application is stored in the dongle mass-storage partition, and loaded in the terminal memory for execution. Upon dongle insertion in the terminal, an opaque area is created in the application data segment in which a set of obfuscated keys are generated. These keys act as master keys to generate session keys for establishing a secure channel with the card. The master keys are computed when the dongle is connected to the host, that is before any application located on the dongle can be run. The application and the smart card must share a common secret that will be used for authentication during this new session keys generation.

4.2 Thumbprints

For this purpose a set of thumbprints is kept in a table by the card. A thumbprint is a section of the code segment that is hashed. Because an attacker may find which section of the code is taken as input for the hash, several thumbprints are processed during the dongle initialization. The smart card keeps all thumbprints in a table together with the corresponding code segment offset and size.

According to a heuristic, the session keys have to be changed after a certain duration. Two equivalent keys set are computed both in the application and in the smart card. New session keys are derived from the master keys with a random value generated by the card and sent to the application.

Together with this random value, the card also sends both offset and size of a randomly selected thumb-print that will be used later for authentication.

The application first generates the new session keys. Then, it computes the thumbprint from the con-sidered code section and uses the new session keys to cipher the thumbprint and prepare a message. This new message is sent to the card that is able to check that the application has retrieved the right thumbprint and has computed the right keys. The communication between the application and the card is still secured by the current session keys. The new session keys replace the old keys upon successful thumbprint verification, first in the card and then in the actual application. This order is important to keep the coherence in case the user randomly and unexpectedly removes the card.

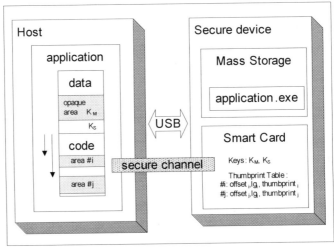

Figure 7: Thumbprint mechanism.

4.3 Block Size

Several options are available to select the number of blocks and the block size, leading to a compromise between higher security and performance. On one side, an option is to maximize the number of blocks. All the application code would be split in blocks of different size, and the corresponding hash values stored into the smart card. The size of the block is correlated with the security level, since the largest size is the whole code segment itself. But for performance reasons, it is not acceptable to hash the whole code segment at each session keys replacement. A compromise is to limit the number of blocks so that performance is not jeopardized.

5 Limitations

There are still many security issues to solve with this design. First, the thumbprint mechanism is not tamper proof. An attacker can maintain a copy of the initial code segment to be executed only for ses-sion keys replacement and then switch to a modified one.

Still, the main weakness is that the application is sensible to attack on the master key values, which breaks everything in case of success. Current research apparently tells us that there is no ideal white-box cryptography algorithm to hide these keys with a high security level. That means that a determined attacker theoretically could always retrieve key values. Lifetime of the keys could be shorten to minimize this risk but still a more effective protection must be found to prevent this attack. One advantage of the current implementation is that master keys are not persistent, and generated randomly at each smart card insertion. An attacker retrieving a master key would only compromise the current session for the current token.

Another possible attack is that at a certain time the master keys are stored in clear in the memory during the key replacement process and in case of hole of security in the application's code an attacker able to take control of the application could directly read the key values. Again there is no perfect protection except making applications more robust by raising the security limit high enough to discourage average attacker. At least when the key values are no more required, the memory buffer should be overridden with random data or other unrelated key values. Careful study of the generated code must be done to check that the optimizer does not remove the scrubbing code.

6 Conclusion

Remote entrusting with advanced smart cards allow to the execution of trusted applications on a terminal without requiring any specific hardware or operating system components. The level of trust is not as high as an end-to-end server to smart card connection, since it is based on white-box cryptography and is only as good as the key obfuscation algorithm. It is assumed that the user is not the attacker that is definitively a different context than the classical use of cards with a payment terminal. It enables however a better level of trust for mass-market applications such as voice-over-IP softphones or Internet authentication.

References

[WyseurB] B. Wyseur, W. Michiels, P. Gorissen and B. Preneel, "Cryptanalysis of White-Box DES Implementations with Arbitrary External Encodings", SAC 2007 - Workshop on Selected Areas of Cryptography, Ottawa, Canada, August 16-17, 2007.

[NagraJ] J. Nagra, M. Ceccato and P. Tonella, "Distributing Trust Verification to Increase Application Performance," PDP2008 - Euromicro Conference on Parallel, Distributed and Network-based, Toulouse, France, February 2008. In D. E. Baz, J. Bourgeois and F. Spies editors, Proc. of the 16th Euromicro Conference on Parallel, Distributed and Network-based Processing 2008, pages 604-610. IEEE Computer Society.

[ScandariatoR] R. Scandariato, Y. Ofek, P. Falcarin and M. Baldi, "Application-oriented trust in distributed computing". ARES 2008 - International Conference on Availability, Reliability and Security, Barcelona (Spain), March 2008.

[CeccatoM] M. Ceccato, Y. Ofek and P. Tonella, "Remote entrusting by run- time software authentication", SOFSEM 2008 - Conference on Current Trends in Theory and Practice of Computer Science,Tatras, Slovakia, January, 2008. In V. Geffert, J. Karhumaki, A. Bertoni, B. Preneel, P. Navrat, and M. Bielikova, editors, Proceedings of the 34th Conference on Current Trends in Theory and Practice of Computer Science (SOFSEM 2008), vol. 4910 of Lecture Notes in Computer Science, pages 83-97, Springer, 2008.

[AusselJD] J-D. Aussel, "Smart Cards and Digital Security," MMM-ACNS 2007 - International Conference Mathematical Methods, Models and Architectures for Computer Networks Security, St. Petersburg, Russia, September 13-15, 2007.

Session 3:
Designing for
the Future:
New Approaches

Future Threats to Future Trust

Herbert Bos[1] · Sotiris Ioannidis[2] · Erland Jonsson[3]
Engin Kirda[4] · Chris Kruegel[5]

[1]Vrije Universiteit Amsterdam
herbertb@cs.vu.nl

[2]FORTH-ICS
sotiris@ics.forth.gr

[3]Chalmers University
jonsson@chalmers.se

[4]Institut Eurecom
kirda@eurecom.fr

[5]TU Wien
chris@cs.ucsb.edu

Abstract

In April 2008, the European 'Forward' initiative organized an experts meeting in Göteborg to discuss future threats to ICT systems. This paper summarizes the conclusions of this meeting and their bearings on trust in future computing systems. In particular, it looks at critical infrastructure and large scale systems, fraud and malware in some detail.

1 The Forward workshops and threats on the net

Only a few years ago, big worms roamed the planet, spreading within hours, or even minutes, to every nook and cranny of the Internet. The damage caused by them was equally impressive; worms have taken out alarm phone centers, train signalling systems, thousands of cash machines, millions of production PCs and servers, and, oh yes, South Korea[1].

No wonder academics and industry scrambled to counter the threat. Indeed, fast spreading flash worms were all the rage among security experts and millions of euros were spent on projects to counter them. Alliances were formed, research grants applied for, projects started, prototype solutions developed, refined, and discarded. Unfortunately, by the time we developed practical counter measures, flash worms had all but disappeared. Instead, we now worry about stealth attacks, botnets, phishing sites, attacks on mobile phones, and whatever new threats emerged in recent years. The problem is that we tend to work on solutions for today's problems and have no time to worry about the threats of the future. The problem is that we are often caught unawares.

---

1 The country virtually dropped off the map as a result of the Slammer worm [BOU03]

D. Gawrock, H. Reimer, A.-R. Sadeghi, C. Vishik (Editors): Future of Trust in Computing, Vieweg+Teubner (2009), 49-54

This need not be the case and there are examples of threats that we saw coming before they hit us. A well-known example is RFID. An RFID tag is a small, extremely low-cost chip that can be used for purposes like identification and minimal processing. By adding RFID tags to everything, from pets to products, industry aims to use RFID technology to create the "Internet of Things". However, researchers have shown that tags can be used to propagate malware, which in turn has led a concerned industry to scrutinize security issues in RFID. All of this happened before any real attacks took place.

For this reason the Forward initiative intends to bring together experts to discuss future threats and develop realistic threat scenarios. As a first step in that direction, a workshop was organized in Göteborg, Sweden, in April 2008, to discuss future threats [FOR08]. The workshop consisted of broad plenary sessions interspersed with focused experts meetings. This paper summarizes the workshop's findings and their bearings on the future of trust. The remainder of this paper discusses the findings of the targeted expert meetings on critical infrastructure and large scale systems (Section 2), fraud (Section 3), and malware (Section 4). Concluding remarks are in Section 5.

2 Trust in critical and large-scale systems

The systems and networks that constitute critical infrastructure are often taken for granted. Many times people only realize their dependence on these services when there is a disruption. Yet, when such disruptions do happen, they may have serious, even dire consequences. Moreover, as witnessed by the Y2K issue in 1999, even the advertized presence of potential problems can be disruptive.

In the past, the systems and networks of the infrastructure were physically and logically independent and separate. They were not connected, and there was little or no interaction between them. With advances in technology, however, this has changed. In each sector, the systems have become automated and interlinked through computers and communication facilities. Furthermore, the trend shows an increase of both automation and linkage, not only within sectors but also between various sectors. Thus, we expect the future will aggravate the interdependencies between systems in general, and systems related to critical infrastructure in particular, leading to a complex "mesh of systems".

While increasing efficiency, interlinked capabilities also render the systems and networks more vulnerable. Not only have the possible vectors for a determined attack or simple harmful influence increased, also the detrimental effects of a service disruption in a single sector have significantly increased. What would have been an isolated incident in the past, can today cause extensive interruptions and/or failures in other sectors as well. In fact,the cascading effects might lead to a more or less global outage or malfunction, affecting systems and networks in even seemingly unrelated sectors. If such cascading effects cannot be contained, they will directly influence both the economy of society and the physical safety of its citizens. In certain cases, adding to the vulnerability of the system may be unacceptable, and we should question whether interlinking the system should be permitted at all.

As mentioned earlier, serious disruptions have already affected such infrastructures as train signalling systems, cash machines and phone systems. Intelligence services have indicated that targeted cyber attacks have caused power-outages in multiple cities in the past [CLA08].

Future vulnerabilities. Even in the absence of attacks, bugs have shown to have devastating effects on infrastructure. A disturbing example is what is known as the Northeast Blackout on August 14, 2003, which affected some 50 million people and caused approximately 6 billion dollars in financial losses [NER04]. The outage had a variety of knock-on effects, such as the break-down of much of the public transport. One of the major causes of the black-out was an unlikely race condition that occurred in the system that dealt with failures in the control system.

This brings us to an important conclusion of the experts meeting in Göteborg. By interconnecting more and more systems and adding more parallelism to individual systems (e.g., by multi-core processors) concurrency is entering all aspects of computing. As a result, the future of trust in computing increasingly hinges on our ability to deal with concurrency vulnerabilities that are extremely hard to find and difficult to trigger.

Another crucial factor is the human one. Members of the expert group shared that in their experience the disruption in interconnected networks is often not caused by a deliberate and malicious activity, but simply by human errors (e.g., router misconfiguration.)

Scale. Most of the challenges in this area are caused by the scale. What we need to deal with is (sets of) large software systems of huge complexity and sometimes heavily distributed. In addition, we have systems with huge numbers of mobile devices (phones, RFID). Problems in the area of large software systems include concurrency, authorization, and integration. In the area of "many devices," the issues revolve around authorization (if people have many devices at home, how do they secure those devices?), sensors that might be fooled, and management of these systems. For both areas, the expert meeting concluded that we must be able to cope with partially compromised systems.

Trusted computing in the form of TPMs is sometimes seen as a panacea for trust in distributed computing. While it is true that TPMs allow one to verify the configuration of remote machines, some inevitable problems come up when applying TPM to large systems. For instance:

- Yes, I can verify that some remote system runs the software that I intend to use, but how do I verify that my own machine is not compromised? The only way to do this is by means of yet another, more trustworthy, device (a mobile phone perhaps?), but how do we make sure that this is not compromised? Yet another, smaller, device? And how do we verify that? Where is the root of trust, and what happens if the dog eats it?

- What do we verify? Systems may run a huge amount of complex software and reliably checking the configuration of a large number of devices is exceedingly difficult. Moreover, as end-users cannot be expected to verify each and every system involved in an interaction with a distributed system, checking has to be delegated in a chain- or tree-like fashion. Any unnoticed compromised system in the hierarchy invalidates the trust in an entire branch of the tree. Worse, this would not be noticed.

- Even if we do notice it, because a remote attestation fails, what does it mean if a chain cannot be verified? Rebooting in a known clean state is often not a solution for mission-critical large scale systems. How can we continue operating when the trust is violated?

- Finally, not all devices are smart enough to be trusted. Phrased differently, they may not have a TPM today, and most likely will not have a TPM in five years time either. Examples include small embedded devices (say the category that sits between between mpeg players and RFID).

Trusting the network. A final conclusion is that the most critical infrastructure of all is the communication system to which the critical system as such is connected. In almost all situations, this is the Internet. A disruption in the network that mediates their interrelations might have more devastating effects than a successful attack on one of the connected systems by itself.

One important issue are threats to the Internet routing infrastructure. Internet routing (BGP) is vulnerable against attacks. In particular, false or spoofed BGP network announcements can be honored by parts of the Internet. This may result in DoS attacks against large parts of the network or hijacking of, for example, well-known web sites during the time the false information is valid.

Other problems arise from mistakes caused by (trusted) operators when configuring routers or entering routing information which could have similar effects on the Internet. Yet another type of problem are DDoS attacks against BGP routers, which may have the effect of making parts of the Internet temporarily inaccessible. A single router can also be attacked and its traffic sent via a tunnel (e.g., GRE) to a remote site that can then act as a man-in-the-middle for arbitrary domains and servers.

The problems arise from the fact that the current protocol, BGPv4, is 12 years old, and it was not designed with the current Internet in mind. Furthermore, BGPv4 is here to stay for a very long time, which means that threats are going to follow us in the near and long term future.

Even though solutions exist, everyone must start using them at the same time, something which is not likely to happen. Countering future threats would involve (i) motivating vendors to implement solutions, and (ii) somehow extending BGP in a backwards compatible way to make sure the new functionality is used.

More secure routing protocols exist (S-BGP, soBGP), and can be used to verify the origin and correctness of the received information. However, BGP signatures are problematic. The solution may be to move this to out-of-band systems, since all routers are CPU-limited. Also, Moore's law does not help router builders, since density and power remain as issues as more capacity is added. It seems that in the future, there will be no need to propose new routing protocols, unless they offer some really great properties, and as mentioned before, old threats will remain.

3   Fraud and the lack of trust

Online scams are a form of online fraudulent activity in which an attacker aims to steal a victim's sensitive information, such as an online banking password or a credit card number. Victims are tricked into providing such information by a combination of spoofing techniques, social engineering, and sometimes advanced exploitation methods.

According to the participants of the expert meeting on fraud, one of the main reasons why online fraud is increasingly gaining in popularity is because Internet-based attacks are difficult to trace back. Furthermore, fraud on the Internet is easy to perform as a high number of users exist that are technically unsophisticated and are still not highly familiar with the Internet technology. For example, the effort required to launch a physical attack against a bank is very high (e.g., breaking in, armed robbery, etc.) in comparison to hosting a phishing web site and waiting for victims to simply enter their sensitive information.

In addition, the meeting concluded that law enforcement agencies are either slow to react or do not have the necessary technical skills to identify the miscreants. With respect to traditional crime, crime on the Internet is much faster and typically more "international." That is, even if the attack takes place in Europe, the servers participating in the attack (e.g., phishing sites) might not necessarily be located in the same region. Hence, cross-border communications is often necessary, which is a time-consuming and tedious process. Miscreants responsible for the attacks are well-organized and know very well how law enforcement and the targeted organizations operate. For example, many attacks are now launched over the weekend because fewer experts are at work during this time (which in turn results in slower responses).

Trust among the good guys. One issue that was discussed in the fraud meeting was whether exchanging data would help mitigate fraud-related attacks. All participants in the expert group thought that this was a good idea and that it could actually help. For example, it is certainly interesting for banks to find out if there are similar attacks happening elsewhere and what solutions other organizations use. Also, organizations are interested in knowing if certain malware specifically targets them before the attack is largely seen in the wild.

However, it was not clear how such a data exchange should be performed. That is, while many organizations are certainly interested in getting information and data, they are less excited about giving away information as they have privacy as well as security concerns. It is clear that a common basis of trust needs to be created among organizations so that they are willing to share sensitive information.

Currently, some organizations (e.g., banks) are not even willing to talk about the problems they face as they are afraid that the information that they give out can be used against them in some way.

The underground economy. One interesting research challenge with respect to online fraud is to be able to understand how the underground Internet economy actually works. For example, if we were to start a botnet business, how would we actually go about and communicate with our "customers"? How would we sell our services and initiate money transfers? Hence, by understanding the way this new type of illegal economy functions, the participants of the fraud group believe that solutions could be created that actually undermine this economy and significantly increase the effort required by the miscreants.

4 Malware

Malicious code (or malware) is defined as code that fulfills the harmful intent of an attacker. Typical examples include viruses, worms, and spyware. One reason for the prevalence of malicious code on today's networks is the rising popularity of the Internet and the resulting increase in the number of available vulnerable machines because of security-unaware users. Another reason is the elevated sophistication of the malicious code itself.

Nature and form of malware. One issue raised in the experts meeting was about the behaviour of malicious code and their sources. Surprisingly, perhaps, the basic functionality of malware has not changed much. The samples that are observed today either steal sensitive information (key loggers, password thieves, Bank Trojans), send spam mails, or can be used to launch denial of service attacks.

The real development is in the way in which the malicious code is written. In addition to obfuscation to evade traditional, signature-based detection, malicious code increasingly tries to evade analysis. That is, by including code that detects virtual machine environments or debuggers, human or automated analysis is made more difficult. Thus, one finding of the meeting was that we expect a significant increase of novel techniques that stealthy, malicious code uses to resist analysis and thwart detection.

Threat landscape. Another question concerns the change in the threat landscape over the last years. There was agreement that most malware is actually coming from a (relatively) small number of criminal groups that have a well-funded development process and a pool of talented developers.These groups use those venues that can be most easily exploited to inject their code on end-user machines. For this, there is a strong trend towards social-engineering-based attacks (such as email) or browser-based exploits compared to exploiting network services. As a result, novel mechanisms for data collection are needed. For example, a traditional honeypot might not be efficient anymore to capture the current threats. This was confirmed by numbers from VirusTotal, which showed a discrepancy between the malware that they see compared to the samples that are collected via traditional honeypots. Moreover, the adversary might have developed techniques to fingerprint and detect honeypots so that they can avoid detection. Finally, mapping out dark (honeypot) address spaces is an emerging threat. As a result, the expert group saw the need to develop techniques that can accurately capture emerging threats, since a good intelligence is a prerequisite for subsequent mitigation efforts.

Related to the previous issue, the group also discussed emerging targets of malicious code. In particular, the question was raised whether mobile devices (phones, PDAs) might become a target. Everybody agreed that the threat has been hyped in the last few years. However, once there is a business model behind attacking phones (i.e., it turns out to be profitable for the criminals), such attacks can be expected to appear. Also, this development will be supported by the significant growth in the number of mobile devices.

5 Concluding remarks

The expert meetings in Göteborg serve as a starting point for developing a research agenda to deal with future threats. Within the FORWARD project the conclusions of the workshop are used to establish working groups, each of which work towards in-depth analysis of a subdomain. So far, the following working groups have been created: (WG1) Smart Environments, (WG2) Malware and Fraud, and (WG3) Critical Systems. Besides analysis in the broad sense, working groups will develop specific threat scenarios in which future threats are worked out in detail. The threat scenarios will be consolidated and worked into a white book.

6 Acknowledgements

FORWARD is sponsored by the European Community's 7th Framework Programme (FP7/2007-2013) under grant agreement no 216331.

References

[FOR08]   The 1st FORWARD workshop, Göteborg, Sweden, April, 2008. http://www.ict-forward.eu/workshop/.

[BOU03]   P. Boutin. Slammed! an inside view of the worm that crashed the internet in 15 minutes. Wired!, 11(07), July 2003.

[CLA08]   T. Claburn. CIA admits cyberattacks blacked out cities. InformationWeek, January 2008.

[NER04]   NERC. Technical analysis of the august 14, 2003, blackout:What happened, why, and what did we learn? Technical report, North American Electric Reliability Council, Princeton, New Jersey, July 2004.

Trusted ⇐ Trustworthy ⇐ Proof Position Paper

Gernot Heiser

Open Kernel Labs and NICTA and University of New South Wales
Sydney, Australia
gernot@nicta.com.au

Abstract

Trusted computing is important, but we argue that it remains an illusion as long as the underlying trusted computing base (TCB) is not trustworthy. We observe that present approaches to trusted computing do not really address this issue, but are trusting TCBs which have not been shown to deserve this trust. We argue that only mathematical proof can ensure the trustworthiness of the TCB. In short: trust requires trustworthiness, which in turn requires proof. We also show that this is achievable.

1 The Security Challenge

There can be little doubt that security, safety and reliability issues in computer systems are becoming increasingly important, even outside the traditional domain of national security uses. One of the reasons is that computer systems, especially embedded systems, are increasingly used in mission-critical, even life-critical scenarios.

Examples where lives are at stake are aeroplanes, cars and medical devices. System reliability and safety are paramount there, and significant effort is generally invested into ensuring this, including certification requirements that focus on software processes and in some cases a degree of formal-method use.

Other devices are treated in a far more nonchalant fashion, yet security violations can have quite significant consequences. Baseband processing in mobile-phone handsets requires approval by certification authorities. Yet, the complete baseband stack may contain millions of lines of code (LOC), and typically all that code executes at the same privilege level in a single, flat address space without memory protection.

A million LOC can safely be assumed to have hundreds (more likely thousands) of bugs, and no-one can seriously expect that the certification process has any significant impact on that amount of defects. Given the programming model, any single bug can, in the worst case, arbitrarily subvert the software. In the case of the phone handset, this could mean jamming the network. If the bug can be triggered externally (or from the user-interface part of the handset software), a distributed denial-of-service attack on the network becomes conceivable, which could within minutes force down the cellular network country-wide. Recovery from such an attack would be very expensive and time consuming.

D. Gawrock, H. Reimer, A.-R. Sadeghi, C. Vishik (Editors): Future of Trust in Computing, Vieweg+Teubner (2009), 55-59

Table 1: Evaluation methods used at the different CC evaluation levels.

Evaluation Level	Requirements	Functional Specification	High-Level Design	Low-Level Design	Implementation
EAL1	Informal	Informal	Informal	Informal	Informal
EAL2	Informal	Informal	Informal	Informal	Informal
EAL3	Informal	Informal	Informal	Informal	Informal
EAL4	Informal	Informal	Informal	Informal	Informal
EAL5	Formal	Semiformal	Semiformal	Informal	Informal
EAL6	Formal	Semiformal	Semiformal	Semiformal	Informal
EAL7	Formal	Formal	Formal	Semiformal	Informal
Trustworthy	Formal	Formal	Formal	Formal	Formal

If this is not disconcerting enough, there are more security issues associated with phone terminals. They are increasingly used to store and access highly-sensitive data and services. Smartphones are used to access the enterprise computing system of the owner's employer, and compromising the device could compromise the corporate IT system. Phones are used for financial transactions (presently mostly small, but there is a tendency to turn them into more full-blown banking terminals), and phones increasingly store sensitive personal information. This implies an increasing reliance on the (even bigger and even less scrutinised) user-interface software stack on the handset. The potential for corporate or personal financial damage and identity theft is clearly mounting.

2 Trust and Trustworthiness

Obviously, as a society we are putting an increasing amount of *trust* in computing systems. Hence, trusted computing is highly relevant for the main stream, not just for specialised "highly secure" systems.

Yet, by and large, the computing systems we routinely trust are far from being *trustworthy* in any real sense. In general they massively violate fundamental security principles, especially the *principle of least authority* (POLA) – their *trusted computing base* (TCB) is far too large. In particular, the operating systems are large (hundreds of kLOC) complex, buggy and impossible to get defect free.

Trusted computing without a trustworthy TCB is a phantasy.

Initiatives such as the TCG's trusted platform module aim at providing a *trust anchor*, which enable secure boot and secure execution of trusted code. This is a (necessary) start, but it does not solve the fundamental problem of the lacking trustworthiness of the TCB.

Having observed the sorry state of the vast majority of systems that are (like it or not) *trusted* to perform security-or safety-critical operations, we would hope that at least our national security is in good hands.

In fact, in the defence sector we can observe that serious attempts are made to establish the trustworthiness of the system (or at least its TCB). Systems used in defence generally require certification under higher evaluation levels of the Common Criteria [ISO99], which appears a very stringent requirement. But is this really true?

First we note that no operating system kernel (always a critical part of the TCB) has been certified at an evaluation level of more than EAL5 (although it seems that at Green Hills Integrity is close to EAL6 certification) [NSA]. The highest level of Common Criteria (CC) evaluation is EAL7, and that has definitely not yet been reached. Hence, even systems used in the most sensitive defence applications are not considered trustworthy at the highest certification level.

Things become even more worrisome if we look at what CC certification really means. For the purpose of security evaluation, the CC distinguish between the *security requirements* of a system, its *functional specification*, its *high-level design*, its *low-level design*, and its *implementation*. The higher evaluation levels (EAL5 and higher) require formal descriptions of the security requirements, as shown in Table 1. However, only a semi-formal representation of the functional specification and the high-level design is required, with a semi-formal argumentation that they meet the formal security requirements. At EAL6, a semi-formal low-level design is also required.

Only at the (so far unachieved) EAL7 do CC require formal functional specification and high-level design, and formal proofs of their correspondence. The requirement for the lowlevel design and its correspondence to the high-level design is only semi-formal. *No formal reasoning whatsoever is required for assessing the actual implementation!* Instead, informal arguments of correspondence between design and implementation are used, and in the end, the CC rely on software processes and testing.

But, as Dijkstra famously remarked, testing can only show the presence, not the absence of bugs. It may therefore not be overly surprising (but is nevertheless scary) that the CEO of a leading vendor of operating systems for military use seems to believe in security by obscurity [O'Dowd08].

> Real trustworthiness cannot be achieved by testing or stringent
> software processes. Trustworthiness requires proof – mathematical
> proof is the only way to gain certainty.

This is our core assertion on the future of trust in computing: we need to enable trusted computing in a real sense, which means that we need real trustworthiness at least in our TCBs. *This can only be achieved by proof.*

And TCBs proved (rather than hand-waved) to be trustworthy are needed just about everywhere, not just in defence. It is needed in everyday devices, such as cars and mobile phones.

3 Requirements

We need to understand what is needed to achieve this level of trustworthiness.

The effort required to build and prove a trustworthy TCB is obviously high, and it must be possible to re-use the results of that effort. This implies that a *general-purpose base* is required on which arbitrary systems can be built, whether for defence use or for commodity articles like mobile phones.

That base must be completely formally verified, providing a complete proof chain from requirements to implementation, as shown in the bottom row of Table 1. The MILS approach [Alves-Foss06] can then be used to build trustworthy systems on top. But we need to keep in mind that *MILS without complete formal verification of the kernel is a fortress built on sand.*

The generality requirement has an important implication: the base must be performant and support the development of well-performing systems on top. This is because it must support systems with tight energy budgets, as many mobile devices are battery powered. Since battery capacity is improving only slowly, the performance requirement will not go away in the foreseeable future. This means that there is very limited freedom to make the security-vs-performance trade offs which are prominent in security-oriented systems available today.

4 Can it be Achieved?

We claim that such a trustworthy base is possible, and the existence proof of such a system is almost complete. It is the essence of a project conducted at NICTA since the beginning of 2004. The project has developed a new operating-system microkernel called *seL4*. seL4 has been formally specified in Isabelle/HOL [Nipkow02], and its performance is at par with implementations of the L4 microkernel, which since more than ten years is the performance benchmark for small kernels [Liedtke97].

Formal, machine-checked proofs have been developed which show that seL4 can satisfy strict isolation requirements [Elkaduwe07]. These proofs do not yet cover a complete set of requirements, such as the CC Separation Kernel Protection Profile [IAD07], but this is now only a matter of time.

seL4 has formal high-level and low-level designs, the latter being a formalisation (in Isabelle/HOL) of an executable specification written in the Haskell programming language. Thanks to its executable nature, the low-level design can simulate the actual implementation and can therefore be used to port and test higher-level software components.

A formal proof of the correspondence between functional specification, high-level design and low-level design has been completed [Cock08]. As such, seL4 goes already well beyond the CC requirements even at EAL7, and it is already the most formally analysed general-purpose operating-system kernel in history.

The final step, the formal proof of the correspondence between low-level design and implementation, is in progress. A formalisation of the implementation (in Isabelle/HOL) exists, and the correspondence proof is to be completed in early 2009. This will result in the first OS kernel that can really support trusted computing.

5 Cost

While it a demonstration that full verification of a high-performance general-purpose OS kernel seems a worthwhile achievement, the issue of cost cannot be ignored. Verification is likely to remain irrelevant if it is unreasonable expensive.

The NICTA project provides a good data point for cost as well. We estimate that by the end of the project (March 2009), the project will have cost around $4–5M. We estimate that on the back of the first project, taking another 10kLOC kernel through full verification will cost no more than $2M. This is to be compared to the industry estimate of $10k/LOC just for CC EAL6 certification, or $100M for 10 10kLOC microkernel! That cost is dominated by the extensive documentation that needs to be created and maintained for CC evaluation, and which is basically irrelevant if the code is formally verified.

In other words, formal verification can be one to two orders of magnitude less expensive than traditional assurance schemes! This experience clearly shows that extending CC by another evaluation level or two, leading up to complete verification, cannot be the right approach. Formal verification must be the basis of an alternative assurance scheme which strips away the need for expensive processes which are irrelevant if the implementation is proved to satisfy its requirements.

6 Conclusions

We observed that the security and safety challenges facing modern computing systems are massive, yet poorly addressed to date. Security assurance even for the the most sensitive military systems is woefully insufficient, and cannot deliver true trustworthiness.

We claim that real trustworthiness is not only required, it is actually *achievable* and cost-effective, and seL4 is a case in point. Real trustworthiness will, in our view, become a central piece of trusted computing.

References

[Alves-Foss06] Alves-Foss, Jim; Oman, Paul W.; Taylor, Carol; Harrison, Scott: The MILS architecture for high-assurance embedded systems. In International Journal on Embedded Systems, 2:239247, 2006.

[Cock08] Cock, David; Klein, Gerwin; Sewell, Thomas: Secure microkernels, state monads and scalable refinement. In Otmane Ait Mohamed, Cesar Munoz and Sofiène Tahar, editors, Proceedings of the 21st International Conference on Theorem Proving in Higher Order Logics (TPHOLs'08), volume 5170 of Lecture Notes in Computer Science. Springer, 2008.

[Elkaduwe07] Elkaduwe, Dhammika; Klein, Gerwin; Elphinstone, Kevin: Verified protection model of the seL4 microkernel. Technical report, NICTA, October 2007. Available from http://ertos.nicta.com.au/publications/papers/Elkaduwe_GE_07.pdf.

[IAD07] US Information Assurance Directorate: U.S. Government Protection Profile for Separation Kernels in Environments Requiring High Robustness, June 2007. Version 1.03. http://www.niap-ccevs.org/cc-scheme/pp/pp.cfm/id/pp_skpp_hr_v1.03/.

[ISO99] International Standards Organization: Common Criteria for IT Security Evaluation, 1999. ISO Standard 15408. http://csrc.nist.gov/cc/.

[Liedtke97] Liedtke, Jochen; Elphinstone, Kevin; Schönberg, Sebastian; H¨artig, Herrman; Heiser, Gernot; Islam, Nayeem; Jaeger, Trent: Achieved IPC performance (still the foundation for extensibility). In Proceedings of the 6th Workshop on Hot Topics in Operating Systems, pages 28–31, Cape Cod, MA, USA, May 1997.

[Nipkow02] Nipkow, Tobias; Paulson, Lawrence; Wenzel, Markus: Isabelle/HOL–a proof assistant for higher-order logic. In Volume 2283 of LNCS. Springer, 2002.

[NSA] National Security Agency: The Common Criteria evaluation and validation scheme. http://www.niap-ccevs.org/cc-scheme/in evaluation/. Accessed May 2008.

[O'Dowd08] O'Dowd, Dan: Linux security controversy. http://www.ghs.com/linux/unfit.html. Accessed May 2008.

An ongoing Game of Tetris: Integrating Trusted Computing in Java, block-by-block

Ronald Toegl · Martin Pirker

Institute for Applied Information Processing
and Communications (IAIK),
Graz University of Technology,
Inffeldgasse 16a, A–8010 Graz, Austria
{rtoegl | mpirker}@iaik.tugraz.at

Abstract

Trusted Computing is a promising approach to improve the security of computer systems. However, current releases of the Java platform do not provide support to utilize the Trusted Platform Module (TPM). This paper presents several building-blocks that lead to the integration of TC into Java. It outlines the issues that arise with multiple TPM-virtualizations in the context of managed environments. Further, it summarizes the design and implementation of Java TC-libraries that support the major operating systems on TPM-enabled platforms, while still considering alternative architectures. The final aspect covered is the ongoing standardization process of a future Trusted Computing API for Java.

1 Introduction

The concept of Trusted Computing (TC) promises an approach to improve the security of computer systems. The core functionality, based on a hardware component known as Trusted Platform Module (TPM), is being integrated into commonly available hardware. Still, only limited software support components exist.

A major share of the software market is utilizing the platform-independent Java™ environment. The Java language provides inherent security features such as type-safety and bounds checking. The runtime environment provides for automated memory management, access control checks and bytecode verification. Performance concerns of Java applications can be mitigated through using just-in-time compilation of Java bytecode. Furthermore, a rich set of libraries covers communication and cryptography. This integrated security by design makes the managed Java environment a natural choice as basis for a Trusted Computing Platform. While the current releases of Java do not provide support to access the TPM by default, there are already multiple usecases demonstrated for TC-enabled Java Applications [DPV+08], [SvDO+06], [VTPW08], [YYE+05].

This paper discusses the integration of TC into the Java platform. Additionally, we reflect on the issues that arise on utilizing multiple parallel TC-aware managed environments (such as Java). We also discuss the associated concept of multiple TPM-virtualizations. It summarizes our implementation efforts on the major TPM-enabled operating systems and platforms, while still considering alternative architectures. Further, experience suggests that the integration of a new concept into a platform is not limited to the provision of software libraries. Hence, this paper also outlines the ongoing standardization process of a future Trusted Computing API for Java.

Figure 1 illustrates those building-blocks of the possible architectures which allow TC integration in Java. This paper is organized as follows: Issues involving basic virtualization and operating system functionality are discussed in section 2.1. The system services and APIs of the TCG are presented in section 2.2. In section 2.3 a discussion of Java libraries, including our jTSS and jTSS Wrapper implementations is provided. The paper continues with an outlook to the upcoming standard Trusted Computing API for Java in 2.4. It concludes in section 3.

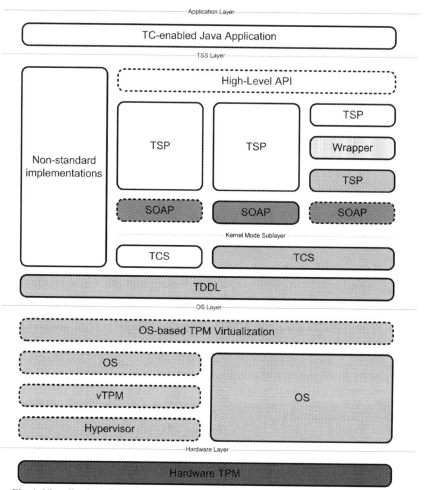

Fig. 1: Virtualization of the TPM may occur at multiple layers of the software stack for Java applications. This causes different requirements for software that provides TPM access, resulting in specific layered architectures. Still, an uniform API should be available on top.

Legend: Hardware is dark gray, native code is light gray and Java code is white. The platform independent SOAP interface is gray. Optional components have dashed lines.

2 The Pieces of the Game

2.1 Hardware and Virtualization

The Trusted Computing Group (TCG) [Trua] has specified the Trusted Platform Module. Much like a smart card it features cryptographic primitives, but is physically bound to the platform. A tamper hardened casing contains low-level functional units for asymmetric key cryptography, key generation, cryptographic hashing and random number generation. With the help of these components and special workflows a TPM is able to enforce strict polices on secret keys to protect them from (remote) attackers. The hardware resources of a TPM are manufacturer implementation specific and typically very limited. For instance, the TPM supplies only a few cryptographic key slots and thus must continually swap keys during operation to and from external storage. It also provides for additional high-level functionality consisting of protected non-volatile storage, integrity collection and reporting (attestation), binding of data to a device or a state (sealing), time stamping and identity management. The state of a system can be evaluated with help of the PCR registers, using the extend operation. A TPM receives measurements x from system software and hashes the input to the PCR with index i and content PCR_i^t with the operation

$$PCR_i^{t+1} = SHA - 1(PCR_i^t \parallel x).$$

For later analysis of the aggregated information, a Stored Measurement Log (SML) must be kept by the system software.

Thus, the current TPM design establishes the need for a singleton system software component that authoritatively manages the TPM device resources and arbitrates concurrent accesses from multiple clients. In our experience, this need is in direct conflict with modern virtualized computer architectures where direct access to hardware is limited.

Virtualization is a methodology of dividing the resources of a computer into multiple execution environments, by applying concepts such as hardware and software partitioning, time-sharing, machine simulation or emulation. Employing virtualization, several operating systems are enabled to share the resources of a single hardware at the same time. A single hypervisor runs directly on the hardware, which it manages exclusively. It then provides a virtualization of it to each operating system. Among the TC aware platforms demonstrated are [GPC+03] and EMSCB[1] . Figure 2 shows a concept sketch of such a virtualization setup.

Virtualized Trusted Computing applications are for instance demonstrated in the OpenTC architecture [KLR+06]. There, based on a choice of the Xen [BDF+03] virtual machine monitor or the Fiasco/L4 [Hoh98] μ-kernel, it allows the creation, execution and hibernation of isolated compartments[2], each executing an unmodified guest OS.

Without explicit TPM virtualization, only one compartment can access the TPM at any given time. Of course, such a limitation is undesirable as it restricts the ability to provide trusted applications. One possible solution is to let the hypervisor provide a separate virtual TPM (vTPM) [BCG+06] for each compartment. A major challenge is to implement these software devices in such a way that they extend the hardware-guaranteed trust of the TPM. [SBHE07] and [BCP+08] propose mechanisms to do so.

---

1 http://www.emscb.com

2 Note that such hardware-emulating compartments are often called "Virtual Machines". In this paper we use the term exclusively for the language-based Java Virtual Machine.

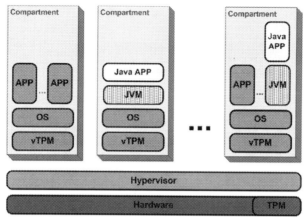

Fig. 2: On a virtualized platform, different operating systems share the same hardware, including the TPM. Within each such a compartment, the Operating System may allow multiple applications to access it. One such application is the Java Virtual Machine (JVM). Legend: Hardware is dark gray, native code is gray and Java code is white.

Even if an operating system is not virtualized, it is still desireable to allow several applications concurrent TPM access within a single instance of an OS. An example of this OS-based Virtualization are the TPM Base Services (TBS) [Mic07] in Windows Vista. As an extension, [EL08] propose TPM paravirtualization where the OS is aware of being virtualized. It is then able to manage e.g. PCR access accordingly in cooperation with the hypervisor.

Currently not all operating systems virtualize the TPM. I.e. in Linux, only a single application with root privileges may access and manage the TPM. In most cases this is a system wide TSS daemon.

2.2 The TCG Software Stack

This section describes an architecture that implements TPM access and management, the TCG Software Stack (TSS) [Trub]. It targets C-based systems and applications and does not consider the requirements of virtualized or managed environments.

The Trusted Device Driver Library (TDDL) abstracts the low-level hardware details into a platform independent interface that takes commands and returns responses as bytestreams. Generic TPM 1.2 drivers are integrated in recent OS releases.

Resource management is implemented in the Trusted Core Services (TCS), which run as a singleton system service. Additional functionalities provided by the TCS are persistent storage of keys, TPM command generation and communication mechanisms. The TCS event manager handles a log file which records PCR extend operations. The upper layers of the software stack may access the TCS in two ways. The first way, intended for development and testing, is a flat C interface that can be accessed directly. An alternative second option is a platform-independent Simple Object Access Protocol (SOAP) interface. It defines a network protocol that manages multiple requests, ensuring proper synchronization. Thus, if the TCS implement SOAP, TPM virtualization at the level of a system service can be provided to applications [CYC+08]. Furthermore, in the case of SOAP based communication client applications do not require root privileges to access with the TPM hardware, but only access to the network protocol stack to communicate with the TCS.

Applications can access Trusted Computing functionality by using the Trusted Service Provider (TSP) interface. It provides a TCG standardized flat C-style interface. A Context object serves as entry point to all other functionality such as policy and key handling, data hashing, encryption or PCR composition. In addition, mechanism for command authorization and validation are provided. Each application dynamically uses a shared library instance of the TSP interface.

The TSS was also designed to allow partial integration in existing high-level APIs libraries, such as PKCS#11 [RSA04] or as Cryptographic Service Provider (CSP) in Microsoft CAPI. This enables the use of the cryptographic primitives provided by the TPM. A limitation of this approach is that these legacy cryptographic APIs do not account for high-level TC concepts such as Sealing.

2.3 Java Libraries and Services for TC

The Java Virtual Machine (JVM) appears as just another user mode application to the OS, but provides an abstraction of the underlying (hardware) platform to Java applications. Applications may not access the TPM hardware device directly. Instead, they require support in the form of libraries, which bridge the gap between the JVM and the specific operating system TC support components, while maintaining a degree of platform independence. A main challenge arises from the complex architecture that occurs in modern Trusted Computing Platforms. Depending on the surrounding environment, a Java library will have to accommodate for different levels of hardware access and to handle different management tasks.

From the preliminaries detailed in sections 2.1 and 2.2 we derive four scenarios:

1. In the case of a non-virtualized environment, the JVM may access and manage the hardware TPM exclusively. As a consequence, all other system and application accesses are blocked. This is sufficient for testing and development purposes, but not suitable for wide deployments.

2. In the case of a non-virtualized environment, where exclusive access to the hardware TPM cannot be guaranteed, the Java environment needs to integrate with existing TPM services, such as a TSS. This system component will handle all TPM accesses.

3. With OS-based TPM virtualization, all applications are given multiplexed and equal access to the TPM. Thus, a Java library may freely access its TPM device instance from within the JVM.

4. As a special case with hypervisor based virtualization, an instance of the JVM may be the only application within a compartment. In this case, different services will not interfere with each other and a Java library can handle its vTPM exclusively.

To enable these scenarios, we have developed two implementations. In scenario two, integration in existing system services is needed for non-blocking TPM access, specifically in Linux. The jTSS Wrapper software package accomplishes this. A thin C-backend integrates the TSP system library. In our implementation we interface with the open source TrouSerS [IBM08] package. The Java Native Interface (JNI) maps the functions of the C based TSP into a Java frontend. There, several aspects of the underlying library, such as memory management, the conversion of error codes to exceptions and data types abstractions. Unfortunately, this wrapping approach results in complex component interactions. For instance debugging across language barriers is a challenging task. Another drawback is that implementation errors in the C-based components may seriously affect JVM stability.

For scenarios one, three and four, a less complex architecture can be used. The jTSS effort closely follows the specification as proposed by the TCG, but implements everything in pure Java. TPM implementations from different vendors and different operating systems (currently Windows Vista and Linux) are supported, demonstrating platform independence. Our Java TCS also synchronizes access from multiple Java applications, where applicable. Such a full Java TSS implementation clearly reduces the number of involved components and dependencies. Consequently, this approach results in less side-effects from incompatible TSS implementations or different interpretations of the TSS specification.

The top-level interface available to application developers is the same in all scenarios, irrespective of the underlying implementation. It defines data types, exceptions and abstract methods – we refer to it as the jTSS API. It closely follows the original TSS C interface and permits to stay close to the originally intended command flows and provides the complete feature set of the underlying library.

Unlike other implementations which do not follow the TCG's split architecture, such as [SRM07], only the TCS need to run as system service. Thus, Java applications may access the TPM via the SOAP interface without root privileges.

A promising alternative approach could involve a hybrid stack with a Java TSP interfacing to a native TCS via SOAP. However, no such SOAP-enabled, C-based stack is openly available yet.

2.4 A Future Trusted Computing API for Java

The original TSP interface closely reflects the detailed hardware command set of the TPM, providing a large set of functions. As a consequence, the resulting API is highly complex. Its adoption by actual applications has been slow [SST08]. Also, it is targeted at C developers, so that a direct mapping into Java results in a non-intuitive API.

We propose that a modern, high-level API for Trusted Computing should go beyond this and provide

- integration in existing cryptographic infrastructures,
- extensive support for the key management capabilities of the TPM and
- easy to use interfaces to high-level TC concepts.

Building on the scenarios and architectures described in section 2.3, such a high-level API can be implemented on top of basic library implementations. Thus it is able to abstract the details and focus on providing complex Trusted Computing mechanisms in a compact way.

We have initiated the standardization [Toe08] of such a modern Trusted Computing API for Java in the Java Community Process (JCP)[3], a program to incubate new industry standards while at the same time ensuring compatibility with Java technology. It is controlled by the Executive Committee, an elected body, representing most major players in the Java industry. The JCP consists of four phases.

1. Initiation: A Java Specification Request (JSR) is created and approved by the Executive Committee.
2. Early Draft: An expert group develops a preliminary draft.
3. Public Draft: The draft is reviewed by the public and feedback given to the expert group. Finally, the Executive Committee votes on approval as a new Java standard.
4. Maintenance: Future updates to the standard are possible by a maintenance process.

For the javax.trustedComputing namespace, the Java Specification Request #321 (JSR321) Expert Group will create a high-level object-oriented API. For instance it will map the key hierarchies to an intuitive object-oriented inheritance hierarchy. The TPM discerns between Sealing, Binding, Identity and Legacy keys, which can either be migratable or non-migratable. It will also be compatible to the existing

---

3 http://www.jcp.org

Java Cryptography Extensions (JCE) architecture. For instance, it will enable the import and export of RSAKey Objects. Finally, it will provide a straightforward interface to high-level TC functionalities.

Besides this API specification, we will also provide a Reference Implementation and a Technology Compatibility Kit. The purpose of the Reference Implementation is to show that the specified API can be implemented and is indeed viable. With the Technology Compatibility Kit, a complete test suite will be provided to enable third parties to build their own, compatible implementations. To increase the transparency and trustworthiness both will to be released as open source software. Even more so, the open source and Java community are invited[4] to take part in the design process as well as in the implementations.

3 Conclusions and Outlook

We have outlined several architectures that allow the integration of TC into Java. Considering modern virtualized computer systems, we derive four scenarios which outline the requirements for Java libraries that access the TPM. Our implementations, jTSS and jTSS Wrapper cover those scenarios and provide an uniform API. Still striving for a better abstraction, we propose design requirements for high-level TC APIs. With those being realized in the upcoming standard JSR321, Trusted Computing applications will be easier to implement than with the interfaces available today. We invite the open source, Java and Trusted Computing communities to actively participate in the design as well as in the implementations. We anticipate that this and the fact that all results will be released[5] under an open source license will foster the use of Trusted technology in research, open and also commercial applications.

Further research will also be directed at minimal-sized compartments for Java services and the formal security analysis of the APIs.

Acknowledgments

The authors thank Michael Steurer and Daniel Hein for comments on an earlier version of this paper and especially Thomas Winkler, who provided the original design and implementation of jTSS and jTSS Wrapper. The efforts at IAIK to integrate TC technology into the Java programming language are part of the OpenTC project funded by the EU as part of FP-6, contract no. 027635. The project aims at providing an complete TC framework. Started as a open source project the results can be inspected by everybody, thus adding towards the trustworthiness of Trusted Computing solutions.

References

[BCG⁺06] Stefan Berger, Ramón Cáceres, Kenneth A. Goldman, Ronald Perez, Reiner Sailer, and Leendert van Doorn. vTPM: virtualizing the trusted platform module. In USENIX-SS'06: Proceedings of the 15th conference on USENIX Security Symposium, pages 305–320, 2006.

[BCP⁺08] Stefan Berger, Ramón Cáceres, Dimitrios Pendarakis, Reiner Sailer, Enriquillo Valdez, Ronald Perez, Wayne Schildhauer, and Deepa Srinivasan. TVDc: managing security in the trusted virtual datacenter. SIGOPS Oper. Syst. Rev., 42(1):40–47, 2008.

[BDF⁺03] Paul Barham, Boris Dragovic, Keir Fraser, Steven Hand, Tim Harris, Alex Ho, Rolf Neugebauer, Ian Pratt, and Andrew Warfield. Xen and the art of virtualization. In SOSP '03: Proceedings of the nine-

---

4 https://jsr321.dev.java.net/
5 Trusted Computing for the Java Platform Website, http://trustedjava.sf.net/

teenth ACM symposium on Operating systems principles, pages 164– 177, New York, NY, USA, 2003. ACM.

[CYC+08] David Challener, Kent Yoder, Ryan Catherman, David Safford, and Leendert Van Doorn. A Practical Guide to Trusted Computing. Number ISBN-13: 978-0132398428. IBM Press, 1st edition, 2008.

[DPV+08] Kurt Dietrich, Martin Pirker, Tobias Vejda, Ronald Toegl, Thomas Winkler, and Peter Lipp. A practical approach for establishing trust relationships between remote platforms using trusted computing. In Gilles Barthe and Cedric Fournet, editors, Trustworthy Global Computing, volume 4912 of LNCS, pages 156–168. Springer Verlag, 2008.

[EL08] Paul England and Jork Loeser. Para-Virtualized TPM Sharing. In Proceedings of TRUST 2008, volume 4968 of LNCS. Springer Verlag, 2008.

[GPC+03] Tal Garfinkel, Ben Pfaff, Jim Chow, Mendel Rosenblum, and Dan Boneh. Terra: a virtual machine-based platform for trusted computing. In SOSP '03: Proceedings of the nineteenth ACM symposium on Operating systems principles, pages 193–206, New York, NY, USA, 2003. ACM.

[Hoh98] Michael Hohmuth. The fiasco kernel: Requirements definition. Technical Report ISSN 1430211X, Dresden University of Technology, 1998.

[IBM08] IBM Corp. TrouSerS an open-source tcg software stack implementation. http://trousers. sourceforge. net/, 2008.

[KLR+06] Dirk Kuhlmann, Rainer Landfermann, HariGovind V. Ramasamy, Matthias Schunter, Gianluca Ramunno, and Davide Vernizzi. An open trusted computing architecture — secure virtual machines enabling user-defined policy enforcement. Research Report RZ 3655, IBM Research, 2006.

[Mic07] Microsoft. TPM Base Services. Microsoft Developer Network, 2007. http://msdn. microsoft.com/en-us/library/aa446796(VS.85).aspx.

[RSA04] RSA Laboratories. PKCS #11 v2.20: Cryptographic Token Interface Standard. RSA Security Inc. Public-Key Cryptography Standards (PKCS), June 2004. ftp://ftp.rsasecurity.com/ pub/pkcs/pkcs-11/v2-20/pkcs-11v2-20.pdf.

[SBHE07] Frederic Stumpf, Michael Benz, Martin Hermanowski, and Claudia Eckert. An approach to a trustworthy system architecture using virtualization, 2007.

[SRM07] L. Sarmenta, J. Rhodes, and T. Müller. TPM/J java-based api for the trusted platform module. http:// projects.csail.mit.edu/tc/tpmj/, 2007.

[SST08] Marcel Selhorst, Christian Stueble, and Felix Teerkorn. TSS Study. Study on behalf of the german federal office for information security (bsi), Sirrix AG security technologies, May 2008. http://www.sirrix. com/content/pages/50590.htm.

[SvDO+06] Luis Sarmenta, Marten van Dijk, Charles O'Donnell, Jonathan Rhodes, and Srinivas Devadas. Virtual monotonic counters and count-limited objects using a TPM without a trusted OS. In STC '06: Proceedings of the first ACM workshop on Scalable trusted computing, number 1-59593-548-7, pages 27–42. ACM, 2006.

[Toe08] Ronald Toegl et al. JSR 321: Trusted Computing API for Java. Java Community Process, 2008. http:// jcp.org/en/jsr/detail?id=321.

[Trua] Trusted Computing Group. https://www.trustedcomputinggroup.org/.

[Trub] Trusted Computing Group. TCG Software Stack Specification, Version 1.2 Errata A. https://www.trustedcomputinggroup.org/specs/TSS/.

[VTPW08] Tobias Vejda, Ronald Toegl, Martin Pirker, and Thomas Winkler. Towards Trust Services for Language-Based Virtual Machines for Grid Computing. In Proceedings of TRUST 2008, volume 4968 of LNCS. Springer Verlag, 2008.

[YYE+05] S. Yoshihama, S. Yoshihama, T. Ebringer, M. Nakamura, S. Munetoh, and H. Maruyama. WS-attestation: efficient and fine-grained remote attestation on web services. In T. Ebringer, editor, Proc. IEEE International Conference on Web Services ICWS 2005, pages –750, 2005.

TrustCube: An Infrastructure that Builds Trust in Client

Zhexuan Song · Jesus Molina · Sung Lee · Houcheng Lee
Seigo Kotani · Ryusuke Masuoka

Fujitsu Laboratories of America
8400 Baltimore Avenue, Suite 302
College Park, Maryland 20740
USA
{zhexuan.song | jesus.molina | sung.lee | houcheng.lee
seigo.kotani | ryusuke.masuoka}@us.fujitsu.com

Abstract

In a client-server environment, typically a lot of sensitive data and/or processes (for clients as well as for the server) are maintained at the server. In order to protect the integrity of the server and prevent leakage of data to unauthorized entities, it is important to make sure that only the authorized person with properly configured authorized platforms can gain the access to the server.

In this paper, we introduce the TrustCube infrastructure. The TrustCube infrastructure is an end-to-end infrastructure that offers measurements of essential elements of clients, including person (or identity), the platform, and the environment; thus, enabling the capability for service providers to make informed decision based on the certifiable report of measurements. Under this infrastructure, a server can accurately evaluate the risk of dealing with a particular client, and handle the requests coming from that client correspondingly.

1 Introduction

Recently, more and more companies move their sensitive data into highly protected servers, and clients are accessing the data over the network. One of the major challenges is to prevent the data from leaking to wrong entities. It requires servers to block requests from unidentified visits and to control the access of authenticated users. One widely used authentication mechanism is username/password: only after a person provides the correct username and password combination, could this person access sensitive information.

However, there are still some issues that need to be addressed. First issue is about the trustfulness of the authentication mechanism. It is widely believed that username/password is a weak user authentication mechanism [Gar02], in the sense that even if the correct username/password combination is provided, it is still difficult to prove that the request is from the rightful owner of that username/password combination. Alternatively, using biometric data is considered to be a much better way to identify a person [AHGBEA07], but using biometric data still comes with its own limitation. One major concern is about its privacy. Unlike username/password, it is very difficult for a person to modify her own biometric characteristics. So once the biometrics data is compromised, there is no easy way to compensate for it.

D. Gawrock, H. Reimer, A.-R. Sadeghi, C. Vishik (Editors): Future of Trust in Computing, Vieweg+Teubner (2009), 68-79

Thus it is always wise not to give the native biometrics data directly to any third parties; or, even better, not to let the data leave the client at all. We will revisit this issue later.

Secondly, after a service provider is persuaded that the request is from the authorized person, how could the service provider trust the platform the person is using? Maybe the person uses a public terminal at internet kiosk, or she plugs her USB storage device to the platform and is making copies of sensitive data files, or she connects a printer to the platform and is printing the documents out. All these cases might be unacceptable in certain applications, but the service provider needs a mechanism to find it out.

Thirdly, even if a service provider is persuaded that the request is from the authorized person, and the person is using the designated platform, without connecting any illegal peripheral devices, how could the service provider trust the environment (OS, applications, and so on) of the platform? She might already be a victim of one of countless worms and/or viruses, or she is running notorious P2P software (e.g. Winny [Fre06]), or a key logger is silently recording all her keystrokes behind the scene.

All these issues, how to trust a person, a platform and the environment of the platform, are becoming more and more important in recent days, as protecting the sensitive data becomes one of the top priorities for government and enterprises alike.

In this paper, we will present our new TrustCube infrastructure. It extensively uses the latest Trusted Computing [TCG08] technologies and addresses well on the previous three issues. The main focus of the TrustCube infrastructure is NOT to directly prevent a bad person (and/or) from using an unknown platform (and/or) that is running malicious software, which is already believed to be very hard. The main focus is to offer various measurements of essential elements of clients, including the person, the platform, and the environment, and provides the capability for *service providers* to make informed decision based on the certifiable report of measurements.

The word TrustCube or T³ means that our infrastructure brings "trust" back to a person, a platform and environment of the platform.[1]

This paper is organized as follows. In the next section, we will introduction related works. Then we will present our TrustCube infrastructure and give a complete workflow to demonstrate how the system works. Next, we will raise some discussion about TrustCube, and finally we will conclude the paper and give some possible future works.

2 Related Works

In this section, we will introduce works that are related to the TrustCube infrastructure. They are Trusted Computing technologies, namely Trusted Platform Module (TPM), Trusted Network Connection (TNC), chain of trust, and remote attestation.

2.1 Trusted Platform Module (TPM)

The Trusted Platform Module (TPM) is a hardware chip that offers facilities for *remote attestation* and the *secure generation of cryptographic keys*, in addition to other capabilities such as hashing, pseudo-random number generation and monotonic up-counters. The TPM is usually deployed as part of a com-

---

[1] Please note that the TrustCube infrastructure is not limited to three aspects and can be expanded to include other aspects as necessary.

puter system's motherboard. Currently, it is estimated that around 230 million PCs are equipped with TPM by year 2009 [Kay05].

Remote attestation allows service provider to detect changes to client's platform. It works by honestly recording changes from hardware to software of the platform, and using Platform Configuration Register (PCR) extension to protect the client-side modification of the record. By looking at the record, along with the corresponding PCR values, service providers are able to know 1) whether the record is tampered, and 2) if not, whether the platform has been changed. The difficult decision about remote attestation is what to measure/verify, which we will discuss in a separate subsection.

Secure generation of cryptographic keys means that the public/private key generation functions are implemented within the TPM. Some private keys (such as Endorsement Key (EK)) never leave TPM and only authorized persons can use keys to encrypt/decrypt and sign messages. Even if a platform is lost or stolen, those keys can never be used by unauthorized persons. It is believed that using TPM key generation function is more secure that similar software solution.

Since the TPM chip only supports limited storage capabilities, inactive keys are encrypted and moved off-chip. Management of the key is performed externally by a Key and Credential Manager (KCM) [TPM08]. Keys are stored in a hierarchy structure. The root of the hierarchy tree is the Storage Root Key (SRK), which is created when creating a new platform owner. Each key has an attribute called migratable or non-migratable. A key is migratable means that KCM can back up the key and later recover it in the same or a different TPM.

Optionally, a key can be protected by a secret. Once a key is protected, only when a person provides the right secret, can she load the key into the TPM and use it. This procedure is called "key authorization." Currently, the existing key authorization mechanism for a TPM is based on a 20 byte shared secret, and is usually created from the hash of a passphrase. Trusted Computing Group has formed the Authentication Working Group to work on a solution that supports a wider range of authentication mechanisms.

In the TrustCube infrastructure, we use bioinformatics to authenticate a person to the TPM. Since the corresponding TCG specification is not available yet, a customized approach is adopted. We will modify our approach when the official specification is published in the future.

2.2 Trusted Network Connect (TNC)

Trusted Network Connect (TNC), an initiative of TCG, addresses and attempts to provide network access control that meets security requirements through open-source, non-proprietary standards. In order to ensure interoperability and compatibility with the existing network infrastructure, TNC is designed to utilize existing industry standards and protocols such as Extensible Authentication Protocol, Transport Layer Security, and RADIUS. The TNC architecture supports commonly used access mechanisms such as VPN, SSL, dial-up remote access and other networking technologies including wired and wireless networks and 802.1x infrastructure.

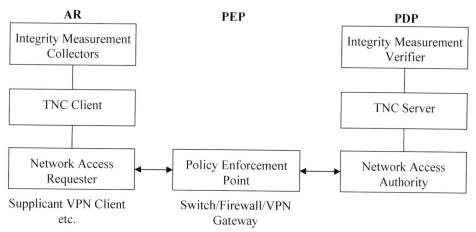

Figure 1: TNC Architecture: This diagram is based on the TNC Architecture Specification

There are three entities in TNC (Figure 1): an Access Requester (AR), a Policy Enforcement Point (PEP), and a Policy Decision Point (PDP). When an AR makes an attempt to access a protected network behind PEP, the access request is passed through an integrity evaluation process in order to determine what level of access should be granted, if any. Based on the measurements collected at the AR and the policy configuration, the PDP makes a decision. The PEP, usually a network access device such as a switch or wireless access point, enforces the decision made by PDP by granting the appropriate access to the AR. The TNC architecture allows for an option to include platform measures such as PCR values from Trusted Platform Module (TPM) of the AR.

In the TrustCube infrastructure, the procedure of building secure communication tunnel between client and server strictly follows the TNC specification.

2.3 Chain of Trust

A chain of trust is established by validating each component of hardware of software from the bottom up. It ensures that only trusted hardware and software can be used while the complete system is still flexible. At the bottom of a chain of trust is the "root of trust component." By TCG definition, root of trust (component) is "a component that must always behave in the expected manner, because its misbehavior cannot be detected."

If a component in the chain cannot validate the component at the next level, we called the chain is broken. When a chain is broken, the component at the next level and the ones at higher levels cannot be trusted, even if some validating result "seems to be correct." In this sense, to trust a measurement report about a high level component, we cannot only look at this level. In fact, we must get a complete report about each component following the chain of trust. Only if all components before this are trusted, can we really start to discuss whether or not this component is trusted.

We will discuss the chain of trust in the TrustCube infrastructure later.

2.4 Remote Attestation

As we discussed previously, remote attestation is one of the key functionalities supported by Trusted Computing technologies. An important research problem consists on determining what data should be used for remote attestation. Several attestation techniques have been proposed.

SignaCert Enterprise Trust Service (ETS) [Sig08] adopts a static scanning based solution. It is a server that can check whether the environment of a platform contains any unknown files. The basic idea is quite simple. At the server (ETS), a huge database is maintained. The database contains a long list of known files and their snapshots (digest values of files). From the client side, the current files in the environment and their snapshots are calculated and sent to the server. The server will compare the submission with the database and check whether the snapshot is correct. If the file is not in the database, or the snapshot of a file is not correct, the file is considered unknown.

TrustedVM, proposed by Vivek Haldar et al. [HVC04], is a dynamic, platform independent solution. It is a virtual machine that can dynamically retrieve enforcement and security policies from the server and execute the attestation on the programs that are running in the virtual machine. The drawback is that this solution will greatly slow down the regular operations in the virtual machine.

The Integrity Measurement Architecture (IMA) [Sai04] for Linux is implemented as part of the operating system. In IMA, a modified operating system (OS) kernel measures all applications, drivers and libraries that are loaded by the OS for verification.

In the current TrustCube infrastructure, we adopt a hybrid solution: SignaCert ETS for static scanning and IMA for dynamic measuring. More discussion will be given later. The bootloader needs to be also modified in order to maintain the chain of trust. For the current TrustCube infrastructure we use TrustedGrub [Tgrub06], which still contains some security problems, as outlined in [Kau07]. In newer version of the TrustCube infrastructure, we plan to support other bootloader such as OSLO [Kau07].

3 TrustCube Infrastructure

In this section, we will give details about the TrustCube infrastructure. First, we will introduce the components appeared in the TrustCube infrastructure, followed by a set of workflows that the TrustCube infrastructure uses to fulfill certain tasks. Finally we will present some discussion.

3.1 TrustCube Infrastructure Architecture

The TrustCube infrastructure includes modules on both the client and the server side. A general architecture is depicted in Figure 2. In this diagram, we assume that a person is using a web browser to view sensitive data in a document server (the web browser and the document server are connected in a dotted line). The diagram is similar for other types of services. In Figure 2, the solid lines mean that the connected components have direct communication while the dash lines means the connected components have logical connection or are corresponding components in client and server.

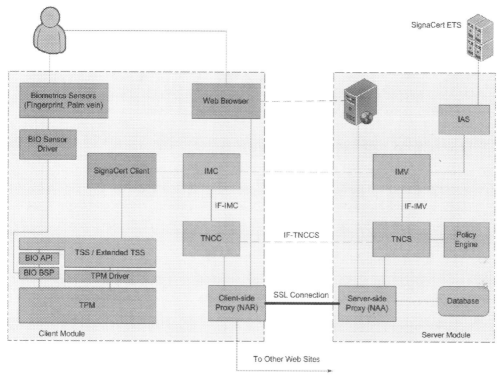

Figure 2: General architecture of the TrustCube infrastructure

The components are described as follows:

- **IMC/IMV, TNCC/TNCS** are standard TNC components. We implemented TNC 1.2 specification using the latest Java binding [TNC08].
- **Biometrics Sensors** are devices that collect person's biometrics characteristics.
- **BIO Sensor Driver, BIO API (Application Programming Interface), and BIO BSP (Biometric Service Provider)** are standard Biometrics application components [Bio05].
- **TPM, and TPM Driver** are standard TCG components.
- **TSS (TCG Software Stack) / Extended TSS.** TSS is one TCG standard component. We extended the existing TSS version 1.2 [TSS08] and added a set of functions to register/handle biometric data.
- **SignaCert client** is a module that collects the snapshots of client-side environment and generates an XML report.
- **Client-side proxy (NAR)** is one implementation of NAR. The component fulfills two functions: it initializes the TNC handshake with server; it serves as a simple proxy that sends server related requests to NAA over SSL tunnel, and relay other requests to external web sites.
- **Server-side proxy (NAA)** is one implementation of NAA. The component also fulfills two functions: it handles TNC handshake requests; it parses the server related requests and relay them to the server.
- **Database** supports Server-side proxy (NAA).

- **Policy Engine** supports TNCS in making decisions about whether or not to give access to a client and/or under which trust level.
- **IAS (integrated authentication service)** helps in the TNC handshake procedure. While a client starts a TNC handshake, it will send the complete report about person, platform and environment. IAS verified the consistency and the correctness of the report. However, IAS will NOT make any decision about whether the request from the client should be approved or not.
- **SignaCert ETS** helps IAS to verify the correctness of the environment section of the report.

3.2 TrustCube Infrastructure Workflow

Before a client is activated, it must complete a one-time registration procedure, which is called "registration phase." Before a client can access any sensitive data in a server, it needs to pass person/platform/environment authentication, we call this procedure "authentication phase." And finally the person starts to work on the sensitive data in the server, and we call this period "operation phase." Figure 3 shows the phase change state diagram.

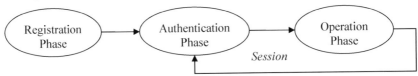

Figure 3: Phase changes in the TrustCube infrastructure

Please note that the communication between the client and the server in all three phases must be secure and must guarantee integrity and authenticity. This can be done using various cryptographic protocols, such as SSL.

3.2.1 Registration Phase

During the registration phase, the information about person, platform and environment is collected and stored in IAS for future authentication purpose. The registration sequence is person first, platform next. Environment registration is optional.

During the person registration, the person's biometric reference data, such as fingerprints, eye retinas and irises, and palm vein patterns, are collected, encrypted and stored in the client platform as a BLOB. Meanwhile, a hash function, such as SHA-1 is applied on the BLOB and the output is used as a secret. Next, the system administrator generates a signing key, which we called person's identity key, or K_{PI}, if the person does not have her identify key created before. If the user already has her identity key in another client, the key will be migrated to this platform. The key, newly created or migrated, is attached under the SRK, and protected by the secret generated from the person's biometric reference data.

If K_{PI} is newly created, it needs to be certified by a Certificate Authority (CA) and a copy of the certificate is stored in IAS for future verification. This step is similar to the AIK registration defined in [SKAE05]. However in the TrustCube infrastructure, we dropped steps related to Privacy CA because the CA we used is controlled by us instead of a public CA mentioned in the specification.

Two steps are involved in the platform registration. The first step is to create and register a signing key which we called platform key, or K_p. K_p is certified by a CA and a copy of the certificate is stored in IAS for future verification. K_p is *not* protected by any secret and any person who has access to the platform can access this key and use it to sign a report. This step needs to be done only once for each platform.

Please note that K_{PI} is migratable and K_p is non-migratable.

The other step of the platform registration is to collect and register certain PCR values (PCR 0 – PCR 6) as the platform's hardware snapshots. This is crucial since it represents the components in the chain of trust before OS. Later, when the hardware setting of the platform is modified, or new hardware is added, we must re-do this step.

The environment registration is to harvest the snapshots of files that will be used in the client. This registration is optional, in the sense that only when the software that will be run in the platform is not known beforehand, is it necessary to register them. When we talk about registering software, we mean to create snapshots (e.g. SHA1 hash value) of all files the software contains. The list of <file, snapshot> pairs is collected, and then added to the white list. For an enterprise setting when multiple platforms are running similar software, this step needs to be done only once.

After the registration, the client is ready to use.

3.2.2 Authentication Phase

The TrustCube infrastructure uses a token based authentication system. Authentication phase happens at the beginning of each session. After a successful authentication, a token is generated and assigned to the client. The token will be attached with any further requests from the same client.

Generally speaking, the authentication phase is a TNC handshake procedure. The procedure is triggered when a person launches the client-side proxy (NAR). As the TNC specification specifies, an IMC will be loaded. This IMC does the following things

- It prompts the person to scan her biometric characteristics (e.g. fingerprint, palm vein), and compares the scanned sample with the biometric reference data using BIO API [Bio05]. If the match fails, the handshake procedure halts. If the scanned data successfully matches the record, using the same hash function we used in the registration phase on the biometric reference data, the secret is calculated and the person unlocks K_{PI}. This step has a potential loophole if the biometric reference data and the hash function are retrieved by a bad person through other channel and the secret is leaked. A possible solution is to store the biometric reference data in hardware (such as advanced security chip or smart card) and to do the matching and secret calculation in the same hardware. Currently, we are working on the smart card approach.

- It retrieves the dynamically scanned snapshots collected by the operation system.

- It launches a separate thread to run a static scanning on the environment. This thread utilizes the SignaCert client module to harvest the snapshots of files at certain directories. The selection of directories to be scanned is defined in a policy file stored in SignaCert ETS and the server can modified the policy file based on its settings. The scanned result is an XML document signed by the SignaCert client.

- It generates a complete report, which includes environment scan report, TPM PCR values, TPM monotonic counter value, the current timestamp, and so on, and signs the report with both K_p and K_{PI}. The counter value and the timestamp are included to avoid the client using the same request more than once.

- The complete signed report is encoded into the TNCC request batch and sent over to the server. After the server verifies the correctness of the batch, the signed report is sent over to IAS through IMV.

- IAS (Integrated Authentication Server) verifies the report and returns the authentication results back to IMV. Please note that IAS does NOT make any decision about whether the request should be accepted or denied. The following methods are used in IAS
- If the report is correctly signed by K_p, the platform is the registered one.
- If the report is correctly signed by K_{PI}, the person is the registered one. This is based on the assumption that only the person which can provide the correct biometrics information can unlock the K_{PI} and use it to sign the report.
- If the PCR 0 – 6 values are identical to the registered ones, the components in the chain of trust before operating system are not compromised.
- If the counter value has been seen before, the request has been used before and will be denied immediately.
- If the difference between the current time and the timestamp in the report is greater than the pre-defined threshold, it will be reported as a potential, but not certain, issue.
- The snapshots collected by the OS are relayed to the SignaCert ETS for verification. Any unknown and/or known malicious measurements will make the environment report untrustworthy.
- The static scanning report is also relayed to SignaCert ETS for verification. Any unknown and/or known malicious signatures will be identified.

The output of IAS is then sent to the policy engine. The policy engine applies the pre-defined policies and determines the following issues.

- Should the current request be approved?
- If approved, which trust level should be assigned to the client?
- If not approved, what is the problem and how the client should fix the problem?

Sample policies include: 1) if the platform or user verification fails, the request will be denied, or 2) if any unknown item in the OS measurements is identified, the request will be denied, or 3) if unknown files are identified, the trust level for the client is 1 (low), or 4) if the correctness of the request cannot be verified (i.e. the signature does not match the request), the request will be denied, and so on. System administrator can always modify the policies after the TrustCube infrastructure is deployed to further tune the system.

Based on the decision of the policy engine, the server-side proxy (NAA) will either assign an access token to the client, or send a deny message which also includes the reason to the client. The access token is a randomly generated unique number. At the server side, this token is linked with the request, the decision from the server, and a valid period. In order for a client to get service beyond the valid period, the client must submit a new authentication request.

3.2.3 Operation Phase

After the client receives the token from the server, it is ready to visit the sensitive data. In this subsection, we are using a browser as the client-side application, but the same idea can be applied to other applications as well.

All HTTP requests from the browser go through the client-side proxy. The client-side proxy and the server are connected by a SSL tunnel. If the destination of the packets is other than the server, the proxy will reply the message to its original destination. Otherwise, the HTTP requests will be put in a special packet and sent to the server-side proxy using the SSL tunnel. The token is attached with the packet.

Once the server received the packet, it will first retrieve the token and validate it. If the token is not valid or expired, a HTTP 401 error message will be returned immediately over the tunnel, then relay to the browser. For a valid token, the initial HTTP requests are rewritten by attaching the token into the request URL. Then, the rewritten HTTP requests are sent to the document server.

The document server retrieves the token from the request URL. From the token, it finds out the trust level of the request. Based on the trust level, the corresponding service is provided. All responses from the document server are sent back to the browser through the server-side proxy, the client-side proxy path.

After the person finishes the browsing, she closes the client-side proxy (NAR). The client-side proxy will send a "bye-bye" message to the server and the server immediately invalidates the token. This concludes the session.

3.3 Discussion

In this subsection, we would like to discuss some issues related to the TrustCube infrastructure.

3.3.1 Chain of Trust

As we discussed previously, it is important that the chain of trust is maintained at the client side in order to provide a certifiable report about the person, the platform, and the environment. In the TrustCube infrastructure, the chain of trust is maintained in the following way.

The root of trust is the TPM. Follow the chain of trust, components below the operating system are measured and corresponding PCR values are extended with the measurement. If the values are identical, we will infer that the platform is not compromised. The operating system is a trusted one, and we are using IBM's IMA [Sai04] on a Fedora system. In a trusted OS, the executed files and loaded libraries are measured before being loaded into memory. Of course, our TrustCube client side modules (include fingerprint drivers) are measured as well. The trusted OS extends the measurement to PCR 8 to make sure that these measurements cannot be compromised without detection. Those measurements are part of the request and sent to the server. The server first checks the measurements and make sure they are identical to what have been saved in IAS, or using third party services, such as SignaCert ETS, to do the check. If the result is positive, the current running environment at the client is trusted, thus the data the client sent is also trusted. Finally the server will do the regular authentication based on the data.

Please note that any mistakes that causes the chain of trust to be broken, such as wrong values of PCR 0 – PCR 6, or unknown files in the operating system, will make the finally request untrustworthy, and cause the request to be rejected by the server.

3.3.2 Authentication of the TPM

In the current TPM specification, using passphrase is the only method for a person to unlock a key in the TPM. However, as we mentioned before, we would like to introduce other mechanisms, such as biometrics, smart card, to receive stronger protection. This requirement is currently being studied by the newly formed TCG Authentication Working Group.

However, currently since the BIO BSP is running as a software module, it is in a different level of the chain of trust from the TPM. If, for some reason, the chain of trust broke in the middle, certain TPM functions will become unavailable.

A possible solution for the problem is to create a "super security chip" or design a smart card which implements both the TPM functions and BIO BSP. In this way, BIO BSP works at the same level as the TPM in the chain of trust and below the operating system. This solution also requires certain extensions from the TSS.

In the current TrustCube infrastructure, we are implementing this idea in a customized way. We will be glad to adopt any specifications from the Authentication Working Group when they become available.

3.3.3 OS Measurements and Static Scanning Report

The TrustCube infrastructure needs both OS measurements and environment static scanning report. The difference is that OS measurements include executable files and libraries that are loaded by OS and environment static scanning report includes the snapshots of disk files at certain directories, no matter if they are loaded or not.

OS measurements are important in the sense that they show the current OS status. If any unknown or malicious measurements are detected, this OS instance is untrustworthy, so are the data it collected. However, only using OS measurement has two drawbacks: firstly, if a malicious file stays in the system but is not loaded yet (this is very common for certain type of virus which comes with infected files), it cannot be detected; and secondly, if the malicious file is a script and the damage is caused after it is executed by a innocent program, it cannot be identified either.

Scanning the whole environment may detect this sort of incumbent malicious files. The problem here is that it is not easy to decide which directories should be includes in the scanning policy. The major bottleneck here is at the disk I/O. One of our experiments shows that just to scan the files in the Windows directory on a standard Windows XP installation takes more than 30 seconds. Among them, 99.99% of the time is to read files from the disk. If we include too many directories in the scanning policy, the initial waiting time might to be too long.

One possible improvement is to implement a background environment scanning function. It runs as a background process and collecting environment report before the real authentication happens. During the scanning, any changes in the directory will be reflected as well. During the authentication phase, the update-to-date environment report will be used without delay.

3.3.4 Dynamic Environment Monitoring

Another possible improvement is to introduce a dynamic monitoring module in the client. Currently, after the client passes the authentication and the token is assigned, any further changes on the client side are not known by the server. If some malicious software is invoked or some unknown devices are connected during the operation phase, the server does not have any control.

A dynamic monitoring module in the client may help. The module will monitor the real-time changes of the platform and environment and report the changes to the server. Based on the changes, the server can either do nothing, or lower the trust level, or deny any future request from the client. Please note that the server will NOT increase the trust level, because the dynamic monitoring module cannot prove that the system is more trustworthy than the module itself.

4 Conclusion and Future Works

In this paper, we introduced the TrustCube infrastructure. The infrastructure extensively uses the Trusted Computing technologies and allows the server to make judgment based on the certifiable report about the person, the platform and the environment. The infrastructure is very flexible and can be used in almost all applications as an independent module to enhance their security.

Future works include a dynamic monitoring module and the improvement of the environment scanning module. Furthermore, we will extend the concept to other platforms, including routers, disk drivers, TV sets, node controllers, sensors, and so on. These platforms are potential stepping stone for Distributed Denial-of-service (DDoS). For a platform, it is tragic to be an accomplice of an evil deed and we believe that our TrustCube infrastructure is a good cure for it.

References

[Gar02] Garfinkel, Simson. Web Security, Privacy and Commerce, 2nd Edition. s.l. : O'Reilly Media, Inc., 2002. ISBN 0596000456.

[AHGBEA07] M1.4 Ad Hoc Group on Biometric in E-Authentication (AHGBEA). Study Report on Biometrics in E-Authentication. Washington, DC : InterNational Committee for Information Technology Standards, INCITS Secretariat, Information Technology Industry Council (ITI), 2007.

[Fre06] Freire, Carl. Virus spreads data, scandal over Winny. MSNBC. [Online] June 12, 2006. http://www.msnbc.msn.com/id/13283771/.

[TCG08] Trusted Computing Group. [Online] https://www.trustedcomputinggroup.org/home 2008.

[Kay05] The Future of Trusted Computing. Kay, Roger. s.l. : GovSec, 2005.

[TPM08] Trusted Computing Group. Trusted Platform Module (TPM) Specification. https://www.trustedcomputinggroup.org/specs/TPM, 2008.

[Sig08] SignaCert. SignaCert Enterprise Trust Server. http://www.signacert.com/products/enterprise-trust-server/, 2008.

[HVC04] Semantic Remote Attestation - A Virtual Machine directed approach to Trusted Computing. Haldar, Vivek, Chandra, Deepak and Franz, Michael. San Jose, California : 3rd Virtual Machine Research & Technology Symposium, 2004.

[Sai04] Design and Implementation of a TCG-based Integrity Measurement Architecture. Sailer, Reiner, et al. San Diego, California : s.n., 2004. 13th Usenix Security Symposium.

[Tgrub06] TrustedGRUB. http://www.prosec.rub.de/trusted_grub.html, 2006

[Kau07] OSLO: improving the security of trusted computing. Kauer, Bernhard. Boston, Massachusetts: 16th USENIX Security Symposium, 2007.

[TNC08] Trusted Computing Group. Specification, Trusted Network Connect (TNC). https://www.trustedcomputinggroup.org/specs/TNC, 2008.

[Bio05] ISO/IEC 19784-1. Information technology - Biometric application programming interface - Part 1: BioAPI Specification (version 2.0, international). 2005.

[TSS08] Trusted Computing Group. TCG Software Stack (TSS) Specifications. https://www.trustedcomputinggroup.org/specs/TSS, 2008.

[SKAE05] Trusted Computing Infrastructure Working Group. Subject Key Attestation Evidence Extension. https://www.trustedcomputinggroup.org/specs/IWG/IWG_SKAE_Extension_1-00.pdf, 2005.

Session 4:
Obtaining Trust
and Modeling
Trust Environments

Trust-based Information Sharing in Collaborative Communities: Issues and Challenges

Barbara Carminati · Elena Ferrari

Department of Computer Science and Communication
University of Insubria, Via Mazzini, 5, 21100 Varese (Italy)
{ barbara.carminati | elena.ferrari }@uninsubria.it

Abstract

Collaborative communities are today one of the emerging trends in the ICT area. This is mainly due to the wide-spread adoption of Web 2.0 related technologies, having, as one of their major goal, that of facilitating user collaboration and knowledge sharing. Clearly, the wide adoption of collaborative tools would take place only if users have assurance that their privacy and security requirements are preserved when sharing information. In this paper, we focus on access control and the related privacy issues. We start by revising the state of the art in the field, then we discuss which are the main requirements for a *privacy-aware* access control mechanism for collaborative communities. Then, we briefly describe some of the results we have achieved in this field.

1 Introduction

Nowadays, we are witnesses of a new era in the web that will deeply impact the way we use it and which will make the web not just an extremely useful tool for our work and/or recreational activities, but also an integral part of our lives. This is mainly due to the emerging of Web 2.0, a new trend in the use of the web that aims to enhance the development of web-based communities to enhance collaborations among users and information sharing. Notable examples of Web 2.0 applications are social-networking sites (WBSNs -- Web-based Social Networks) [SD+05], a particular example of collaborative communities, which make users able to publish resources and to record and/or establish relationships with other users, possibly of different type ('friend', 'colleague', etc.), for purposes that may concern business, entertainment, religion, dating, etc. To have an idea of the relevance of the social networking phenomena, MySpace (www.myspace.com) attracted more than 114 million global visitors age 15 and older in June 2007, representing a 72-percent increase versus one year before. Facebook (www.facebook.com) experienced even stronger growth during the same time frame, reaching 52.2 million visitors with an increase of 270 percent. Bebo (www.bebo.com) also increased by orders of magnitude, reaching 18.2 million visitors.[1]

What is also very important to point out is that collaborative tools and, more precisely, the social networking paradigm is today more and more used not only by single users, but also at the enterprise level to communicate, share information, taking decisions, and doing business. This is in line with the emerging trend known as Enterprise 2.0 [McAfee06], that is, the use of Web 2.0 technologies,

---

[1] Social Networking goes Global, ComScore Inc., www.comscore.com.

D. Gawrock, H. Reimer, A.-R. Sadeghi, C. Vishik (Editors): Future of Trust in Computing, Vieweg+Teubner (2009), 83-92

like blogs, wikis, and social networking facilities, within the Intranet, to allow for more spontaneous, knowledge-based collaboration.

Clearly, the wide adoption of social networking tools, as well as of all the other Web 2.0 related technologies, would take place only if users have assurance that their privacy and security requirements are preserved when sharing information. As an example of this trend, some concerns among social network users have recently began to emerge. For instance, in 2006, Facebook receives the complaints of some privacy activists against the use of the News Feed feature [Chen06], introduced to inform users with the latest personal information related to their online friends. These complaints result in an online petition, signed by over 700,000 users, demanding the company to stop this service. Facebook replayed by allowing users to set some privacy preferences. More recently, November 2007, Facebook receives other complaints related to the use of Beacon [Berteau07]. Beacon is part of the Facebook advertising system, introduced to track users activities on more than 40 web sites of Facebook partners. Such information is collected even when users are off from the social-networking site, and is reported to users friends without the consent of the user itself. Even in this case, the network community promptly reacts with another online petition that gained more than 50,000 signatures in less than 10 days. These are only few examples of privacy concerns related to WBSNs. All these events have animated several online discussions about privacy in social networking, and government organizations started to seriously consider this issue [Canadian07, Hogben07]. Even more urgent is the development of adequate security and privacy services when collaborative community facilities are used at the enterprise level. It is true that one of the major goal of Enterprise 2.0 is to facilitate sharing of information, but it is also true that such sharing should be regulated by proper access control policies, on the basis of the sensitivity of the protected information and the environment where the sharing of information takes place.

A further relevant feature of collaborative communities (and, in particular, of social networks), which may impact how security and privacy are enforced, is that some of them provide to their members the ability of specifying how much they trust other members. This can be done either by expressing a recommendation, or by rating other users according to a scale. An analysis of the literature related to trust modelling and computation is out of the scope of this paper, however it is widely accepted that there does not exist a unique definition of trust, in that it may vary depending on the context and for which purposes the trust is used. For instance, in P2P (Peer-to-Peer) systems, trust is mainly related to the reliability of a peer in providing a given service, whereas in WBSNs supporting collaborative rating (e.g., movies, books) trust is mainly a measure of how much a user is an expert of a particular topic (*topical trust*). We believe that trust can play a key role in a controlled sharing of information in collaborative communities in that it can be one of the main factors to determine whether a user has the right to access a given information. Clearly, this requires the definition of new models for trust representation and computation in that, in this case, trust should convey information about how much a user is compliant with the specified access control policies. For instance, a user is trusted if he/she does not release information to other users which are not authorized by the specified access control policies.

In this paper, we focus on access control requirements arising in collaborative communities and on the privacy concerns associated with access control enforcement. In particular, we consider the privacy concerns related to access control policies, trust and relationship disclosure when performing access control. Besides discussing the requirements of an access control service for collaborative communities, we discuss possible solutions for access control enforcement, able to trade-off between efficiency of access control, confidentiality and privacy guarantees.

Table 1: WBSNs comparative analysis

WBSN	Purpose	Relationships	Trust	Protection Options
Bebo	general	friend	none	public, private, 1st degree contacts, selected contacts
FaceBook	general	friend	none	public, private, 1st-2nd degree contacts, selected contacts
Friendster	general	friend	none	members from selected continents, private, 1st-2nd degree contacts
MySpace	general	friend	none	public, members > 18 years old, private, 1st degree
Multiply	general	various	none	public, private, 1st and nth degree contacts, 1st degree but not online buddies, selected contacts
Orkut	general	friend	personal	public, private, 1st-2nd degree contacts
Flickr	photos	friend/family	none	public, private, 1st degree (friends or family)
Last.fm	music	friend	none	public, private, 1st degree contacts (and profile neighbors)
Xing	business	generic	none	public, private, 1st-4th degree contacts
LinkedIn	business	various	business	public, private, 1st and nth degree contacts
RepCheck	reputation	generic	personal, business	none

The remainder of this paper is organized as follows. Next section briefly surveys the stat of the art, whereas Section 3 discusses the main access control and privacy issues related to information sharing in collaborative communities. Sections 4, 5 and 6 describe some of the research results we have achieved in the field of trust-based information sharing. Finally, Section 7 concludes the paper and outlines future research directions.

2 State of the art

To understand the need for access control services for collaborative communities, let us start to overview which is the state of the art. Up to now, most of the research has focused on web-based social networks. However, in this context so far research has mainly focused on privacy-preserving techniques aiming to allow statistical analysis on social network data without compromising WBSN members' privacy [LDGK0807]. In contrast, access control and the related privacy issues is still a new research area and only few work have been done in this field. If we examine what is provided by current WB-SNs (cfr. Table 1) we see that most of them provide very simple access control mechanisms. Indeed, most of today WBNSs enforce access control according to a very simple model, according to which the owner of a resource has only 3 options wrt its protection: 1) defining it as as public, 2) defining it as private, or 3) defining it as accessible only by his/her direct neighbours. For instance, besides the basic settings, Bebo (http://bebo.com), Facebook (http://facebook.com), and Multiply (http://multiply.com) support the option "selected friends"; Last.fm (http://last.fm) the option "neighbours" (i.e., the set of WBSN members, computed by the SNMS, having musical preferences and tastes similar to mine); Orkut (www.orkut.com) supports the option "friends of friends" (2nd degree friends), Xing (www.xing.com) the options "contacts of my contacts" (2nd degree contacts), and "3rd" and "4th degree contacts"; whereas LinkedIn (www.linkedin.com) gives the possibility to choose between "my connections" (i.e., the WBSN members which I am directly connected to, that is, 1st degree contacts) and "my network" (nth degree connections— i.e., all the WBSN members to whom I am either directly or indirectly connected, independently from how distant they are). All these approaches have the advantage of being easy to be implemented, but they lack in flexibility in terms of the access control requirements that can be specified.

As far as trust is concerned the majority of the considered WBSNs do not support it. The only exceptions are represented by Orkut, LinkedIn and RepCheck (www.repcheck.com). In Orkut and RepCheck trust can be expressed according to a numeric scale. In LinkedIn, a free text label can be associated with a user, explaining why he/she is recommended by another user. The semantics of trust varies depending on the specific purposes of the WBSN: for instance, Orkut supports personal trust, whereas RepCheck supports both personal and business trust. However, trust is not used as a parameter to perform access control.

To our knowledge, apart from our research that we will describe in Sections 4, 5 and 6, the only other research proposals trying to overcome the restrictions of the access control mechanisms provided by today WBSNs are the ones by Hart et al. [HJS07] and Ali et al. [AVM07]. However, [HJS07] deals only with access control policy specification, without considering the problem of access control enforcement, nor the related privacy issues. In contrast, Ali et al. [AVM07] propose a mandatory access control model, where trust is used to determine the security level of both users and resources. However, even in this case privacy issues arising when performing access control are not addressed. Moreover, both the two proposals adopt a very simple access control model, which is almost the same as the simple access control model provided by today WBSNs. In contrast, we believe that there is the need of an access control model able to express more articulated access control requirements and a related mechanism which is able to trade-off between efficiency, confidentiality and privacy guarantees. In the following section, we discuss which are the main requirements related to access control.

3 Access control requirements

In this section, we briefly discuss some of the main access control issues that need to be addressed in the field of information sharing in collaborative communities, by also focusing on the related privacy issues. Then, in the following sections we briefly describe the research results we have achieved in this field. The reference scenario for what is discussed and described in the remainder of the paper is a collaborative community used at the enterprise level, either for enhancing knowledge sharing and information exchange at the intranet level, or used at the internet level as a way to increase the enterprise outcome.[2] In what follows, we model a collaborative community as a graph where nodes represent users or organizations whishing to collaborate and edges represent relationships between nodes. For instance, if Alice is a friend of Bob, then there is an edge from the node representing Alice to the node representing Bob. The edge is labelled with the relationship type and the trust level.[3] An example of collaborative community is reported in Figure 1.

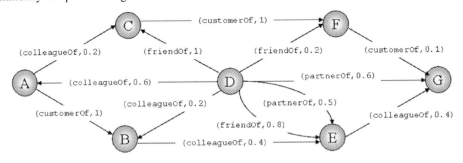

Figure 1: A portion of a collaborative community

---

2   Cfr. the definition of Enterprise 2.0 given in Section 1.
3   Here, we do not go into the details of trust computation, see Section 6 for more details about this topic.

Let us start to examine which are the main issues related to access control.

Trust-based information sharing. The availability of huge amount of information within a collaborative community obviously raises important confidentiality issues. There is thus the need of devising suitable models and mechanisms able to enforce the variety of access control requirements that collaborative community users may have. These models should be able to overcome the limitations of the simple model provided by today WBSNs (cfr. Section 2). In defining these models, trust should be considered as a fundamental parameter to decide the result of an access request. Besides devising suitable policy languages to express access control requirements, architectural issues related to the efficiency of access control are also crucial. Indeed, the decentralized and highly dynamic nature of collaborative communities makes the traditional client-server architecture used by most of current data management systems not well suited. Therefore, alternative ways of performing access control should be investigated (see Section 4 for more details on this topic).

Privacy-aware access control. In a collaborative community, established relationships are one of the key factors to enforce a selective sharing of information. Indeed, access control requirements are usually expressed on the basis of the relationships a user should have with other users, and their maximum depth and trust level, in order to get access to a resource. Establishing relationships in a community implies, in some sense, an exposure of personal information of the users involved in the relationships, which may give rise to some relevant privacy concerns. For instance, being aware that a given user participates to a network of consultants of a company X, makes one able to discover that the user is a consultant of that company. Thus, in general, a user might prefer to keep private some of his/her relationships, or make them available only to selected users. The issue is therefore to devise *privacy-aware* access control mechanisms, able to enforce users privacy preferences on the established relationships when performing access control (see Section 5 for more details on this topic).

Trust modelling, computation, and protection. Given the key role of trust to enforce a controlled information sharing in collaborative communities, a fundamental issue is to define suitable trust models. These models should keep into account that, in this scenario, the semantics of trust should be also related to the compliance with the specified access control policies and privacy preferences. Another important point is how to compute trust. Indeed, it is quite evident that assigning a wrong trust value to a potential malicious user could imply unauthorized releasing of information or unauthorized disclosure of personal relationships. Therefore, some mechanisms and strategies should be devised to help in trust computation. Finally, similar to relationships, there is also the need of protecting trust when performing access control. Indeed, a user may not want to disclose to everybody the trust he/she assigns to other users in the community. Similar to relationship disclosure, the user preferences wrt to trust disclosure should be enforced when performing access control (see Section 6 for more details on this topic).

In the following sections, we briefly describe for each of the above-mentioned issues, the research results we have achieved so far.

4 Trust-based Information Sharing

In [CFP06] we have defined an access control model, which extends the basic access control model provided by current WBSNs (cfr. Section 2). Our XML-based policy language allows one to specify access control requirements through a set of access rules. Access rules express access control restrictions in terms of relationship types, depths and trust levels. For instance, consider the collaborative community in Figure 1, B can specify that a particular document, say d_1, can be seen only by his direct or indirect colleagues whose distance is not greater than 3 and with a trust level greater than 0.4; or, he can decide not to specify any constraint on the depth and/or trust level, according to the protection requirements of the considered resource. Policies are specified by each node in the network by using a GUI provided by our prototype [CFP08].

However, besides the definition of a suitable policy language, one of the key issues is related to the architecture according to which access control should take place. Here, the main goal is to trade-off between efficiency, privacy and confidentiality concerns of collaborative community users. As mentioned in Section 3, the traditional way according to which access control is performed in data management systems (see Figure 2(a)) does not fit very well with the collaborative community scenario. In a traditional data management system, there is a trusted module, called *reference monitor*, which mediates each access request submitted to the system, and decides whether it can be granted or not, on the basis of the specified access control policies. The access control policies specified by all the users are stored into a centralized policy base, managed by the database server. We believe that this architecture is not appropriate for a collaborative community environment for two main reasons. The first is that in a dynamic and highly decentralized environment like collaborative communities, a centralized service in charge of performing access control may become a bottleneck for the whole system. The second reason is that adopting centralized access control enforcement implies to totally delegate to the community manager the administration of user data and the related access control policies and this may lead to some privacy and confidentiality concerns. For instance, a community user might not want that the community manager knows the policies regulating access to his/her resources. Additionally, the increasing privacy concerns about the management of personal information by the community manager (cfr. Section 1) lead us to believe that a centralized access control solution is not the most appropriate one, since we believe that, in the next future, collaborative community users would like to have more and more control over their data and the way access control is enforced over them. In view of this, we believe it is necessary to investigate alternative ways of enforcing access control, which make users not totally dependent from a centralized service.

The alternative way to perform access control wrt the centralized solution is to adopt a fully *decentralized solution* (see Figure 2(b)), according to which each node locally stores its access control policies and is responsible for performing access control. Since access control is based on the relationships existing among collaborative community nodes, it is necessary to ensure that relationships are not forged to obtain unauthorized access to resources. Therefore, relationships are encoded into certificates signed by both the nodes establishing the relationship. The relationship certificate also contains the trust level of the corresponding relation. If a fully decentralized solution is adopted, each node stores the certificates corresponding to the relationships he/she has established in the community. The advantages of this solution are that each node keeps locally his/her policies and data, without revealing them to a third party and that the workload due to access control enforcement is distributed among the community nodes. The drawback is that answering an access request may require software and hardware resources more powerful than those typically available to collaborative community participants. Indeed, since access to a resource is granted on the basis of the direct/indirect relationships the requestor node has with other nodes in the network, answering an access request requires to verify the existence of specific paths within a WBSN. Additionally, since the trust level of an indirect relationship is usually computed by taking into account all the shortest paths connecting the two nodes (or a subset of them), this task may be very difficult and time consuming in a fully decentralized solution.[4] For this reason, we have adopted a *semi-decentralized* solution (cfr. Figure 2(c)), according to which certificates are managed by a *Certificate Server (CS)*. This server acts like a certificate repository in charge of storing into a central certificate directory all the relationship certificates specified by community nodes, and enhanced with the functionalities for retrieving certificate paths. In contrast, access control enforcement is in charge of nodes (as in the fully decentralized solution). This solution has several benefits in term of efficiency and scal-

---

4 In the literature, there exist several different methods to compute the trust value of indirect relationships [GH06], but most of them consider all the shortest paths (or a subset of them) to perform the computation.

ability with respect to the fully decentralized one. Indeed, introducing the certificate server makes the overall framework more efficient, in that the burden of certificate management and path discovery is on the *CS*, which obviously performs this task more efficiently than any other single node in the collaborative community. Moreover, the framework gains in scalability, in that a collaborative community could exploit several (external) certificate servers, on the basis of the number of its participants. Furthermore, this solution might be extensible to interactions among different collaborative communities. Indeed, users of a given collaborative community could interact with participants of another community, under the assumption that there exists a mutual agreement between the corresponding certificate servers. Finally, the last two solutions, i.e., the fully decentralized and the semi-decentralized, can be further classified into *owner-side* and *requestor-side* access control. The owner-side paradigm is the one usually adopted by data management systems. According to this paradigm the resource owner is in charge of checking whether the access can be granted or not (possibly interacting with the *CS* for path retrieval), on the basis of the specified policies. In contrast, according to the requestor-side approach, the burden of answering an access request is mainly on the requestor node. More precisely, according to this paradigm, which is the one we adopt in our system [CFP08], the owner sends to the requestor node the policies h/she has to satisfy in order to gain access to the requested resource. The requestor node should then provide the owner with a *proof*, certifying that he/she satisfies the requirements specified by the received policies. The proof, which is built by interacting with the *CS* to obtain the required certificate paths, consists of a set of relationship paths, as well as a trust level. Moreover, the resource owner receives some additional information that makes him/her able to check the correctness of the proof. We refer the interested readers to [CFP06,CFP08] for all the details of the access control protocol.

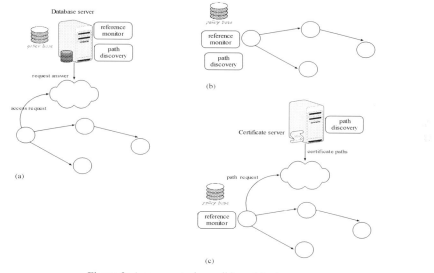

Figure 2: Access control: possible architectures

5 Privacy-aware Access Control

In a collaborative community, access requests are mainly granted on the basis of the relationships existing among nodes in the community. Therefore, answering an access request mainly means verifying the existence of certain relationship paths within the network. An important aspect that should be taken into account is that a node in the community may have some privacy preferences on the disclosure of his/her relationships. For instance, a given node may wish that only a subset of the other nodes in the collaborative community can be aware of a specific relationship he/she participates in. Since relationship information is fundamental in order to regulate access to shared resources, techniques should be devised to perform *privacy-aware access control*, that is, to protect relationship information leakage while enforcing access control. To this purpose, a naive solution applicable in semi-decentralized architecture is to let the *CS* enforce the privacy preferences of the community users wrt relationship disclosure. However, for those environments where relationship privacy is a primary need, we believe that relying on a *CS* having the right to know all the relationships existing in the community is not appropriate. Therefore, a decentralized solution should be, in this case, preferred.

To this purpose, one option, that we have explored in [CFP07], is to adopt a cryptographic based solution, according to which certificates are encrypted and the corresponding keys are delivered only to those users authorized according to the specified preferences. In this scenario, the *CS* acts only as a repository of encrypted certificates, and it does not receive the corresponding decryption keys. Therefore, it cannot infer information on the relationships established by collaborative community users. Clearly, the main drawback of this approach is related to the cost of key management and distribution. Another problem is related to the fact that the *CS* must be trusted wrt certificate revocation enforcement. Indeed, when a relationship does not exist anymore, the community users should be informed because the relationship should not be exploited anymore to get access to a resource. To overcome this problem, according to the architecture proposed in [CFP07], the central node maintains a certificate revocation list which must be updated to reflect social network topology changes.

An alternative option to cryptographic-based solutions can be that of exploiting a collaborative protocol [CF08]. This approach has the benefit of not requiring the management of the ceriticate revocation list by the *CS*. The idea of a collaborative solution is that the path (and the corresponding trust level) necessary to obtain access to a resource is built through a collaboration of selected nodes in the community. The collaborative process is started by the resource owner which tries to build the required path by contacting his/her neighbours and asking them whether they have a relationship of the required type with the resource requestor. If a path satisfying the specified requirements is found, the process halts, otherwise the node receiving the request for collaboration propagates it to his/her neighbours, with which it has a relationship of the required type. This process is iterated until the request cannot be further forwarded (i.e., the process reaches a node that does not have relationships of the required type) or the path is found, that is, the process reaches a node having a direct relationship of the required type with the requestor. During the collaborative process, information on the traversed path (i.e., traversed relationships and corresponding trust levels) is gathered. When the path is found, all this information are sent back to the resource owner, which is then able to locally verify whether the found path satisfies the depth and trust level requirements specified in the access rule. It is relevant to note that according to this collaborative process information on relationship a node inserts in the path (i.e., relationship type and trust level) are available to all the nodes that subsequently take part to the collaborative process. To overcome this privacy concern, we propose a collaboration driven by the specified preferences wrt the release of relationship information: only the neighbours that satisfy the preferences associated with the relationships in the path built so far are contacted to take part to the collaborative process. The use of cryptographic techniques and of a particular digital signature data structure (called *onion signature*) ensure that relationship privacy is guaranteed during the collaborative process. We refer the interested reader to [CF08] for more details about the protocol.

6 Trust Modelling, Computation and Protection

As we mentioned in Section 1, trust plays a key role when performing access control in collaborative communities in that it is one of the fundamental parameters to decide whether the access can be granted or not. When trust is used for access control purposes, its semantics is mainly related to the compliance with the specified access control policies and   the specified preferences wrt relationship disclosure, if any. In this scenario, it is fundamental to devise mechanisms that help the user to objectively assess the compliance of a user wrt the specified access control policies and privacy preferences. This is still an open issue, and many alternative options can be devised. In what follows, we briefly present our proposal.

A possible solution is to adopt the same rational   applied in the real world: the trust value assigned to a person is estimated on the basis of his/her reputation, which can be assessed taking into account the person behaviour. Indeed, it is a matter of fact that people assign to a person with unfair behaviour a bad reputation and, as a consequence, a low level of trust. Thus, a possible solution is to estimate the trust level to be assigned to a user in a collaborative community on the basis of his/her reputation, given by his/her behaviour with regards to all the other users in the community. In our scenario, this can be done by making a user   able to monitor the behaviour of the other users wrt the release of private information or resources. Obviously, this naive solution to this problem implies to log all the access control decisions into an audit file that can be inspected by the other users in the network. However, this solution raises serious privacy concerns, because a participant might not agree in releasing information about the decisions he/she has made, even if these are signals of good behaviour. For instance, a participant might prefer not to make public that he/she released some resources related to his/her private life (e.g., the Mexico.jpg file) to a given participant in that, he/she would prefer not to reveal at all to others the existence of that resource. To overcome this problem, there is therefore the need to investigate methods making available information about access control decisions and actions performed by collaborative community users in an anonymous version. Here, the challenge is that of devising anonymization strategies of the audit file, such that details about the performed decisions/actions are kept private but, at the same time, it is possible to determine whether the decision underlying the action is a correct or not, with regards to the specified access control policies and privacy preferences. In [NCFT08], we have defined a method exploiting the property of the ElGamal cryptosystem, which allows one to inspect the audit file, without violating user privacy. In particular, each node in the community is equipped with an audit file, which reports all the user decisions wrt the release of resources and relatioship certificates. The audit file is built by a trusted module, which is downloaded from the community manager site when the user joins the community. The audit file contains, in addition to each decision made by a node wrt the release of a resource or a certificate, also some additional information that makes the other nodes in the network able to evaluate whether the decision is compliant or not with the specified policies and preferences. In particular, the audit file is made available to other community nodes in an anonymized version, that avoids to reveal the details of the performed actions by still being able to determine their compliance with the specified policies and preferences.

Finally, another relevant issue related to trust is to devise methods to protect the trust level encoded into relationship certificates. Like for relationships, this issue is tricky because on the one hand there is the need of protecting trust level disclosure, on the other hand the resource owner has to know the trust level of relationships in order to decide whether the access can be granted or not.

7 Conclusion

As Web 2.0 tchnologies are more and more used by single users as well as enterprises there is the need of securing one of its key representatives, that is, collaborative communities. In this paper, we have focused on access control requirements of collaborative communities, with a particular interest on privacy protection during access control enforcement. We have also presented some techniques that can be used to address the identified requirements.

The area of security and privacy for collaborative communities is new and therefore a lot of research issues still remain open. For instance, one important issue, which we have mentioned at the end of Section 6, is related to trust protection when performing access control. Also, the use of trusted computing technologies for privacy-aware access control enforcement is an interesting research direction. Finally, other security services, besides access control, should be re-designed to better fit in the collaborative community scenario, such as for instance, identity management, authentication, or integrity enforcement.

References

[AVM07]   Ali, B. Villegas, W. Maheswaran, M: A Trust based Approach for Protecting User Data in Social Networks. In: 2007 Conference of the Center for Avanced Studies on Collaborative Research (CAS-CON'07), 288–293, 2007.

[Berteau07] Berteau, S: Facebook's Misrepresentation of Beacon's Threat to Privacy: Tracking Users who Opt out or are not Logged in. Security Advisor Research Blog. Available at: http://community.ca.com/blogs/securityadvisor, 2007.

[Canadian07] Canadian Privacy Commission. Social Networking and Privacy. Available at: http://www.privcom.gc.ca, 2007.

[CF08]   Carminati, B. Ferrari, E: Privacy-aware Collaborative Access Control in Web-based Social Networks. In: Proc. of the 22nd IFIP WG 11.3 Working Conference on Data and Applications Security (DB-SEC2008). Springer, London, UK, July 2008.

[CFP06]   Carminati, B. Ferrari, E. Perego, A: Rule-based Access Control for Social Networks. In: Proc. of the OTM Workshops. Springer, Montpellier, France, November 2006.

[CFP07]   Carminati, B. Ferrari, E. Perego, A: Private Relationships in Social Networks. In: Proc. of the ICDE 2007 Workshops. IEEE CS Press, Istanbul, Turkey, April 2007.

[CFP08]   B. Carminati, E. Ferrari, A. Perego. Enforcing Access Control in Web-based Social Networks. ACM Transactions on Information and System Security, to appear.

[Chen06]   Chen, L: Facebook's Feeds Cause Privacy Concerns. the Amherst Student. Available at: http://halogen.note.amherst.edu/astudent/2006-2007/issue02/news/01.html, October 2006.

[GH06]   Golbeck, J. Hendler, J.A: Inferring Binary Trust Relationships in Web-based Social Networks. In: ACM Trans. Internet Techn. 6(4): 497-529, 2006.

[HJS07]   Hart, M. Johnson, R. Stent, A: More Content - Less Control: Access Control in the Web 2.0. In: Proc. of the Web 2.0 Security and Privacy Workshop, 2007. Available at: http://seclab.cs.rice.edu/w2sp/2007/papers/.

[Hogben07] Hogben, G: Security Issues and Recommendations for Online Social Networks. European Network and Information Security Agency (ENISA), position paper, 2007. Available at: http://www.enisa.europa.eu/.

[LDGK0807] Liu, K. Das, K. Grandison, T. Kargupta, H: Privacy-Preserving Data Analysis on Graphs and Social Networks. Next Generation Data Mining, to appear.

[McAfee06] McAfee, A.P: Enterprise 2.0: The Dawn of Emergent Collaboration. In: MIT Sloan Management Review, 47(3):21-28, 2006.

[NCFT08]   Nin, J. Carminati, B. Ferrari, E. Torra, V: Dynamic Reputation-based Trust Computation in Private Networks. Technical Report, University of Insubria, 2008, submitted for publication.

[SD+05]   Staab, S. Domingos, P. Mika, P. Golbeck, J. Ding, L. Finin, T. et al: Social Networks Applied. In: IEEE Intelligent Systems, 20(1): 80-93, 2005.

Can Economics Provide Insights into Trust Infrastructure?

Claire Vishik

Intel Corporation UK
claire.vishik@intel.com

Abstract

Many security technologies require infrastructure for authentication, verification, and other processes. In many cases, viable and innovative security technologies are never adopted on a large scale because the necessary infrastructure is slow to emerge. Analyses of such technologies typically focus on their technical flaws, and research emphasizes innovative approaches to stronger implementation of the core features. However, an observation can be made that in many cases the success of adoption pattern depends on non-technical issues rather than technology– lack of economic incentives, difficulties in finding initial investment, inadequate government support. While a growing body of research is dedicated to economics of security and privacy in general, few theoretical studies in this area have been completed, and even fewer that look at the economics of "trust infrastructure" beyond simple "cost of ownership" models. This exploratory paper takes a look at some approaches in theoretical economics to determine if they can provide useful insights into security infrastructure technologies and architectures that have the best chance to be adopted. We attempt to discover if models used in theoretical economics can help inform technology developers of the optimal business models that offer a better chance for quick infrastructure deployment.

1 Introduction

With the advent and proliferation of Internet-based communications and electronic commerce, there was also a burst in research in modeling economic attributes of the emerging realities of digital commerce. Economic assessment of the elements of the digital economy focused on several directions: economics of (digital) information and its distribution [PRIE94], productive business models for electronic commerce, and economics of supplemental areas of digital economy, such as security and privacy or Business-to-Business systems. Although some theoretical studies have appeared during the last fifteen years (e.g. [ANDE01], [GORD02], [VARI95]), the emphasis in assessing economics of security and privacy continues to be on the analysis of the cost of supporting different aspects of security, economic effects of vulnerabilities on more general aspects of business [CAVU07], and attitudes of users faced with security threats ([HERR06], [GALO05], [POIN06]). There is very little research on economics of technology elements of security or privacy, such as authentication or PKI, using economic theory to explain success or failure of some of the security and privacy mechanisms.

The purpose of this paper is to explore the ability of some ideas in theoretical economics to obtain useful insights into design and deployment of authentication and verification infrastructure that we call "trust" infrastructure for the sake of simplicity. This infrastructure is needed to support the ability of users, devices, and digital artifacts to be reliably authenticated and their rights established and verified in single or multiple domains. This infrastructure is also necessary to ensure that elements of transactions can be reliably verified in order to be trusted. Infrastructure of this type, including CAs (Certificate Authorities), directories, identity management, policy management, and other systems, is necessary to

D. Gawrock, H. Reimer, A.-R. Sadeghi, C. Vishik (Editors): Future of Trust in Computing, Vieweg+Teubner (2009), 93-101

carry out such functions as remote attestation in Trusted Computing, single sign-on (SSO) as described by Liberty Alliance specifications, and to implement similar schemes proposed for payment transactions and communications among heterogeneous networks.

2 Problem Statement

Viable technologies have been designed for authentication of users and devices in various environments and for verification of the validity of the credentials used in a variety of procedures such as digital signatures. New approaches continue to emerge, sometimes promising considerable improvements for the currently used procedures, e.g. "Identity Based Encryption" that attempts to alleviate complexity of key management commonly associated with asymmetric cryptography. Analysis of recent US patents and patent applications indicates that these technologies continue to be of significant interest to industry and academia.

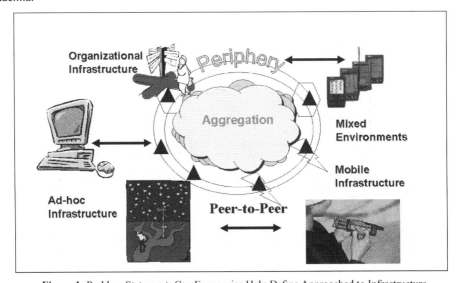

Figure 1: Problem Statement: Can Economics Help Define Approached to Infrastructure

Standards have been developed addressing aspects of the "trust" environment, from the format of credentials to associated transport and communication protocols. Moderate successes can be reported, in adoption of PKI by various governments, growing proliferation of secure email, emergence of more secure connections between different types of networks, or examples of SSO systems going beyond one organization. Yet these successes did not lead to the establishment of the global and ubiquitous trust infrastructure that could be used to support authentication and verification on a significant scale.

It is clear that technology limitations of various approaches to trust infrastructure could be eliminated if compelling reasons existed to build global verification infrastructure. These reasons are likelier to be economic or organizational than technical. They need, therefore, to be studied outside of the technology domain alone. Figure 1 above illustrates the interdependencies in the problem being studied.

We observe that credentials presented and exchanged for verification or authentication can be compared, in some cases, to money or fiat money – a recognized equivalent of value. Consequently, we ask the following questions: could theoretical economics and, specifically, theory of exchange and monetary economies provide guidance with regard to the types of technologies that will be the most successful to be employed for building "trust infrastructure"? Could theoretical economics and analysis of related technologies inform us of the organizational or government support necessary for the emergence of the global "trust infrastructure?"

The paper starts with the description of economic theories of monetary, exchange economies, and intermediation, discusses their applicability to economics of security, analyzes the benefits of using these theories to assist in defining architectures and business models for trust infrastructures, and ends with conclusions on the viability of this approach. The paper doesn't discuss technologies used in trust infrastructures: the assumption is made that the readers are familiar with the essential features of these technologies, but it attempts to provide some background in economics useful to technology developers.

3 Verification and Authentication Infrastructure

There are multiple ways, in which elements of the trust infrastructure are built and trust is established. In peer-to-peer systems, credentials exchanged in the course of a transaction can be linked to a third party performing verification or contained on the devices exchanging information. If proof of validity can be established on each device with the levels of trustworthiness that are sufficient for participants in peer-to-peer connections, credentials can be exchanged to the satisfaction of both parties. However, the rules for the propagation of trust to other participants in peer-to-peer network are difficult to establish and impossible to maintain and verify in this environment. Although many peer-to-peer systems that attracted a large population of users focused on their primary functionality (e.g. file exchange) and didn't invest heavily in trust or security, today's social or marketing networks that follow models similar to classic peer-to-peer are more concerned about establishing and preserving trust. Consequently, a body of research is beginning to emerge that defines optimal trust in this environment that is likely to contribute to the development of new technologies for various types of peer-to-peer networks.

Mobile and ad-hoc networks that have become increasingly pervasive over the last decade are designed in a fashion somewhat similar to peer-to-peer. They don't rely on fixed infrastructure for authentication and verification ([MERW07]), and all network functions are performed by the nodes forming the network. Consequently, verification is carried out in a manner similar to the procedures in peer-to-peer networks.

In organizations, extensive internal infrastructures for authentication and verification have been developed that may include PKI and other elements, such as identity management or policy management systems. As organizational computing becomes more complex, multiple infrastructures supporting verification are created, and attempts to merge or integrate them are part of ongoing IT efforts. These infrastructures are based on the same principles of managing risks as their predecessors: issuance of IDs and credentials (including keys and certificates) is governed by complex rules that also define the domains where these rules are allowed to operate. Similar efforts focusing on extending infrastructures are undertaken in standards organizations, such as OASIS work on Enterprise Key Management Infrastructure, an XML based protocol to provide symmetric key management framework over TCP/IP networks.

In electronic commerce, several types of verification and authentication accompany transactions: those supported by internal infrastructures of e-commerce entities, those related to external payment systems, and, frequently, those linked to the environment of individuals accessing systems, such as system parameters collected from their devices, IP addresses, or hardware tokens. Individuals and organizations, therefore, have to rely on multiple systems guaranteeing varying levels of assurance and trust when determining rights to access systems and perform transactions. Exchange of credentials is the foundation of these transactions, and artifacts connected with the user's or provider's "trustworthiness" are exchanged for rights to access information or obtain goods.

With concerns about privacy growing, more systems are designed based on verification of credentials instead of the identification of individuals and/or their devices. . Although these models are more frequently a subject of research rather than commercial implementation, it is clear that they will influence the design of "trust" infrastructures in the near future.

The very brief overview of some of the available methods of designing infrastructures for key and credentials' management and verification demonstrate that they follow diverse models: peer-to-peer non-centralized exchange of credentials, centralized organizational models, and aggregated models where several infrastructures are connected.

4 Exchange Economies, Monetary Economies and Asymmetric Information

Let us now examine in general terms how various types of economies operate. Differences between monetary and exchange economies have been a subject of study since the 19th century. Among the factors affecting direct exchange of goods, double coincidence of wants can be seen as the core source of inefficiency in exchange markets. First described by Jevons in 1875 [JEVO20], double coincidence of wants means that both agents involved in an exchange transaction without a recognizable currency need to find the other agent's offering useful and desirable. Instead of simply obtaining the objects that is needed, an agent has to locate another agent that not only has the desirable commodity, but also wants to exchange it for the commodity that the first agent offers. These requirements increase the waiting periods before transactions can occur, according to Jevons, and therefore make transactions less efficient.

However, it is not double coincidence of wants alone that leads to limited efficiency of exchange markets. In order to mitigate, to some extent at least, the consequences of double coincidence of wants in exchanges, the economy can create special markets where pairs of products or artifacts can be exchanged [BANN96]. This method increases the number of markets and is costly, but it is possible.

This is the predominant model in today's trust infrastructure: multiple credentials' exchange "markets" have emerged, permitting the agent's credentials to be verified by infrastructures specifically created for each transaction type. Current trust market is therefore costly and inefficient and requires a greater effort on the part of the users and operators to establish their trustworthiness. If credentials used by these systems are time-sensitive and need to reflect changes in the positioning of the agent and the verifier, the weaknesses of this model become even more apparent.

But low efficiency is not, according to some researchers, the main problem with exchange economies. Banerjee and Maskin [BANN96] believe that the main issue is asymmetric information, unequal knowledge of buyers and sellers about the value of artifacts offered in exchanges. Because of the lack of expertise and ability to recognize intrinsic and market value of artifacts in a market, agents assume that there is a high risk associated with a transaction [AKER73]. The increased perception of risks can eventually result in a situation when no transaction happen [AKER73]. Figure 2 below illustrates some aspects of asymmetric information in markets.

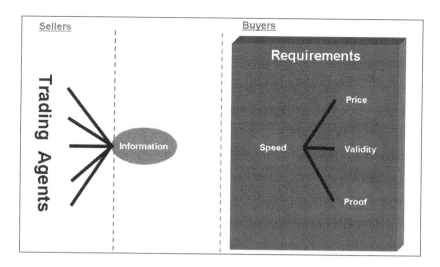

Figure 2: Asymmetric Information and Market Requirements

Asymmetric information of the parties involved in transactions using trust infrastructure is certainly the largest inhibitor of the emergence of global and ubiquitous systems. A look at vulnerabilities of digital commerce systems (e.g. phishing) demonstrates that asymmetric information is inevitably present in markets for informational products and strongly affects security artifacts. The full value (in this case, trustworthiness) of these assets can be determined only when the exchange has been completed and the value transferred to the other party [BHAT89], [PRIE94].

As shown by Akerlof [AKER73], in many cases, the quality of a product or artifact is difficult or impossible for the agents to verify without access to additional infrastructure. Since low quality goods (in this case, unreliable verification or fraudulent credentials), although easier to implement or obtain, are less desirable and frequently not acceptable, no transactions at all may take place in a market that is believed to contain higher risks relative to perceived value of the product, in this case access to systems in exchange for disclosure.

Intermediation is one of the tools helping information markets resolve the issue of asymmetric information. Marketing theory views intermediaries as "organizations that support exchanges between producers and consumers, increasing the efficiency of the exchange process by aggregating transactions to create economies of scale and scope" [WILL87], [WILL94]. Williamson [WILL94] contends that a very important role of intermediaries is increasing quality in a market, a role that is extremely important in a market where the product is verification of credentials presented in support of a transaction.

According to Bose and Pingle [BOSE95], the main function of intermediaries is to eliminate friction in markets and therefore increase trust among participants. Bhattacharya and Hagerty [BHAT89] see the role of intermediaries as regulators between agents in a market.

5 Are Models and Approaches of Theoretical Economics Applicable to This Context?

Trust infrastructure can be presented as a market, with credentials acting as a product or currency, depending on the model, and agents involved in transaction exchanging these credentials for the right to use or access systems. Parallels with economic models of exchange, monetary, and intermediated markets are striking.

But the similarities are incomplete: credentials do not need to obey the laws of supply and demand, nor does the supply of credentials need to depend directly on the frequency and volume of transactions and portfolio of products.

As a result, while using parallels describing the effects of introducing the universal equivalent of value in economic models and proof of validity of credentials and verifiers in trust infrastructures can lead to new interesting insights, direct re-use of most modeling techniques or models from economics for the analysis of trust infrastructure is not possible. The models and their assumptions need to be adapted to the new problem.

An informal test of the validity of this approach in general is to establish if new information about trust infrastructures can be gained by using economic models to define the design of verification protocols and architecture of infrastructures that are proved to be viable by these models, but are not currently used because there appears to be no evident technological gain.

It would be especially valuable if models specifically created to study "trust" infrastructures could assist in examination of more complex situations where validity, efficiency, and need for privacy are included in the analysis.

5.1 Detecting and Integrating New Business Models

New business models tend to emerge through the inventive spirit of innovators who found new companies based on new concepts. Occasionally, new business models are theoretically developed and then successfully introduced into markets. Vickery auctions, currently used in spectrum auctions, are an example of such top-down introductions. Although some examples of this approach can be found, introducing new business models based on theory is rare.

There is abundant literature claiming that the process of innovation has changed in the Internet economy. Many papers, from the last decade or more recent, allude to aspects of this paradigm shift ([DRUC94], [ARTH96]). However, many fundamental questions about the greater responsiveness of today's computing environment to the introduction of new business models remain unanswered. In fact, even the general trends in the emergence of the new models for the Internet-influenced environment continue to be elusive [MORO02]. There is evidence that "disintermediation" and direct transactions among agents are growing in importance [ANTH06], but there is also proof that the trend towards intermediation is essential [KLOS05]. It is possible to find examples that independent markets are likelier to emerge quickly in today's more dynamic environment, and it is also easy to find strong testimony of the crucial need for cooperation among markets. Although the big picture may not appear consistent, seemingly opposing trends are not necessarily at variance with one another.

In the case of building infrastructures, an undertaking that requires considerable investment and a substantial level of trust from the participants rather than spontaneous technology emergence tested by the viability of the business model, we believe that economic modeling offers significant benefits. This is because substantial investments are required to start significant infrastructure projects, limiting the usefulness of the market test that many technologies are expected to undergo. In addition, non-technical requirements for such infrastructures, including already mentioned support for privacy features, special rules for user enrollment, or requirements for interoperability with other legal entities ensure that the design is founded on a number of characteristics that technology alone cannot properly define. Finally, the fact that many of the new frameworks (e.g. Liberty Alliance or Trusted Computing) rely on infrastructure to implement their full vision, makes evaluation of viable operational models much more important than in an average case of technology deployment.

5.2 How to Build "Trust" Infrastructures

As mentioned in previous sections, theoretical economics can provide elementary insights into the business models used for trust infrastructures.

For instance, peer-to-peer or similarly designed mobile or ad-hoc "trust" infrastructures offer little efficiency from the economic point of view and can only guarantee a limited level of trust. Models used for studying exchange economies could be adapted for this area, demonstrating that search for an acceptable "transaction agent" providing requisite levels of proof as well as asymmetric information of the parties in the transaction about the validity of credentials continue to be strong inhibitors of the wide-scale deployment of these technologies. Although efforts in increasing flexibility and portability of credentials' systems are necessary to move the field forward, it is also important to work on models that increase efficiency for deployment.

Centralized organizational "trust" infrastructures, analogous with monetary economies where the value of a currency is universally recognized, offer a better level of efficiency and can support higher levels of verification requirements. However, given the growing need to bridge isolated systems, organizational infrastructures remain insufficient to support diverse verification needs of modern computing environments. While the level of trust within the system can be maintained, whenever multiple isolated systems have to exchange verification units, asymmetric information among verifiers will negatively affect the efficiency of transactions. In addition, search effort for transactions requiring greater universal coverage will continue to be significant. And friction among participants, caused, for example, by differing privacy requirements or regulatory mandates in isolated trust infrastructures will continue to be an impediment for wider deployment.

Finally, aggregated infrastructures, with intermediation, while expensive to build, appear to offer the highest level of efficiency for the diverse and pervasive verification (trust) infrastructures. This model permits to alleviate the negative influences of asymmetric information in the systems and also devise more effective mechanisms to eliminate friction among participating nodes and agents.

In addition to outlining general architectures for trust infrastructures, re-using the models of theoretical economics permits us to examine the influence of non-technology factors on optimal architectures. Productive and interesting research in this area can be carried out by studying methods and developing technologies to reduce friction in transactions among different "trust" infrastructures. Effects of privacy requirements on architectures and design of optimal regulations to support ubiquitous trust infrastructures are some of the areas of research that could conducted using the methodology described in this paper.

6 Conclusions

Building verification and authentication infrastructures that support trust in diverse environments is very important for the progress of computing. Literature analysis points to a gap in the research in this area. While technology-related research is very active, theoretical examination of economic influences on architectures is minimal, with the substantial body of research focusing on the more general study of the economics of security and/or privacy. Although there are significant differences in the models used in theoretical economics to study exchange and monetary economies, there are sufficient analogies that permit to use this approach to study some features of "trust" infrastructures. The general insights in the optimal architectures in this area may not lead to complete constructive practical recommendations for deployment, but modeling of the elements of friction caused by non-technical elements of trust infrastructures can increase our understanding of the important issues that new technologies alone cannot resolve.

Bibliography

[AKER73] Akerlof, G. A. The Market for "Lemons": Quality Uncertainty and The Market Mechanism. Quarterly Journal of Economics, 1973, 488-500.

[ANDE01] Anderson, R. 2001. Why Information Security is Hard-An Economic Perspective. In *Proceedings of the 17th Annual Computer Security Applications Conference* (December 10 - 14, 2001). ACSAC. IEEE Computer Society, Washington, DC, 358.

[ANTH06] Anthias, T. and Sankar, K. 2006. The network's new role. *Queue* 4, 4 (May. 2006), 38-46. [3] Arrow, K .J. The Economics of Information. In Dertouzos, M. and Moses, J, ed. The Computer Age: A Twenty Year View. Cambridge, MA: MIT Press, 1979.

[ARTH96] Arthur, W. B. "Increasing Returns and the New World of Business." *Harvard Business Review,* July-August 1996, 74(4), pp. 100-109.

[BHAT89] Bhattacharya, S. & Hagerty, K. Dealerships, training externalities, and general equilibrium. In Prescott, E.C.and Wallace, N. (eds.). *Contractual Arrangements for Intertemporal Trade. Minnesota Series in Macroeconomics,* Minneapolis: University of Minnesota Press, 1989.

[BANN96] Bannerjee, A and Maskin, E. Fiat Money in the Kitoyaka-Wright Model. Quarterly Journal of Economics, 111 (4) 1996, p. 9551005.

[BOJA08] Bojanc, R. and Jerman-Blaič, B. 2008. Towards a standard approach for quantifying an ICT security investment. *Comput. Stand. Interfaces* 30, 4 (May. 2008), 216-222.

[BOSE95] Bose, G. and Pingle, M. Stores. Economic Theory, 6 (1995), p. 251-262.

[CAVU07] Cavusoglu, H., and Raghunathan, S. 2007. Efficiency of Vulnerability Disclosure Mechanisms to Disseminate Vulnerability Knowledge. *IEEE Trans. Softw. Eng.* 33, 3 (Mar. 2007), 171-185.

[DRUC94] Drucker, P.F. The Theory of Business. *Harvard Business Review*, September/October 1994, pp. 95-104.

[GALO05] Gal-Or, E. and Ghose, A. 2005. The Economic Incentives for Sharing Security Information. *Info. Sys. Research* 16, 2 (Jun. 2005), 186-208.

[GORD02] Gordon, L. A. and Loeb, M. P. 2002. The economics of information security investment. *ACM Trans. Inf. Syst. Secur.* 5, 4 (Nov. 2002), 438-457.

[HERR06] Herrmann, P. and Herrmann, G. 2006. Security requirement analysis of business processes. *Electronic Commerce Research* 6, 3-4 (Oct. 2006), 305-335

[JEVO20] Jevons, William Stanley. Money and the mechanism of exchange. New York:D. Appleton, 1920.

[KLOS05] Klos, T. B. and Alkemade, F. 2005. Trusted intermediating agents in electronic trade networks. In *Proceedings of the Fourth international Joint Conference on Autonomobus Agents and Multiagent Systems* (The Netherlands, July 25 - 29, 2005). AAMAS '05. ACM, New York, NY, 1249-1250

[MORO02]Morowitz, H. J. 2002, The Emergence of Everything: *How the world became complex*, Oxford University Press, New York.

[POIN06] Poindexter, J. C., Earp, J. B., and Baumer, D. L. 2006. An experimental ecnomics approach toward quantifying online privacy choices. *Information Systems Frontiers* 8, 5 (Dec. 2006), 363-374.

[PRIE94] Priest, W. C. An information framework for the planning and design of the information highways. Center for Information, Technology, and Society, February, 1994.

[MERW07] van der Merwe, J, Dawoud, D, and Mac Donals, S. A survey on peer-to-peer key management for mobile ad hoc networks. ACM Computing Surveys (CSUR) v. 39 , Issue 1 (2007)

[VARI95] Varian, H. R. Economic Mechanism Design for Computerized Agents. In *The First Usenix Workshop on Electronic Commerce*, New York: Usenix Association, 1995, p. 13-21.

[WILL87] Williamson, S. D. Recent developments in modeling financial intermediation. *Federal Reserve Bank of Minneapolis, Quarterly Review*, 11, Summer (1987), 19-29.

[WILL94] Williamson, S. and Wright, R. Barter and Monetary Exchange under Private Information. The American Economic Review, March (1994), p. 101-123.

Reviewing Privacy during Design – Voluntary Technology Dialogue System

Kathryn Whelan · Kevin Fisher

Intel Corporation (UK) Ltd.
{Kathryn.Whelan | Kevin.Fisher}@intel.com

Abstract

This paper introduces a framework proposal encouraging industry and regulators to conduct data protection and privacy technology design reviews early in the design process, as driven by the 2008-2009 Comité Européen de Normalisation/Information Society Standardization System (European Committee for Standardisation, known as CEN/ISSS) Data Protection and Privacy ("DPP") Workshop[1] work programme. Included are a description of the proposed project, working method and approach, precedents and previous work, as well as the rationale, objectives and consequences of not developing such a model, concluding with comments regarding policy relevance and market impact.

1 Project Description

The objective of this project is to use the standardisation process to help organisations comply with data protection and privacy obligations under the "Data Protection" Directive 95/46/EC[2] ("the Directive") and relevant national legislation. Such compliance is to be encouraged by facilitating harmonisation of practice, improving understanding of sector requirements and encouraging consistency of assessment and oversight.

The proposal aims to assist organisations of all sizes in complying with their data protection and privacy obligations and monitoring their data protection compliance. The recommendations are intended to improve the level of awareness of data protection and privacy issues in general and of issues specific to particular business sectors and/or related to the development of new products and technologies.

The proposal is based on one of the three of the key recommendations put forward by the Initiative for Privacy Standardisation in Europe (IPSE) in it's 2001 report[3]. IPSE, which was launched to analyse the status of privacy protection arrangements and to determine whether standardisation of actions could assist business in implementing the Directive, identified several standardisation opportunities that could aid implementation.

Recommendation 6 concerned the establishment of a coordination and early-warning system for new developments in technology to assist data protection commissioners and business to liaise on technological developments and ensure independent data protection expertise and analysis for new technologies.

D. Gawrock, H. Reimer, A.-R. Sadeghi, C. Vishik (Editors): Future of Trust in Computing, Vieweg+Teubner (2009), 102-108

1.1 Precedent/Previous Work

Historically data protection and privacy reviews have taken place on a mostly informal basis between industry and the Article 29 Working Party ("WP29") [4] or an individual Data Protection Authority ("DPA"). However, this has never developed into a systematic process, remaining simply an informal review. In addition, any outcome has not been seen as a binding opinion. However, this existing dialogue can be seen as a template for this proposal, though it is clear that such a process is not scalable and would not be capable of serving the needs of all companies, nor of providing a level playing field.

Meanwhile, momentum builds in cross border collaboration efforts, recognition of the needs of today's interconnected and increasingly complex technological world. Examples can be cited, such as regulatory investigations of industry sectors across borders, the development of a Binding Corporate Rules (BCRs) approvals framework[4] or the Data Privacy Subgroup of Asia Pacific Economic Cooperation's (APEC) Electronic Commerce Steering Group (ECSG) Cross-Border Privacy Rules (CBPRs) [5], and international discussion and development in subject areas such as Privacy Impact Assessments (PIAs) [5], audit frameworks[1], standardisation[1][7], best practices[1] & guidance[4].

2 Voluntary Technology Dialogue System

The CEN/ISSS (European Committee for Standardisation/Comité Européen de Normalisation [CEN] –/Information Society Standardization System [ISSS]) Data Protection and Privacy Workshop[1] ("CEN/ISSS WS/DPP") has received funding from the European Commission ("EC") for the 2008-2009 work programme.

The CEN/ISSS Workshop Agreement ("CWA") for the Voluntary Technology Dialogue System[1] proposes the creation of a voluntary framework for dialogue and will outline processes between industry and regulators, with the aim of ensuring new products, technologies and services comply with the Directive.

2.1 Rationale

Ensuring new products, technologies and services comply with the relevant Data Protection and Privacy laws as transposed in all European Union ("EU") member states can be a challenging task for industry. In addition, regulators find themselves somewhat unaware of potential new technologies likely to reach the market in the near future.

In an effort to help both industry and regulators overcome these hurdles it is proposed to develop a voluntary systematic process enabling companies of all sizes (small and medium sized enterprises through to multi national corporations) to work more closely with regulators during the development cycle of new products.

There are clear benefits for Industry arising from closer liaison with regulators at a very early stage of product development. Such liaison will help determine design specifications and help companies to become more familiar with obligations under existing data protection legislation.

It is hoped that European regulators would welcome the opportunity to be briefed on future technology roadmaps via the dialogue system which may assist regulators to meet their obligations to provide "better regulation".

While in the past, there have been a number of new technology discussions between industry and the Article 29 Working Party, such discussions have never been a standardised and systematic process, the discussions have simply operated as an informal review. The experience of these discussions may be seen as one basis for a dialogue system, however, it is clear that existing informal arrangements are not scalable and would not be able to serve the needs of all companies nor provide an equal opportunities playing field.

It is proposed to develop a formal voluntary framework for dialogue and outline processes between industry and regulators. This voluntary process would enable fast and effective reviews of new design concepts between an industry player (or group of players) and EU regulators.

The primary purpose is to ensure new technologies are not inappropriately delayed from reaching the market and thereby providing benefit to EU citizens, and to protect against privacy invasive technologies unwittingly being launched on the EU market.

The secondary purpose is to provide education of both parties on regulatory expectations and new technology developments.

The framework will be defined, documented and agreed with regulators and industry and include agreements and processes on, for example, lead times, documentation requirements, escalation procedures, confidentiality practices and the dialogue process itself.

2.2 Objectives

From an industry perspective the following three requirements of a design review with regulators are clear:

- a voluntary one-stop shop review process;
- no after the event surprises;
- a documented "opinion" issued by the regulator(s) at the end of the process.

Likewise, from a regulator perspective, three different requirements must be considered:

- the provision of an opportunity to improve technical and market knowledge;
- the ability to prioritise reviews for those technologies with a greater perceived data protection and privacy impact;
- the education in and respect of data protection and privacy requirements in technology design.

For the users of technology the implied requirements are that continuous improvement is evident in:

- industry and regulator understanding of issues surrounding data protection and privacy in technology;
- features and functionality which does not threaten or may even protect the data protection and privacy rights of individuals in their use of technology.

This process will not provide a "label of approval" nor will it eliminate uncertainty completely. It is all about reducing risk for all parties (industry, regulators and users) by increasing levels of trust and comfort for the use of technology in the digital economy.

2.3 Consequences of not developing a new model

Industry will continue to bring new technologies to market. Many of these technologies hold the potential for significant privacy enhancements for the consumer (PETs - privacy enhancing technologies for example). However, there is always the chance of a privacy invasive technology reaching the market.

The WP29 will continue to be the primary focus of major industry players. Problems of capacity within the WP29, if not already obvious, will become clear in a short period of time. In addition, it is likely that smaller industry players (SME's) will lose out.

By maintaining the status quo we risk the potential for:
- privacy invasive technologies reaching the market
- new privacy enhancing or enabling technologies being delayed from entering the EU market
- the EU consumer missing out on the benefits of these new technologies
- WP29 inundated with design review requests
- poorly briefed EU regulators with respect to technology developments
- increased product development costs resulting in higher prices for the consumer
- a potential stalling of innovation of consumer-friendly data protection practices and promotion of better compliance.

2.4 Working method/approach

The work identified in the proposal will be carried out by the re-convened CEN/ISSS WS/DPP during 2008 and 2009. Within CEN/ISSS WS/DPP the work of the proposal will be divided into three separate streams.

The project structure consists of the Secretariat (project management and administrative support), the Workshop Chair, Workshop voluntary experts and a Project Team of paid experts, with editor and writer for each of the three streams.

The Project Team assists the WS/DPP members in drafting and editing the technology dialogue framework. The Project Team has been appointed under CEN/ISSS Workshop rules.

The coordination will be ensured by the plenary chair of the Workshop, with the help of the secretariat. It is anticipated that the plenary Workshop will meet three times a year with additional meetings being held by the separate work stream team as necessary. Voluntary experts from the ICT industry, the national regulators and consumer representations will take part. Participants from other EU projects on Data Protection and Privacy are involved (Article 29 Working Party[4], PRIME – PRivacy and Identity Management for Europe[8], EuroPriSe[9])

Draft materials will be subject to peer review and a public consultation process. A public conference will be held at mid-term to inform a larger audience of the current work of the Workshop. The CWA will be made available on the CEN/ISSS WS/DPP website.

In order to address all types of organisations in view of their background from different sectors and industries and to assist them to use DPP best practices and enhancing DPP awareness - the approach via standardisation would provide a common framework platform hence facilitating communication among the various actors. It is seen as the appropriate work approach in this work phase, also considering that multinationals are multi-sector. However this focus should not limit the standardization work to be just generic.

The approach taken will be based on the general principles contained in the directive, and add sector specifics on a maximum possible number of issues. The horizontal principles in the directive will thus be complemented by additional practices and examples addressing specific privacy issues as they should apply according to the needs and risks of such sectors. The CWA will thus rely on the common elements in the directive which apply to all sectors, and pay high attention to the sector specific privacy issues and give practical advice to users in an easy understandable way.

During the past three years of existence of the WS/DPP, strong links have been established with organisations representing all interested parties. The WS/DPP members show such an interest in the development of CEN reference documents in the field of privacy and data protection that, though there was no public budget for 2006, some of them have asked CEN to maintain the WS open in 2006, on a private funding basis and with a restricted work programme. This has allowed the WS to develop links with new members, from the academic world, the industry (both from ICT and users businesses), and governmental data protection officers. Moreover, all former and actual members of the WS have been contacted on the occasion of this proposal, and they have shown interest in the proposed 2007-2008 work programme. In all phases of the project each work stream will maintain regular contact with the respective interest groups on best practice, audit tools and technology reviews. This will be accomplished through open contact communications and personal contacts by Workshop members who are also members of these associations.

3 Conclusion - policy relevance and market impact

The Voluntary Technology Dialogue System will offer clear benefits for industry resulting from closer liaison with regulators at a very early stage of product development thereby avoiding regulatory obstacles early in the production process, time-to-market delays, and reducing the risk of privacy invasive technologies unwittingly being placed on the EU market. In addition regulators will benefit from improved awareness of new areas of technological development.

It is envisaged that the "lead country" concept envisaged under the Binding Corporate Rules framework will be a requirement in making this dialogue process work. However, during research and development of the CWA it is likely that additional opportunities or requirements for review frameworks will become apparent.

The CEN/ISSS WS/DPP is an open forum and comprises members from IT companies, legal firms, national data protection authorities and European industries and the work is informed by input from consumer associations and the academic world.

The CWA to be completed under this proposal aims to help businesses, product designers and data managers comply with obligations under the Directive and, where possible and appropriate, the diverse European national laws and additional requirements. The CWA's provide frameworks, tools, data protection guidance and introduce a liaison system to improve communications during the product design stage between industry and the regulators.

The current process for technology reviews (ad hoc via the WP29) is not scalable, nor does it provide an equal opportunity for all industry. Continuing the present status quo may delay the introduction of technology to the European market, add cost to industry which will be passed on to the consumer, maintain market in-equalities within industry and consume exponentially more of the WP29's time.

Self-assessment in combination with the introduction of a data protection best practice management system will help firms comply with their legal obligations more effectively at lower cost. This will enhance the dissemination of consumer-friendly data protection and privacy practices, while promoting better compliance.

References

[1] CEN/ISSS DPP Workshop http://www.cen.eu/cenorm/businessdomains/businessdomains/isss/activity/ws-dpp.asp

- 2006 ICT Standardisation Work Programme Application for a Grant - Organisation: CEN - Title : Workshop Data Protection and Privacy
- Voluntary Technology Dialogue System EC proposal - Jan06
- CEN 2008-2009 Work Programme - WS DPP N002
- Call For Experts - WS DPP N003
- CWA 15499:2006 - Personal Data Protection Audit Framework (EU Directive EC 95/46) Part I: Baseline Framework - The protection of Personal Data in the EU Part II: Checklists, questionnaires and templates for users of the framework - The protection of Personal Data in the EU
- CWA 15263:2005 - Analysis of Privacy Protection Technologies, Privacy- Enhancing Technologies (PET), Privacy Management Systems (PMS) and Identity Management systems (IMS), the Drivers thereof and the need for standardization

[2] Data Protection Directive 95/46/EC Directive 95/46/EC of the European Parliament and of the Council of 24 October 1995 on the protection of individuals with regard to the processing of personal data and on the free movement of such data http://ec.europa.eu/justice_home/fsj/privacy/law/index_en.htm

[3] Initiative on Privacy Standardisation in Europe (IPSE) Report (2001) http://www.edis.sk/ekes/ipse_final-report.pdf

[4] Working Party 29 (WP29)

- 2008-2009 Work Programme http://ec.europa.eu/justice_home/fsj/privacy/docs/wpdocs/2008/wp146_en.pdf
- Opinion 1/2002 on the CEN/ISSS Report on Privacy Standardisation in Europe http://ec.europa.eu/justice_home/fsj/privacy/docs/wpdocs/2002/wp57_en.pdf
- WP74 - Working Document on Transfers of personal data to third countries: Applying Article 26 (2) of the EU Data Protection Directive to Binding Corporate Rules for International Data Transfers, June 2003 http://ec.europa.eu/justice_home/fsj/privacy/docs/wpdocs/2003/wp74_en.pdf
- WP107 - Working Document Setting Forth a Co-Operation Procedure for Issuing Common Opinions on Adequate Safeguards Resulting From "Binding Corporate Rules", April 2005 http://ec.europa.eu/justice_home/fsj/privacy/docs/wpdocs/2005/wp107_en.pdf
- EC call for tender - Comparative study on different approaches to new privacy challenges, in particular in the light of technological developments http://ec.europa.eu/justice_home/funding/tenders/2008_S087_117940/invitation_tender_en.pdf

[5] APEC (Asia Pacific Economic Cooperation)

- Data Privacy Subgroup of Asia Pacific Economic Cooperation's (APEC) Electronic Commerce Steering Group (ECSG) http://www.apec.org/apec/apec_groups/committee_on_trade/electronic_commerce.html
- APEC Data Privacy Pathfinder Projects Implementation Work Plan http://www.apec.org/apec/apec_groups/committee_on_trade/electronic_commerce.html#Activities

[6]   Privacy Impact Assessments (PIAs) – examples of initiatives

- Information Commissioner's Office (UK) – Privacy impact assessment handbook http://www.ico.gov. uk/upload/documents/library/data_protection/practical_application/pia_final.pdf
- Privacy Commissioner (of New Zealand) – Privacy Impact Assessment Handbook http://www.privacy. org.nz/privacy-impact-assessment-handbook
- The Office of the Privacy Commissioner (Australia) – Privacy Impact Assessment Guide http:// www.privacy.gov.au/publications/#G
- U.S. Department of Homeland Security (USA) – Privacy Impact Assessments (PIAs) - Guidance http:// www.dhs.gov/xinfoshare/publications/gc_1209396374339.shtm

[7]   ISO/IEC JTC 1/SC 27/WG 5 "Identity Management and Privacy Technologies" (International Standards Organisation/ International Electrotechnical Commission Joint Technical Committee 1/ Sub Committee 27 (IT Security Techniques)/ Working Group 5 "Identity Management and Privacy Technologies")

- Structure http://www.jtc1sc27.din.de/cmd?level=tpl-bereich&menuid=63157&cmsareaid=63157&languageid=en
- Programme of Work http://www.jtc1sc27.din.de/cmd?level=tpl-bereich&menuid=64847&cmsareaid=64847&languageid=en http://www.jtc1sc27.din.de/sixcms_upload/media/3031/WG5_PoW_Oct2007.pdf

[8]   PRIME - Privacy and Identity Management for Europe project https://www.prime-project.eu/

[9]   EuroPriSe - European Privacy Seal http://www.european-privacy-seal.eu/

Session 5:
Applications: Trust
in Health Systems

Trust and Privacy in Healthcare

Peter Singleton · Dipak Kalra

Centre for Health Informatics & Multi-professional Education (CHIME)
University College London, Holborn Union Building, Highgate Hill, London, N19 5LW
United Kingdom
peter.singleton@chi-group.com | d.kalra@chime.ucl.ac.uk

Abstract

This paper considers issues of trust and privacy in healthcare around increased data-sharing through Electronic Health Records (EHRs). It uses a model structured around different aspects of trust in the healthcare organisation's reasons for greater data-sharing and their ability to execute EHR projects, particularly any associated confidentiality controls. It reflects the individual's personal circumstances and attitude to use of health records.

This model is extended by considering the relative gains and risks from greater data-sharing as viewed by population segments to give a range of 'attitudes': positive, negative, ambivalent/marginal, or contingent.

The model is compared with results from a recent literature survey by the authors published by the UK General Medical Council (GMC) on Public and Professional Attitudes to Privacy.

Various policy options are considered which may modify attitudes to make the proposal more or less attractive to patients, recognising that there are those that have little to gain or will always view the proposition of EHRs negatively, and that time and experience may be needed to resolve doubts.

The paper does not consider legal questions of privacy and medical confidentiality, although the authors are very familiar with these, preferring to focus on how to meet public expectations and concerns.

1 Introduction

This paper examines trust and privacy in healthcare from the perspective of the patient in sharing, or permitting the sharing, of the medical data recorded about them. This is in contrast to the more frequently discussed topic of trust relationships across healthcare between different providers, though a lack of clear and acceptable solutions to this may contribute to a dilution of trust by the patient in the system as a whole, as wider record sharing becomes possible.

Much of this trust depends on conformance in practice with the 'social contract' surrounding access to healthcare. The 'social contract' is usually implicit rather than explicit, except in private care or the USA where the regulations in the Health Insurance Portability and Accountability Act (HIPAA) make certain aspects explicit and subject to express consent. The 'social contract' would cover aspects such as:

- How the data would be used – to help the patient themselves, to help others, to provide more effective safer healthcare
- How the data will be protected – accuracy, safety, appropriate access, preventing abuse, punishing misuse

D. Gawrock, H. Reimer, A.-R. Sadeghi, C. Vishik (Editors): Future of Trust in Computing, Vieweg+Teubner (2009), 111-121

- What choices the data subject may have – to prevent data being recorded, to prevent data being shared beyond immediate care needs, to stay with the past ways of doing things
- How conformance will be reviewed against these promises – Information governance, rights and remedies

We need to establish some sense of particular terms that are used, sometimes interchangeably, in this area:

- *security* – covering protection and assurance of availability of the data, including access controls, encryption, disaster recovery, and data integrity
- *privacy* – the personal right to keep matters private - a unary power to prevent use, sharing, or retention of data
- *confidentiality* – appropriate sharing by mutual agreement around protecting the person's interests – a professional 'duty of care'- this may allow discretion over when to share/not to share
- *trust* – in this context, an expectation of these requirements being met: security is a 'hygiene factor' – people will expect this as a minimum; privacy is key for some people; whereas confidentiality is what most people want – but often ranking after high quality and safe healthcare

We also need to consider how different parties might 'trust' a healthcare IT system, and what would need to be done to meet the expectations:

- system users – Clinicians, administrators, service managers – data accuracy and reliability are the main factors, though it is critical that users are aware that information may not be 100% accurate
- wider stakeholders, such as indirect users of data from systems, e.g. managers and planners, epidemiologists – mainly data quality; is the data at least consistent and are errors within acceptable bounds
- service users/ patients, including patients, family, and carers – can they trust the system to deliver and also protect their interests, e.g. privacy and confidentiality?

It is for the last group that issues arise. Increased data-sharing, especially through EHRs, should improve the quality of healthcare delivery and medical knowledge through better exploitation of the data. However, it does change the 'social contract' of how data is used as it is commonly understood, though this is often expressed in terms of 'my doctor' and 'my record' may be rather out-of-date concepts given that much of modern care is often delivered by a number of care teams and through a number of disparate medical records, some electronic and some paper-based.

We should note that loss of trust may result in patients withholding information from their clinicians, or avoiding treatment altogether if they believe or fear that their privacy might be compromised

Trust is a complex issue and often a practical compromise between assurance and expediency. Assurance is expensive and time-consuming to effect, and may not be 100% guaranteed (like security!). Game theory shows that trust in other parties is an effective strategy where there is a win-win outcome – depending on balance of options; punishment for breach of trust is usually part of the strategy.

2 Trust in the Healthcare system

The MORI polls [MORI07a] and other surveys [MORI07b] have continued to show a high degree of public trust in doctors as against governments or commercial companies, and even to be higher than teachers and judges. Caveats probably apply – patients' relationships with doctors can often have an element of Stockholm syndrome because of their dependence on the doctors for cure or treatment, and may be influenced by a perceived consensus (and by media portrayal in the news and through fictional stereotypes) rather than being based on personal experience.

Some of the survey questions are about a generalised 'trust' rather than a trust to 'do something' specifically – the MORI polls for the British Medical Association and RCP concerned trusting doctors to 'tell the truth', though the 2007 Royal College of Physicians poll showed that while 90% of the interviewees trusted doctors to tell the truth this fell to 82% in terms of recommending the most effective treatment. As a sort of base level, the 'average man/woman in the street' is trusted to tell the truth by only 52% of the interviewees.

Trust 'to do something' has two components: a trust in the 'intent' to do something and secondly a trust in the 'ability to execute' that objective, so perhaps not surprisingly the public trust doctors to tell the truth as they have little reason to lie (indeed, in these days of more defensive and accountable medicine there may even be too much truth) and telling the truth is fairly simple to do, though telling it in a kindly manner may be rather more difficult. Recommending the right treatment may be harder to execute as doctors may be constrained by public policy and local budgetary constraints as well as their own interests (for example, if they are themselves budget-holders for treatment costs).

In the context of healthcare data-sharing, the trust that most needs to be considered is in using data effectively and in sharing it appropriately and confidentially, which leads to a Boston matrix of four obvious positions, illustrated in Figure 1 below:

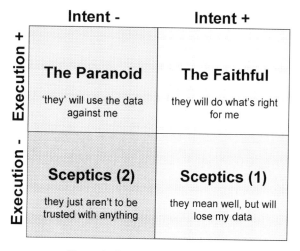

Figure 1 – Matrix of Trust positions

We use the term 'paranoid' in a very loose sense of people who are distrustful of the ways in which their data may be used; however, the term 'distrusters' is too vague and is too easily confused with the 'sceptics'.

Does this help us understand people's concerns over privacy and data-sharing? Perhaps it will if we tie it in with how people will gauge the risks of data-sharing for healthcare.

3 Risk positions in data-sharing

Generally patients share personal information with their doctors and other members of their heath care teams in order to help diagnose a condition and to ensure the right treatment. This is the immediate personal gain from data-sharing. There is the wider gain from medical research and clinical audit of using medical data to improve the science and delivery of medicine, but this is rarely a conscious part of the decision-making process – though it may be part of the 'social contract' that a patient would expect – if they thought about it. A similar view might be considered for teaching, and certainly many patients with a sense of loyalty or gratitude to a specialist or to a care organisation show willingness to assist in student teaching, examinations, etc. This includes both their time and person, and a willingness for their records to be used as a teaching resource. Anecdotally, few such patients request for their records to be only used anonymously.

There are threats from data-sharing too – particularly for taboo or sensitive subjects. There is plenty of evidence [PRINC99], [HOSL77], [HARR07] that patients will avoid or defer treatment for such sensitive conditions – HIV sufferers may find that *where ignorance is bliss, tis folly to be wise*' – at least in terms of their own status. Information may not be socially sensitive, but may have economic repercussions for the individual, health problems may make it difficult to get a job or would increase insurance premiums, so that the individual will prefer to keep such information away from interested parties (hence concerns about commercial companies having access to medical data). At times a patient might wish to seek health care privately in order to keep a condition or procedure away from their NHS medical notes.

However, others may have little 'harmful' or embarrassing information that they need to keep private, but are simply sensitive to the idea of their health data being shared – a position explicitly supported in the EU Data Protection Directive (95/46/EC).

Others, possibly a sizeable segment of the population, may have nothing to hide (perhaps through fortunately being healthy) and few concerns about the sharing of their health data.

So when a patient needs to consider issues around data-sharing they will look to the benefits and risks.

Patients will generally be happier to share information with their immediate clinicians as that brings them the most immediate benefits – though that does not mean that they will not be reluctant to share some information. They can judge the level of need for disclosure based on their trust in the clinician and the apparent relevance of the information, based on the clinician's responses and questions. They can to some degree negotiate around the level of privacy ('please don't note this down' or 'please don't tell anyone else').

Wider sharing is often less apparent, less negotiable, and may rely on the clinician's discretion over the need to share information further. Generally, patients will be unaware of what 'event data' is recorded and shared about the basic interactions with the health system (the fact that a GP prescribed medication and needs to be reimbursed). However, in the UK patients now receive routinely a copy of referral letters made by their GP so that they know what is being communicated and also have assurance that a referral has actually been actioned. It is not yet clear if future extensions to the NHS Choose and Book system will increase the information about referrals that is shared with patients.

When considering whether to trust healthcare staff to use their information, patients are likely to weigh up what they may 'gain', either directly in terms of getting effective treatment for their condition (assuming they have one) or indirectly through better-run healthcare or more effective medical science, against any possible 'pain' from the release of information that may embarrass them or lead to possible harm (e.g. lost job, refused or more expensive insurance, personal or social problems when others get to know something secret). Some, of course, will see the possible sharing as intrusion by state agencies or a breach of their personal rights – this we have considered as 'concerns' and treated as a form of 'pain' to be weighed against any possible 'gain'.

This leads us to broadly six situations for patients:

• healthy/no secrets	• mainly small 'gain' (as healthy) and little or no pain from sharing (as no 'secrets' that might be revealed)
• healthy/concerned	• some gain, but principles can be ranked very high, and may offset the possible perceived benefits
• healthy/with secrets	• some immediate gain, but a considerable risk from disclosure
• ill/no secrets	• clear gain and little or no pain from sharing
• ill/concerned	• clear gain, may compromise on principles in order to get best treatment
• ill/with secrets	• clear gain, but will want to limit revealing secrets

The gain-pain balance for each of these six situations is illustrated in Figure 2 below.

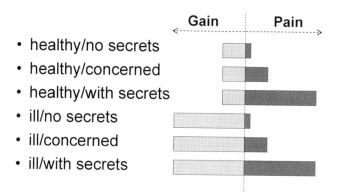

Figure 2 - Gains and losses from sharing

4 Risk Appraisal model

This model takes the two dimensions of trust and risk/reward to look at how each of the four patient segments defined in the Boston Matrix are likely to approach the question of data-sharing, where the trust position in intent and execution will modify the individual's perception of the risks and rewards. Figure 3 below shows this model for the paranoid patient:

The Paranoid: -intent/+execution
'they' will use the data against me

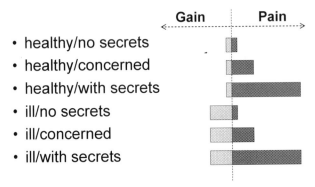

Figure 3 – The Paranoid: Gains and losses from sharing

The key thing is that the 'paranoid' don't expect much by way of benefits (as they anticipate that the execution of the data-sharing project will be poor and do little to improve either their own care or health-care generally) and fear that the worst will always happen, viz. that their data will be lost or misused, so generally (but not universally) will perceive little to gain from increased data-sharing from their point of view.

Figure 4 applies this model to the faithful patient's perspective:

The Faithful: +intent/+execution
they will do what's right for me

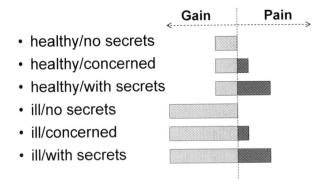

Figure 4 – The Faithful: Gains and losses from sharing

The 'faithful' are not blindly trusting, there is still a resolution between possible gains and risks to be made, but they will presume that the benefits are forthcoming and trust that possible risks should not occur because their interests will be protected rather than abused. In this sense their view of the balance between pain and gain is an optimistic one.

Figures 5 and 6 show the model for sceptics:

Sceptics (1): +intent/-execution
they mean well but will lose my data

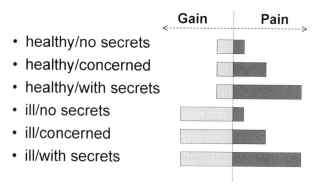

Figure 5 – Sceptics (1): Gains and losses from sharing

The first set of sceptics will tend to scale down the perceived benefits and uprate the risks to reflect their view of possible incompetence in protecting their data – such as the loss of CDs in the post[1]!

Sceptics (2): -intent/-execution
they just aren't to be trusted with anything

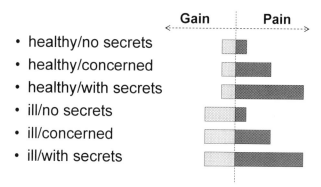

Figure 6 – Sceptics (2): Gains and losses from sharing

The second set of sceptics will downgrade the benefits much more as they do not think that enough effort will be put into realising them, and will still assume the worst in terms of the risks.

---

1 A loss of CDs by the UK Revenue & Customs in November 2007 which hit the headlines: http://news.bbc.co.uk/2/hi/programmes/moneybox/7076106.stm

5 Overall attitude to Data-sharing

Applying the pain/gain measures leads to a very crude matrix of perceptions of the overall risk/reward outcome:

Table 1: Matrix of Risk/Reward Perceptions

	Healthy			Ill		
	n/s	conc	w/s	n/s	conc	w/s
The Paranoid: -intent/+execution	✗	✗	✗	✓	?	✗
The Faithful: +intent/+execution	✓	✓	✗	✓	✓	✓
Sceptics (1): +intent/-execution	?	✗	✗	✓	+	✗
Sceptics (2): -intent/-execution	?	✗	✗	✓	-	✗

A tick (✓) represents an overall positive balance, whereas a cross (✗) indicates a likely overall negative position; a plus (+) suggests an only slightly positive approach and similar a minus (-) a slightly negative position; the question mark (?) is used where the balance is possible very fine. "n/s" means "no secrets", "conc" means "concerned", "w/s" means "with secrets". This table is not intended to be taken as scientific or precisely quantifiable – but it may illustrate that there are different factors to be taken into account and will, in different balance, give rise to very different reactions to particular data-sharing propositions.

While this table may seem to indicate that there are more negatives and uncertains than positives, we must remember that the groupings are unlikely to be evenly distributed (see next section). Furthermore, the attitudes observed in practice can be influenced by circumstances and by design and, of course, to some degree by spin and propaganda.

It is important to recall that initially much of the public was very uncertain or negative about online shopping and its risks, but as the level of risk became clearer (and banks offered guarantees against fraud) and the benefits became better established, overall attitudes have progressively changed – although some people inevitably still prefer the immediacy of physical shopping. Conversely, data disasters such as the UK tax authorities' loss of CDs with tax-payers details may adversely affect the public perceptions, particularly over the ability to execute (deliver against commitments made).

We also need to realise that these are 'default' positions, which may be modified based on greater understanding and options for controlling the use of their data – the 'Faithful with secrets' may be happy (or at least happier) to share data if there is a facility to restrict access to what they consider their 'secrets' and a guarantee only to share non-secret data.

We should also note the fact that being ill can greatly change people's choices, which is part of the rationale for the Article 29 Data Protection Working Party paper on EHRs [AR2907] suggesting that any consent to have an EHR would be coerced to some degree by circumstances and so not valid in law (even though it leads to the conundrum that you could never validly choose anything that was good for you; only if it was bad or of no relevance for you could you validly choose it!)

6 Evidence from the literature

In 2007, the authors produced a literature survey for the UK General Medical Council into Public and Professional Attitudes to Privacy [SILE08]. While most of the surveys took very different approaches, based on some of the information gleaned, a slightly different but related model was used to estimate how many of the population fall into different attitude categories:

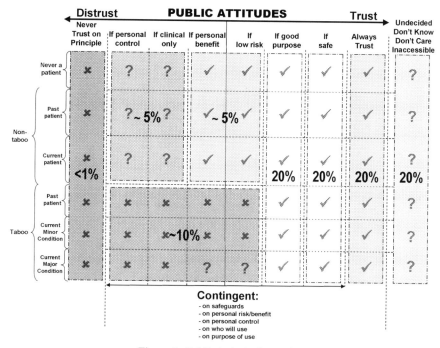

Figure 7 - Public Attitude Categories

The figures are approximate – the left-most column is based on actual numbers of people opting-out of various EHR projects, though it should be noted that this result is a combination of 'attitude' and 'incentive to action', so many more might object in principle, but are too busy or lack sufficient motivation to actually opt out. Similarly the second-to-last column of the right could perhaps be similarly split into a small number who would actually be bothered to opt-in – the current French EHR project suggests that few people see enough benefit to take the trouble to opt-in.

This diagram attempts to reflect negotiable elements in the data-sharing 'contract' with the public: what aspects are important to individuals and what options might offered to offset concerns or possible 'pain', so that the public and the healthcare system can benefit from better and more effective data-sharing.

7 Effect of countermeasures to reduce risk and improve trust

Where security countermeasures are known to be in use, the individual's perception of possible 'pain' may change, hopefully improving the overall balance of benefits against risk. Countermeasures may be institutional or personal – viz. access controls, security, audit and sanctions vs. personal choices and privacy settings.

Measures such as transparency and some degree of personal control over the release of or access to the data will reduce doubts about any subversive intent behind the increased data-sharing, mitigating concerns about 'government databases' or 'Big Brother' surveillance. We should, however, note that providing total personal control may undermine the viability of an EHR project by so delaying benefits (particularly 'network effects' such as benefits of an EHR for emergency or unscheduled care), such that it may not be possible to justify starting or continuing the project.

Particularly, information provision about security measures, access controls on staff, and deterrence of possible abuse will help to provide evidence that risks are small (or at least smaller than feared). However, sceptics are likely to play 'Doubting Thomases' waiting until there is more substantial proof. This proof could be developed by simply putting more emphasis (including publicity) on the control of existing paper and electronic records [ANDE01], in preparation for the roll-out of an EHR system.

Linking access to clinical workflow/care pathways[2] so that fears about unrestricted access by all and any healthcare staff can be reduced seems particularly important and addresses one of the increased risks brought on by the advent of EHRs. However, these measures may not be easy to communicate to the public at large, in part because it has been difficult to provide convincing success stories of access control measures that can accommodate the tremendous inter-patient variations in clinical pathway.

Clearly where people doubt the trustworthiness of organisation itself then they are likely to doubt any security measures being taken by it, but it is possible that being made aware of the range of controls may serve as some level of proof that the organisation has a definite intent to protect data, although trust in its ability to apply them successfully may take longer to achieve.

Offering personal choices and tailored privacy settings are likely to radically change the individual's perception of risk, though those with greater doubts may well assume that these are mere sops to the public which will simply be overridden in practice.

The provision of facilities, such as 'sealed envelopes', to protect an individual's secrets should help significantly in addressing the 'pain' side of the equation. However, significant thought needs to be put in place to decide how clinical practice can continue where data is withheld – and whether this withholding is made apparent to the clinicians (so perhaps either revealing that secrets exist or some indication of the nature of the secret simply by revealing there is one).

8 Conclusions

Transparency/openness: It is important that public concerns are recognised as perfectly reasonable when developing literature or public information campaigns – any form of glossing over concerns are likely to be viewed negatively, probably creating more distrust than might already exist.

Personal control: – at some level at least – provides some measure of reassurance in being able to control risks and demonstrating that the public are being involved in disclosure decisions. Being permitted to say 'No', even if this is never exercised, provides much reassurance – as does being able to change ones mind at any time, so that people do not feel 'locked into' a decision (in which case they usually opt for the least risky option, often foregoing possible benefits in order to avoid potential risks).

Complexity: There is a danger that by providing too many options it may become difficult to communicate and administer the range of options, especially where different controls are combined so permutations may increase exponentially with different implications in relation to the delivery of care.

---

2 For example, the use of 'Legitimate Relationships' in the English National Programme

Delivering a service: Clearly it is important that it is still possible to provide an effective healthcare service, preferably better than the approach currently delivered despite poor use of medical information; where patients wish to withhold information or prevent data-sharing, then their individual care may suffer (as less effective processes have to be followed) and may impact the care of others (by displacing resources to inefficient pathways or restricting knowledge about particular conditions – consider if many people with HIV were able to insist that their HIV status were hidden, would we be able to plan to deliver effective care?)

Basic conflict of interests between the common good and individual 'rights': as the previous paragraph touches on, there may be conflicts of interests between the desire of an individual to restrict possible sensitive information, the need to provide an efficient quality healthcare service, and the wider need to understand health and healthcare for the benefit of all. It is not possible to side-step this conflict, though a suitable choice of options and clear information may reduce the apparent conflict – the alternative would seem to be the rather draconian approach suggested by the Article 29 Data Protection Working Party whereby laws are passed to support the creation of EHRs on a statutory basis

References

[MORI07a] MORI: Trust in Professions, 2007: www.ipsos-mori.com/_assets/polls/2007/pdf/trust-in-professions-2007.pdf

[MORI07b] MORI: The Use of Personal Health Information in Medical Research, Medical Research Council, 2007, www.mrc.ac.uk/Utilities/Documentrecord/index.htm?d=MRC003810.

[PRINC99] Medical Privacy and Confidentiality Survey by Princeton Associates: www.chcf.org/documents/healthit/survey.pdf

[HOSL77] Holahan CJ, Slaikeu KA., Effects of contrasting degrees of privacy on client self-disclosure in a counselling setting. J Couns Psychol 1977;24: p. 55–9.

[HARR07] Harris Polls: The Harris Poll #27, 2007: Many U.S. Adults are Satisfied with Use of Their Personal Health Information www.harrisinteractive.com/harris_poll/index.asp?PID=743

[SILE08] Singleton P, Lea N, Tapuria A, Kalra D. Public and Professional attitudes to privacy of healthcare data: a survey of the literature. General Medical Council 2008 www.gmc-uk.org/guidance/news_consultation/GMC_Privacy_Attitudes_Final_Report_with_Addendum.pdf

[AR2907] Article 29 Data Protection Working Party of Data Protection: Working Document on the processing of personal data relating to health in electronic health records (EHR), European Commission, 2007, http://ec.europa.eu/justice_home/fsj/privacy/docs/wpdocs/2007/wp131_en.pdf

[ANDE01] Anderson, RJ. Security Engineering, Wiley 2001 - measures to avoid 'blagging' and other social engineering attacks [p167-168]

Protecting Patient Records from Unwarranted Access

Ryan Gardner[1] · Sujata Garera[1] · Anand Rajan[2] · Carlos V. Rozas[2]
Aviel D. Rubin[1] · Manoj Sastry[2]

[1]Johns Hopkins University
Computer Science Department, Baltimore, MD
{ryan | sgarera | rubin}@cs.jhu.edu

[2]Intel Corporation
Corporate Technology Group, Hillsboro OR
{anand.rajan | carlos.v.rozas | manoj.r.sastry}@intel.com

Abstract

Securing access to medical information is vital to protecting patient privacy. However, Electronic Patient Record (EPR) systems are vulnerable to a number of inside and outside threats. Adversaries can compromise EPR client machines to obtain a variety of highly sensitive information including valid EPR login credentials, without detection. Furthermore, medical staff can covertly view records of their choosing for personal interest or more malicious purposes. In particular, we observe that the lack of integrity measurement and auditability in these systems creates a potential threat to the privacy of patient information. We explore the use of virtualization and trusted computing hardware to address these problems. We identify open problems and encourage further research in the area.

1 Introduction

Costs and needs of healthcare are increasing on a global scale. Many healthcare organizations are migrating to more electronically based information systems with hopes to increase quality of care and to help reduce expenses. These electronically based systems are accessed by employees from a diverse set of roles and include systems for physician order entry, patient management, billing, and many others. Each has access to large amounts of patient health information. While an open platform policy on the systems increases flexibility, the lack of dedicated and contained applications and hardware introduces security issues and creates a potential threat to the privacy of personal information. In order to protect the privacy and confidentiality of patient data, it is important to ensure that these vastly heterogeneous systems access medical information in a secure manner.

The Electronic Patient Record (EPR) is an integral component of the medical infrastructure and represents a chronological record of a patient's interaction with the doctors at a hospital. This record includes personally identifiable information (PII) and information about each patient visit such as lab results and diagnosis, for example. To date, several security breaches related to the EPR have occurred [Win05, LeKe97]. As one example, a state employer in Pennsylvania obtained access to an employee's prescription records for AZT (a drug used for treating AIDS) and shared them within the agency. Furthermore, the University of Washington Medical Center's computer system was invaded by a hacker who stole 5,000 cardiology and rehabilitation patients' records. As such, adversarial attempts ranging from identity theft, blackmail, and even insurance issues may represent significant threats in the medical field.

D. Gawrock, H. Reimer, A.-R. Sadeghi, C. Vishik (Editors): Future of Trust in Computing, Vieweg+Teubner (2009), 122-128

The previous security breaches [Win05, LeKe97] clearly demonstrate that the EPR system, in general, is vulnerable to threats from inside and outside. In particular, machines accessing the patient record using the EPR application (EPR clients) could be compromised and malicious code may be installed on them. Furthermore, the EPR system lacks a monitoring technique capable of alerting administrators to probable illegitimate accesses. In this paper, we explore possible approaches to protecting confidential patient information and identify open problems.

2 The Electronic Patient Record System

As discussed previously, the Electronic Patient Record (EPR) represents a chronological view of a patient's interaction with the hospital. When a patient makes his first visit, he is assigned a record number and his EPR is created. The information from each of his visits thereafter is recorded as well as laboratory tests and results and any other medical data. This record also persists after the patient's death. That is records are never deleted.

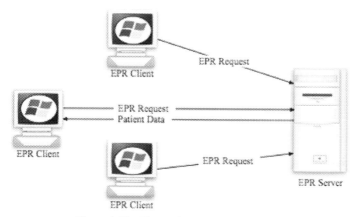

Figure 1: The Electronic Patient Record System

A typical EPR system is illustrated in Figure 1. It is comprised of an EPR server that maintains all patient records and a client that allows users to view the records. The EPR server also maintains the access policy associated with the records. The client, on the other hand, allows users (doctors, nurses, lab technicians, etc.) to access records through the EPR application installed on the client machine. It requests information from the server and displays it to the user. Once a user is authenticated into the system, she can view every patient record and all data contained within it. While such a view everything policy enhances flexibility and availability, it does not imply that a hospital employee may legally view arbitrary records. However, as mentioned, no monitoring is in place to prevent or detect such breaches of privacy.

2.1 Threats Against EPR

The EPR client is typically a workstation with a Windows OS. For example, it may be a home computer used to access patient information over a VPN connection. Since the client is more accessible to an adversary and is more vulnerable than the EPR server, we limit our discussion to inside and outside threats against the EPR client system.

Inside threats assume an adversary who has the credentials necessary to gain legitimate access to the EPR system. This class of adversaries includes employees such as nurses or doctors of a hospital. A classic example of such an adversary is represented by the recent privacy breach of George Clooney's personal health record. A hospital worker at the Palisades Medical Center was suspended for inspecting Clooney's health record and revealing some of its information to the THEM Weekly Internet site [Hamm07].

Outside adversaries, on the other hand, may try to exploit an EPR client and run malicious code to obtain a variety of information. For example, such an adversary may install a key-logger on the client machine to capture username and password keystrokes as they are entered by a user. The adversary could then use these credentials to retrieve patient information of choice from the EPR server. Similarly, such an adversary might attempt to compromise a machine to obtain sensitive patient information accessed by that machine or resident on it.

In the section that follows, we discuss methods for administering protection against inside and outside adversarial attempts through appropriate monitoring and integrity measurement frameworks.

3 Protecting Patient Records

In the medical field, it is essential that the security solutions applied do not impact the usability of the systems they protect. An increase in the time a doctor has to spend at the computer may mean delayed response to patients in critical conditions and ultimately even a decrease in the number of patients that can be treated and seen. Because the optimal treatment of patients almost always takes a greater priority than their assured privacy, developed security mechanisms must not negatively impact the quality of medical care. In what follows, we suggest several possible approaches to preventing privacy breaches by adversaries without and with legitimate access to the EPR system. We aim to enable each of these techniques to be as transparent to medical staff as possible, leaving many open research problems.

3.1 Outside Adversaries

We fist consider adversaries who are not legitimate users of the EPR system but may try to gain access to it. To prevent privacy breaches from such adversaries, we need to ensure that machines compromised by them cannot access EPR and also ensure that (potentially stolen) machines cannot be configured to record massive amounts of personal health data as it is downloaded from the server.

A natural approach to verifying the nature of the code running on the client is to apply well known techniques of trusted computing [Task81, GPC+03, SJZvD04]. Suppose we have a client machine containing a Trusted Platform Module (TPM) [Trus06] and a processor with a security extension such as Intel Trusted Execution Technology (TXT) [Inte07]. We can provide reliable attestations of this client's code by using the hardware to provide signed, unalterable hashes of chosen portions of the client's memory [SJZvD04, GPC+03, SPvD05, SZJvD04, MPP+08]. As these security hardware devices and facilities are becoming more ubiquitous, the solution's platform requirements are rapidly becoming realistic.

While the attestation process using a TPM is well known [SJZvD04, GPC+03, SPvD05, SZJvD04, MPP+08], we summarize it here for completeness. It is illustrated in Figure 2.

- The attesting machine loads a small portion of code into its processor. It computes a hash of this code, which is sent to the machine's TPM through a special pin. The TPM stores the hash in a specific register that is only accessible for writing through the pin. The processor then passes execution onto the hashed code.

- That running code, which has now been attested, computes a hash over other portions of code, such as the bootloader, and further stores the hashes on the TPM in a manner such that the hashes can be chained with other hashes, but never erased.
- The bootloader computes a hash over additional code, such as the operating system, and attestations are chained up the software stack. Each computed hash is hashed with the existing hash in the TPM register in a hash chain.
- The machine provides external entities with attestations of its running code on request by having the TPM sign its stored hash values using an internal, inaccessible private key.

Although this solution seems straightforward, many challenges remain to practically and securely deploying it. One of the challenges arises from the dynamic nature of the operating system [MSWM03]. Operating systems draw their code and data from a variety of locations, and scattered portions of the data are typically inconsistent between booting or hash measurements. This lack of consistency makes measurements difficult to interpret since the hashes generally need to be compared against a known white-list. Furthermore, these measurements do not scale well considering that new modules and applications are constantly installed on the operating system. In an environment of vastly heterogeneous systems, such as a hospital, new techniques need to be explored for obtaining integrity measurements that can be meaningfully interpreted by the EPR server.

One characteristic of EPR clients of which we may be able to take advantage in this regard is the fact that, on a large timescale, they can be stateless. For this reason, and to prevent persistence of sensitive information, we propose the exploration of an architecture where the EPR client is run inside a virtual machine. This architecture is illustrated in Figure 2. The statelessness of the EPR client allows us to spawn a new, *clean* image of the client for each instance of the application. Since the image is clean, the hypervisor can hash it before each VM is spawned, and the hashes will remain identical for that VM. Furthermore, compromises of a VM will not persist to the next VM instance. The physical machine can also be used for other, completely isolated applications without affecting the security of the EPR by running other, non-EPR VMs as in Terra [GPC+03].

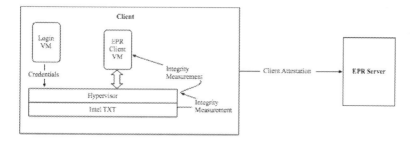

Figure 2: Process for Attesting an EPR Client's Software

Another challenge arises in the medical field results when a client is found to be compromised. Due to the critical nature of medical care, in this case, we cannot, in general, simply deny information to a compromised machine. If only the virtual machine is compromised, we may be able to develop a method to spawn a new, uncompromised virtual machine on demand. However, rather than simply spawn a new, raw machine, it would be ideal if the new machine could pull some state from the compromised one. For example, doctors and medical staff would be saved significant time if the new machine could be spawned almost transparently, continuing to present information on the patient of interest. New methods to enable secure transfer of such data must first be explored and developed, however, to ensure that the compromise is not spread as well.

Lastly, techniques that spawn new VMs cannot be applied when an adversary is able to compromise the hypervisor. The machine cannot even be guaranteed to display a message to the doctor or nurse asking them to use an alternate machine since an adversary in control may prevent the display of such messages. Additional research is also needed to detect and determine the best ways to respond in such scenarios

3.2 Inside Adversaries

Secondly, we consider threats from adversaries who have legitimate access to the EPR system. As indicated in Section 2, EPR accesses are not monitored, and no alerts are raised on a breach of privacy. Furthermore, while each access is logged with the accessed record, the large size of these audit logs and lack of contextual search parameters hampers the ease of finding and tracking privacy breaches. Increasing the tractability of searching the logs could deter potential invasive activity by enabling more effective identification. Similarly, it would be beneficial to devise methods of automatically monitoring the EPR record accesses and raising alarms under suspicious activity.

Monitoring EPR accesses at the server and detecting privacy breaches involves differentiating legitimate accesses from illegitimate ones based on the context of the accesses involved. In particular, under certain situations, for instance in an emergency, accessing a colleague's EPR may not constitute a privacy breach. Furthermore, patients' records may be accessed by innocent accident from time to time without any significant inspection of the information. In such settings, the context of the EPR access must be carefully examined before declaring a privacy breach.

A natural approach to detecting privacy breaches involves careful examination of which records are accessed and when. However, we may also be able to increase the accuracy of privacy breach detection through collaborative monitoring between the server and client. Contextual information on each patient record access may also be indicative of possible privacy breaches. When the client is established as trusted, we may be able to use the client to record and send such contextual information to the server. For example, the time spent viewing a record and the actions performed by the respective user may be indicative of legitimate, accidental, or malicious accesses of EPR. The location of the client being used may also provide useful information. Additionally, one may even wish to restrict the actions that specific clients may take, such as printing, for example.

One of the challenges of designing such a collaborative framework is maintaining efficiency. The collaboration between the client and server may mandate a rich client that needs to keep track of a considerable amount of contextual information. As a result, it is possible that the performance of the client and timeliness of response to the user may deteriorate. We seek to explore methods to implement such a collaborative monitoring framework while maintaining usability and efficiency at the client end.

4 Related Work

There has been considerable research in the area of trusted computing. Tasker [Task81], Tygar [TyYe94] and Yee [YeTy95] are some of the pioneers of this field. A trusted computer system was defined by Tasker [Task81] in the early 1980s as one that deployed hardware and software integrity measurement techniques to protect sensitive information. In this section, we describe some of the hardware based integrity measurement techniques that have developed since then.

Tygar and Yee [TyYe94, YeTy95] explored methods of establishing trust remotely using secure processors. Their system, Dyad, allows one to verify stored data on a system and allows for authenticated and encrypted communication channels with a remote system. The authors argue that this system is widely suited to electronic commerce applications.

Independently, Sailer *et al.* developed a technique of establishing load time integrity remotely using trusted platform modules [SJZvD04, SZJvD04, Trus06]. In addition to providing integrity measurements from the BIOS to the application layer, these authors' system also tries to enforce a security policy by aborting the execution of software that has an incorrect fingerprint.

Authentication of the platform's software stack was also explored previously by Gasser *et al.* [GGKL89]. In this architecture, each machine is equipped with trusted hardware and a public/private key pair. The key pair is used to create signed attestations of all code loaded on the system. As described previously, this attestation chain recursively attests code at higher levels. The standard TPM machine architecture [Trus06] is similar to that proposed by Gasser *et al.*.

Subsequently, Garfinkel *et al.* introduced Terra [GPC+03], a system that uses virtualization to isolate sensitive code and produces attestations of software running in several, individual virtual machines. The measurements produced by Terra are taken at the partition block level and can, therefore, be more difficult to interpret than the selective measurements produced by a system by Sailer, Jaeger, Zhang, and van Doorn [SJZvD04, SZJvD04]. Microsoft NGSCB, [CJPL02, EnPe02, ELM+03] is similar to the Terra system, but it only attests software at the application level.

Marchesini *et al.* [MSWM03] explored the usage of the TPM to transform a desktop Linux machine into a virtual secure coprocessor. The authors demonstrate proof of concept by building a system using TCPA/TPM architecture to bind an Apache Web server's SSL private key to the service it provides. They identify several open problems faced when building and deploying such a framework.

Copilot [PFMA04], introduced by Petri *et al.*, makes use of a method that requires an additional PCI card. It performs integrity measurements of the Linux kernel memory at periodic intervals. The PCI card cannot read the state of the machine's processor, however, so it is vulnerable to a kernel relocation attack where the memory mappings used by hardware are altered [SLS+05].

Arbaugh *et al.* proposed AEGIS [AFS97]. It is unlike the above hardware solutions in that it is designed only to boot when the machine is in an expected state rather than simply indicating when it is not. Its framework authenticates the code loaded on the machine at boot time using a PROM card and a modified BIOS. Any violations in integrity result in the system being unable to boot, which is referred to as secure boot. Arbaugh *et al.* further explore this problem [AKFS97] and describe a method for recovery in the situation of a failed integrity check.

5 Conclusion

We have identified security weaknesses and open problems in the electronic patient record system considering threats from both inside and outside adversaries. We encourage the exploration of virtualization to prevent persistence of sensitive information and to allow for consistent integrity measurements using trusted computing hardware. We further suggest the possibility of collaborative monitoring between an EPR client and server to improve the auditability of the EPR system and identify several open research problems.

References

[ArFS97]   Arbaugh, William, Farber, David, and Smith, Jonathan: A secure and reliable bootstrap architecture. In IEEE Symposium on Security and Privacy, 1997.

[AKFS97]   Arbaugh, William, Keromytis, Angelos, Farber, David, and Smith, Jonathan: Automated recovery in a secure bootstrap process, 1997.

[CJPT02]   Caroll, Amy, Juarez, Mario, Polk, Julia, and Leininger, Tony: Microsoft Palladium: A business overview, August 2002.

[ELM+03]   England, Paul, Lampson, Butler, Manferdelli, John, Peinado, Marcus, and Willman, Bryan: A trusted open platform. In IEEE Spectrum, 36(7):55-62, 2003.

[EnPe02]   England, Paul and Pienado, Marcus: Authenticated operation of open computing devices. In Australasian Conference on Information Security and Privacy, 2002.

[GGKL89] Gasser, Morrie, Goldstein, Andy, Kaufman, Charlie and Lampson, Butler: The digital distributed system security architecture. In NIST/NCSC National Computer Security Conference, 1989.

[GPC+03]   Garfinkel, Tal, Pfaff, Ben, Chow, Jim, Rosenblum, Mendel, and Boneh, Dan: Terra: A virtual machine based platform for trusted computing. In ACM Symposium on Operating Systems Principles, 2003.

[Hamm07] Hammel, Sara: George Clooney addresses the leak of his medical records, In People, October 2007.

[Inte07]   Intel Corporation: Intel Trusted Execution Technology. 2007. Available at http://www.intel.com/technology/security/.

[LeKe97]   Leahy, Patrick and Kennedy, Edward: Setting information age parameters for medical privacy. November 1997. Available at http://leahy.senate.gov/press/199711/s1368.html.

[MPP+08] McCune, Jonathan , Parno, Bryan, Perrig, Adrian, Reiter, Michael, and Isozaki, Hiroshi: Flicker: an execution infrastructure for TCB minimization. In SIGOPS: Operating Systems Review, 42(4):315–328, 2008.

[MSWM03]   Marchesini, John, Smith, Sean, Wild, Omen, and MacDonald, Rich: Experimenting with TCPA/TCG hardware, OR: How I learned to stop worrying and love the bear. Technical Report, Dartmouth College. December 2003. Available at http://www.cs.dartmouth.edu/~sws/pubs/TR2003-476.pdf.

[PFMA04] Petroni, Nick, Fraser, Timothy, Molina, Jesus, and Arbaugh, William: Copilot – a coprocessor based kernel runtime integrity monitor. In USENIX Security Symposium, 2004.

[SJZvD04] Sailer, Reiner, Jaeger, Trent, Zhang, Xiaolan, and van Doorn, Leendert: Attestation based policy enforcement for remote access. In ACM Conference on Computer and Communications Security, 2004.

[SLS+05]   Seshadri, Arvind, Luk, Mark, Shi, Elaine, Perrig, Adrian, van Doorn, Leendert, and Khosla, Pradeep: Pioneer: Verifying code integrity and enforcing untampered code execution on legacy systems. In Symposium on Operating System Principles, 2005.

[SPvD05]   Shi, Elaine, Perrig, Adrian, and van Doorn, Leendert: Bind: a fine grained attestation service for secure distributed systems. In IEEE Symposium on Security and Privacy, 2005.

[SZJvD04] Sailer, Reiner, Zhang, Xiolan, Jaeger, Trent, and van Doorn, Leendert: Design and implementation of a TCG-based integrity measurement architecture. In USENIX Security Symposium, 2004.

[Task81]   Tasker, Peter: Trusted computer systems. In IEEE Symposium on Security and Privacy 1981.

[Trus06]   Trusted Computing Group: TPM main part 1 – design principles, specification version 1.2 revision 94, March 2006.

[TyYe94]   Tygar, J.D. and Yee, Bennet: Dyad: A system for using physically secure coprocessors. In IP Workshop Proceedings, 1994.

[Win05]   Win, Khin: A review of security of electronic health records. Health Information Management, 34(1), 2005. Available at http://www.mja.com.au/public/journal/34-1-2005/win.html.

[YeTy95]   Yee, Bennett and Tygar, J.D.: Secure coprocessors in electronic commerce applications. In USENIX Workshop on Electronic Commerce, 1995.

Challenges in Data Quality Assurance in Pervasive Health Monitoring Systems

Janani Sriram[1] · Minho Shin[1] · David Kotz[1] · Anand Rajan[2]
Manoj Sastry[2] · Mark Yarvis[2]

[1]Institute for SecurityTechnology Studies
Dartmouth College, Hanover, NH, USA
{Janani.C.Sriram | mhshin | dfk}@cs.dartmouth.edu

[2]Intel Corporation Hillsboro, OR, USA
{anand.rajan | manoj.r.sastry | mark.d.yarvis}@intel.com

Abstract

Wearable, portable, and implantable medical sensors have ushered in a new paradigm for healthcare in which patients can take greater responsibility and caregivers can make well-informed, timely decisions. Health-monitoring systems built on such sensors have huge potential benefit to the quality of healthcare and quality of life for many people, such as patients with chronic medical conditions (such as blood-sugar sensors for diabetics), people seeking to change unhealthy behavior (such as losing weight or quitting smoking), or athletes wishing to monitor their condition and performance. To be effective, however, these systems must provide assurances about the quality of the sensor data. The sensors must be applied to the patient by a human, and the sensor data may be transported across multiple networks and devices before it is presented to the medical team. While no system can guarantee data quality, we anticipate that it will help for the system to annotate data with some measure of confidence. In this paper, we take a deeper look at potential health-monitoring usage scenarios and highlight research challenges required to ensure and assess quality of sensor data in health-monitoring systems.

1 Introduction

The advent of portable computing devices and miniature sensing devices presents many new opportunities for personal healthcare. Formerly, most medical sensing devices were used in a hospital setting under the care of trained medical and technical personnel; soon, many devices will be worn throughout a patient's daily life or installed at home and in assisted-living settings. These devices will collect health related data for many purposes, by patients with chronic medical conditions (such as blood-sugar sensors for diabetics), people seeking to change behavior (e.g., losing weight or quitting smoking), or athletes wishing to monitor their condition and performance. The resulting data may be used directly by the person, or shared with others: with a physician for treatment, with an insurance company for coverage, with the adult children of elderly parents, or by a coach.

Clearly, to be useful these systems must assure that high-quality information reaches the data user – or, at least, the system must be able to express some level of confidence in the data being presented. Failure to consider the confidence level can directly lead to incorrect medical and financial decisions. For example, if a physician bases a medical decision on information that is inaccurate, stale, or irrelevant to the patient at hand, he could end up prescribing incorrect medication to a patient, or even worse, perform surgery on the wrong patient. Similarly, an insurance company could collect fees or render payments that do not accurately reflect the patient's health status and treatments. Confidence in data in the area of emerging pervasive medical applications can return to medical providers some of the same assurances available in a personal interaction with the patient.

Outside the hospital setting, in particular, the sensors may be applied by the patient or family members; the data may be gathered through a personal mobile device (such as a mobile phone), over a personal network (such as a wireless network at home), or over the public Internet. Clearly, the accuracy and availability of sensor data is difficult to ensure. To evaluate the trustworthiness of medical data gathered in this manner, we need a holistic system view that inspects contributions to risk and error in medical data as it flows from the patient to the caregiver.

We motivate this topic area with three use cases in Section 2. We list several factors involved in data quality (Section3) and describe research challenges related to each factor (Section 4). We survey related work in Section 5. Finally, in Section6 we summarize.

2 Use cases

We set the stage for our discussion by presenting three scenarios that motivate many of the research challenges.

2.1 Scenario 1

Jack's doctor suspects that Jack has episodes of low blood-glucose levels not immediately visible from the manual measurement method and recommends a five-day glucose sensor test. The test uses an implanted glucose sensor and an electronic recorder to continuously monitor glucose levels, allowing physicians to study patterns over an extended period using more frequent samples.[1]

The doctor inserts the sensor under the skin of the patient's abdomen and connects the wire from the sensor to the recorder. A nurse calibrates the sensor by entering the blood-glucose level obtained from the manual method into the recorder. Jack is advised to always carry the recorder, and to keep it from getting wet.

During the five-day test, the sensor takes glucose readings every five minutes and sends it across the wire to the recorder. Jack also records glucose levels using the manual method four times a day, along with insulin injection times, meals, and exercise.

After the five-day test is complete, the doctor removes the implanted sensor and uploads data from the recorder to the doctor's computer. The doctor compares results from both types of tests to diagnose the condition or prescribe changes to insulin type or dosage and diet.

2.2 Scenario 2

Following minor surgery Jane awoke in a hospital room. A nurse applied a suite of sensors to her, including electro-cardiogram, blood oxygenation, and blood pressure. The nurse waved each device in

---

1 This scenario is based on a real "Five-Day Glucose Sensor Test" program at the Dartmouth-Hitchcock Medical Center (http://tinyurl.com/6y2tk6).

front of a barcode reader on the bedside monitor. This step helped ensure that the monitor was receiving data wirelessly from the right set of sensors; the barcode also encoded the date of the last calibration of each sensor. Any sensor due for periodic maintenance would be automatically rejected. Soon her vitals were continuously being displayed on the bedside monitor.

Back at the nurse's station, telemetry from the room monitor was flowing into a display that monitored all patients on the floor. Validating against the vitals she had just seen in the room, the nurse uses the nurse's station computer to enter Jane's identity, associating the data stream with Jane. Data entering the database could now be routed to Jane's medical record. From the nurse's station, the nurse is able to view sensor data from all of the patients on the hospital ward. Each display includes patient identifying information as well as confidence information to reduce false alarms (false positives) and missed alarms (false negatives).

Meanwhile, on the floor of the ward, a physician is making rounds. When he approaches Jane's bed, his mobile tablet associates with Jane's bedside monitor and sensor and displays Jane's medical record as well as her current vitals. A built-in confidence indicator assures the physician that this is indeed Jane's data and that the sensors are relevant, accurate, functional, and correctly applied.

Concerned about her recovery, Jane's doctor refers her to a cardiologist for an expert opinion. Rather than traveling to see Jane, the cardiologist first reviews her medical record. Via a telepresence capability built into her room, the cardiologist is able to speak with Jane, viewing her condition first-hand and discussing her symptoms, while simultaneously viewing her continuous vitals stream. Based on this information, and a built-in trust assessment of the data, the doctor prescribes medication for Jane with confidence.

2.3 Scenario 3

John's insurance company promises to reduce his insurance rates if he would quit smoking. The insurance company provides a wrist-mounted device that contains sensors to detect heart beats, blood oxygenation, accelerometers, and a smoke sensor to ensure that John is true to his word. The device includes several tamper-evident features that would allow the insurance company to determine at periodic intervals that the device (sensors, processor, and software) have not been modified.

A nurse visits John to program the sensing device by connecting it via a temporary wire to her own trusted device. During this training phase, the device measures small changes in John's heart rate, establishing a signature for John's heart-rate variability. Then John was asked to perform several tasks, including mimicking his smoking behavior, to calibrate an activity inference. Before the nurse left, she reminded John to wear the device at all times, to avoid smoking or being around others who smoked, and to periodically connect it to his PC for data upload. John was told that if he did not wear his device, or if he gave the device to a friend to wear, he would not receive his discount.

The device constantly monitored its sensors, ensuring that John was wearing it and there were no telltale signs of smoking, such as detection of smoke in the air, drops in blood oxygenation without corresponding exercise activities, or detection of smoking gestures. Every week, John would connect the device to his PC to upload data to his insurance company.

John's insurance company input the periodic data from John into a validation algorithm to assess the probability that he was smoking. The algorithm includes correlation across multi-modal sensors, such as detecting smoke in the air or changes in physiological data, and recognizing smoking gestures, to determine the probability that John is smoking. In addition, the results indicate the probability that John has applied the sensors correctly, based on both a qualitative assessment of the data as well as self-test features in the sensor. Finally, the algorithm assesses the probability that John is trying to actively cheat, testing the authenticity of the devices that originated the data, validating the attestable state of the devices, and matching patterns in the sensor data (e.g., signatures of activity and heart rate variability) against John's previously recorded patterns.

3 Data Quality

Health-monitoring scenarios like those above require high-quality data from medical sensing devices or sensors. *Data quality* refers to the accuracy, authenticity, and appropriateness of a set of data for a given purpose. Ideally, a pervasive health-monitoring system assures high-quality data through a design and implementation that *ensures* the authenticity and integrity of the sensor data. Since it is impossible for a system to ensure perfect data quality, it is important to be able to *assess* the degree of confidence in the data, and to express that confidence in a way that allows the user to interpret the data in context. *Confidence* in sensor data represents the belief that the sensor reading accurately reflects the desired value; by *assessing quality* we mean quantifying confidence in sensor data and effectively presenting the results of the assessment to the user of the sensor data.

In this context, *facts* are data that are presumed correct a priori, not obtained from any of the sensors in question. For example, facts include information from the patient's medical history.

Finally, we define *trust* as the system's belief that a person or component will behave as expected.

3.1 Factors

An assessment of data quality entails an understanding of the various factors that might affect data quality; we consider six sensor factors, two human factors, and three system architecture factors. Ultimately, in future research, we hope to find a quantifiable metric or rubric for each factor.

3.1.1 Sensor factors

(Factor S1) Sensor design: Each sensor is characterized by a baseline measurement error inherent in the engineering, design, type, and purpose of the sensor. Confidence depends on both the *precision* (granularity of its reading) and *accuracy* (potential deviation from the true value).For example, a household bathroom scale may report weight in tenths of pounds (precision) and may be expected to be within two pounds of the correct weight (accuracy).To ensure high-quality sensor data, well-designed sensors with fine precision and high accuracy must be selected with due consideration to the medical needs of the situation, cost, and convenience. In Scenario 1, for example, the implanted sensor provides higher temporal precision (many readings per day) and possibly higher accuracy than the manual method.

(Factor S2) Sensor manufacture: Quality of manufacture reflects the trust in the sensor manufacturer and its manufacturing process; confidence may be based on past interaction or reputation.

(Factor S3) Sensor calibration: Sensor accuracy degrades with time, requiring periodic recalibration. Confidence in the sensor's calibration depends on the time since the last calibration, rate of drift away from calibration, and the reliability of the calibration authority.

(Factor S4) Sensor application: Many medical sensors must be applied correctly to provide meaningful results. For example, a thermometer may need to be applied directly to bare skin; a pulse oximeter may need to be applied to a specific part of the body. Confidence derives from trust in the patient or car-

egiver's ability and reliability in applying the sensor (see below) or from corroborating evidence (e.g., by secondary sensors that confirm the proper application of the primary sensor).

(Factor S5) Sensor integrity: In some settings, such as Scenario 3, there may be concern that the patient or another party may tamper with the sensor or the sensing system. Confidence in the sensor's integrity may derive from tamper-resistant or tamper-evident hardware, including trusted-platform modules that can attest to the integrity of the sensor system software.

(Factor S6) Sensor data correlation: One mechanism to assess confidence in sensor readings is to compare those readings against other data. *Redundant sensing* correlates a sensor reading against other sensors of the same type, with sensors from different parts of the body (spatial correlation), or with historical values from the same sensor (temporal correlation). *Multi-modal sensing* correlates a sensor reading against other sensors of different types, building on known correlations between sensor types. In Scenario 3, for example, a smoking event creates smoke in the air, a drop in blood oxygenation, and smoking gestures by the patient. *Fact checking* correlates a sensor reading with facts, such as information (e.g., age) from medical records.

3.1.2 Human factors

Any health-monitoring system involves human participants (patients and caregivers) and must necessarily trust these participants to carry out specific roles in each usage scenario [8], [24]. Some participants may be more trustworthy than others, for certain roles. Confidence in the sensor data derives from the level of trust in the participant(s), specifically, the system's ability to believe in the participant's identity (authenticity), responsibility (performing the role when expected), competence (performing the role correctly), and motivation (willingness to perform the role).

(Factor H1) Trust in patient: Consider the role of applying the sensor, which raises the following fundamental trust issues. Identity: are we sensing the right patient? Responsibility: does the patient regularly apply the sensor? Competence: does the patient tend to apply the sensor correctly? Motivation: does the patient have incentives to cheat? In some usage scenarios the patient may be the only participant involved, monitoring his own health. These trust issues ultimately affect the quality of data from the patient's sensor.

(Factor H2) Trust in caregiver: One or more caregivers are responsible for the initial configuration of a sensor, and (in some cases) for the periodic application or adjustment of the sensor. For instance, in the smoking cessation scenario data quality is affected by trust in the nurse who calibrates and provides the sensor to the insured. In other settings, a caregiver may be a physician, a technician, or a lay person such as a family member. The trust issues mirror those with patients.

3.1.3 System architecture factors

Some envision a three-tiered architecture for pervasive health monitoring: sensing, storing, and delivering health data [16]. The specific architectural choices will depend substantially on the needs of the situation. An architecture suitable for use in an emergency room is likely to be different from that used in an assisted living environment or a personal health monitoring system for an athlete. Regardless, the architecture must be robust and available to ensure timely delivery of data and secure to ensure data quality; we highlight three common factors here.

(Factor A1) Networking: From patient to caregiver, sensor data may travel on many networks: the patient's home network, public networks such as the Internet, or private networks such as coffee-shop

Wi-Fi networks. Despite the threats to sensor/system communications we desire data to arrive intact and without delay.

(Factor A2) Device platform: We anticipate that devices other than health sensors, such as the patient's mobile phone, will be involved in a typical deployment to provide computation and storage for the sensors. Data quality may be affected by the choice of device hardware and software platforms; for example, a platform with higher computation power can afford more sophisticated data-protection mechanisms. Confidence depends on the robustness and integrity of the device.

(Factor A3) Data pre-processing: System components pre-process sensor data for various purposes. *Data aggregation* combines multiple sensor values into a new statistical value (such as an average over time), or into an informative metric (such as an activity level from accelerometer data). *Data fusion* combines sensor data from multiple noisy sensors to derive information that is more concise and less noisy. Confidence in sensor data depends on the choice of aggregation or fusion methods and the location of the data processing along the data path.

4 Challenges

Were visit each of the factors described above, identifying the key challenges (denoted by [C]) involved in ensuring and assessing data quality and recognizing some of the technical wrinkles (denoted by [W]) that may have to be ironed out. The common research challenge across factors is assigning a metric to each. And, given some metric for each factor, how do we derive concise confidence metrics from multiple factors— and how does the passage of time modify our earlier confidence estimates? The resulting confidence level could expressed by a single metric (number between 0 and 1) or multiple metrics. How would the system present data confidence alongside data values, in a display meaningful to the data user?

4.1.1 Sensor challenges

(Challenge S1) Sensor design: We assume that a sensor's designed-in quality metrics (precision and accuracy) can be measured by an accredited lab that publishes the results as facts. [C1] When receiving the data, then, assessment reduces to a question of identification: how can the system authenticate the source of the data as being from a specific sensor model? [W1] If sensor data are collected in a storage device for later retrieval, what confidence do we have in the chain of custody for that device, and its integrity against tampering? [W2] If sensor data are cryptographically signed by a remote sensor, then what confidence do we have in the validity and integrity of the signing key? See also Challenge S5.

(Challenge S2) Sensor manufacture: The best solutions presumably rest on professional engineering standards and quality-metrics organizations. Similarly, the methods to assess confidence in a given manufacturer are non-technical, based on reputation or on a history of high-quality products. [C2] The technical challenge, however, is to find a way to *quantify* confidence in manufacturers, at least as far as needed to assess this factor alongside the others. [W3] How do we evolve our confidence measures, particularly on historical data, when there is new information about the manufacturer? [W4] How does quality of manufacture affect factory calibration of the sensor and how can this be factored into our belief in the calibration state of the sensor?

(Challenge S3) Sensor calibration: Calibration is necessary to configure a sensor to achieve its design specifications for precision and accuracy, and is initially performed by the manufacturer. Most sensors require periodic re-calibration, however, to accommodate natural drift in the sensor's capability or the effects of temperature, air pressure, or other environmental factors. Hospitals have trained technical

staff and a careful inventory system to ensure that all medical devices are tested and calibrated often. At home, the responsibility of getting the sensor recalibrated may rest on a patient or caregiver (Challenges H1, H2). Confidence in the calibration state of a sensor, then, reduces to the authentication of a calibration authority and the time since the most recent calibration.

If active mechanisms are possible, the system can trigger an instantaneous self-test in which a test signal is given to the sensor; the system can verify that the sensor detects the test signal or use the results of the self test to dynamically adjust future readings. How can the system accomplish this test in an environment with potential for adversaries to interfere? [C3] The key challenge is: how do we assess the confidence in the calibration state of the sensor? How do we know that the sensor been calibrated correctly and sufficiently recently? [W5] How do we represent the calibration results? If a sensor attaches a digital certificate with its sensor data, how should calibration results be encoded? How should the system validate this certificate and assess confidence from it? [W6] How do we assess our confidence in the calibration process? How do we model the accuracy of calibration, trust in the calibration authority and rate of calibration drift? How do we model environmental effects, and use input from auxiliary sensors (see Challenge S6)?For sensors that include a self-calibration mechanism, such as a scale that "zeroes" itself before use, how do we assess our confidence in the sensor's self-calibration, and the risks of tampering in that process (Challenges S4, S5)?

(Challenge S4) Sensor application: The sensor must be applied correctly and its position stabilized when the patient is mobile. To ensure proper application requires training of (and trust in) the medical personnel, caregiver, or patient who applies the sensor (Challenges H1, H2). [C4] The key challenge is: How can we validate that the sensor is applied correctly and remains stabilized in position? One approach is to use auxiliary sensors to validate correct application of the primary sensor. They might be packaged with the primary sensor or worn separately, or be embedded in the room (to measure ambient temperature or light). For example, the wrist device in Scenario 3 can make use of tilt sensors that ensure that the device is oriented correctly; pulse oximeters can be coupled with contact pressure sensors to ensure that optimum contact is maintained for reliable estimation of blood oxygenation. Another approach is to identify causal relationships between incorrect sensor application and lack of sensor data correlation[23].For instance, in Scenario 2 if one of the vital sign sensors exhibits a physiologically impossible change from past values the system can prompt the nurse to reapply the sensor. [W7] How can the assessment of sensor application be represented internally? Correct application of the sensor may depend on several parameters such as skin contact, orientation, lack of motion, pressure, or even environmental factors (for example, ambient light levels for pulse oximeters). If so, how can we combine individual assessments? [W8] Is the assessment static or dynamic? If dynamic, how does the time since last assessment factor into the metric? How do we trigger reassessment balancing the overhead involved with the need to ensure that the sensor is in place since it was applied? Do we reassess periodically or reassess when an event (e.g., motion) occurs? [W9] How do we know who applied the sensor and how does trust in the person who applied the sensor factor into the assessment of sensor application?

(Challenge S5) Sensor integrity: There is always the risk that a sensor, or its associated computing and communications capabilities, may be damaged or even manipulated to produce incorrect results. [C5] How can we ensure sensor integrity, using tamper-resistant hardware and secure embedded software? [W10] How can the sensor attest to its integrity, for example, through cryptographic statements made under the protection of a trusted hardware platform [32]? [W11] How can the system assess and quantify confidence in the sensor values, say, based on the attestations of the sensor's integrity? For devices that store data for later retrieval, how can we assess the integrity of the data while stored, and assess evidence of tampering with the sensor or device?

(Challenge S6) Sensor data correlation: Although assessment of the above factors may provide some degree of confidence in the sensor data, ultimately it is important to determine whether a given sensor value is somehow corroborated by other sensor values: either redundant sensors of the same type, complementary sensors of a different type, or known facts about the patient or the environment. [C6] How do we identify and model the correlations, and quantify confidence from the correlations observed? This requires a thorough understanding of the usage scenario, careful physiological study with human subjects, and a collaboration between bio-engineers and medical practitioners. Context awareness introduces possibilities for correlation. Context information such as patient motion or environmental changes can be used to correlate or correctly interpret the sensor data [33], [7], [20]. For example, if the motion sensor detects activity this information can be used to rationalize a sudden increase in sensed heart rate. [W12] How can we assess the degree of correlation among redundant sensors? Complementary multimodal sensors? How do we assess confidence in the sensor data across time? Measurement error or patient activity may disrupt one set of readings, but the prior and subsequent readings may fit the general trend. [W13] How can we combine these assessments into an assessment of overall correlation? How does the assessment weigh the relative importance of each correlation method? [W14] How do we represent the results of correlation to the system? Do we report the data with low confidence or reject non-correlating data? Correlation may also be used to address the challenges involved in some of the other factors such as the use of multi-modal sensors for ChallengeS4.Or,a non-correlating sensor may indicate a need for recalibration. How can we assess the reliability of these mechanisms?

4.1.2 Human challenges

A key question, involving both technical and non-technical considerations, is how the system should balance *trust* (expecting good behavior from the actors), *enforcement* (ensuring good behavior through sensor design or cryptographic protocols), and *assessment* (expecting good behavior, but assessing the results carefully). The right balance depends on the nature of the scenario, the motivations of actors, and the risk of incorrect decisions based on invalid data. The following discussion highlights some of the trust issues that impact data quality.

(Challenge H1) Trust in patient: We cannot *ensure* that the patient will be trustworthy, that is, that the patient will fulfill her role properly. We must therefore trust the patient to fulfill her role, whatever it might be, and then *assess* our confidence in the patient based on a priori information (such as the patient's prior history of compliance or capability with sensor devices) and based on dynamic information (such as data from contextual sensors that corroborate the primary sensor). [C7] How do we quantify confidence in the data based on fuzzy notions of trust in the patient [38], [30]?

[W15] What we may be able to ensure, to some degree, is the identity of the patient. How can we ensure that the sensor is applied to the correct patient, or that the sensed data is labeled with the correct identity when stored or transmitted? Regarding assessment, how can we determine whether the sensed data indeed comes from the desired patient? These challenges may be easier in some settings than others. In Scenario 2, for example, the identity of patient is established with bar-coded sensors and a one-time validation of observed vital signs of the patient. In Scenario 3, however, John may try to cheat by having someone else wear the sensor. In such settings, we may be able to use health-sensor data as a biometric identifier [6], [15], [14]. [W16] The patient's role may be minimal (e.g., an in-patient laying in a hospital bed may simply be expected not to remove the sensor device), or extensive (e.g., the glucose-monitor patient who must conduct the finger-prick test four times daily, and keep the embedded sensor dry). How can we assess whether the patient has fulfilled his or her roles responsibly and competently? How can we leverage information about past experience with this patient to do so? [W17] In settings where the patient may be motivated to provide incorrect data, how can we model these risks and use other evidence to validate that she has fulfilled her roles? [W18] Do we evolve trust in the patient based on new information about the patient? If so, how does this affect data quality? In the case of long-term monitoring, for instance, if we know nothing about the patient *a priori* we may decide to make only minimal trust assumptions about her behavior and later evolve the trust as we learn from later interactions. For short-term monitoring, however, we may have to make an active effort to get useful information about the patient to establish a basis of trust.

(Challenge H2) Trust in caregiver: [C8] Ultimately, how do we model these different roles, and how do we assess and quantify the effects on our confidence in the data quality? How would the system know which caregiver is involved, and in what way? It may be hard to identify, let alone authenticate, a caregiver assisting the patient. [W19] As with the patient, above, how do we quantify confidence in the data based on fuzzy notions of trust in the caregiver? How do we relate this confidence to other factors, such as our confidence in the sensor's calibration state?

4.1.3 System architecture challenges

(Challenge A1) Networking: Since health information is sensitive, health-care providers are required to comply with HIPAA privacy policies [12]. Thus, the system should have no weak links that leak health information or that are susceptible to side-channel analysis, for example, discovering the number and nature of health sensors or medical servers in use by traffic analysis. [C9] How can we ensure the confidentiality and integrity of health-sensor communications in low-resource devices? [W20] How do we ensure availability of network links for timely arrival of data? How do we ensure robustness of the network in the face of faulty links, network latency or malicious denial of service attacks? [W21] Sensor devices may use a wireless network to communicate, such as Bluetooth or Wi-Fi. These network protocols (and their implementations) have known vulnerabilities; can we prevent (or at least detect) an adversary who cracks into a sensor device through one of these vulnerabilities? How can we provide high availability and low latency in the face of adversaries who jam wireless networks?

(Challenge A2) Device platform: [C10] The challenge is to develop mechanisms to protect data quality on the mobile platform and to assess their state when the device is used, and protocols for communicating that state to the system. [W22] How can trusted hardware(such as a Trusted Platform Module[32]) be used to secure the mobile platform?

[W23] How can the platform attest its state to the system? Remote attestation mechanisms on the device can significantly improve the reliability of the device and hence the system's confidence in the data quality. The precise form of attestation depends on the system's methods for assessing data quality.

(Challenge A3) Data pre-processing: Data pre-processing techniques can reduce false alarms that may be caused by outliers. For example, the inaccuracies introduced in certain physiological signals due to bodily motion, known as motion artifacts, can be modeled in different ways [35], [37]. These models help to recover the original physiological signal from the motion-distorted sensor data. [C11] What pre-processing techniques are useful, and how do we assess confidence in the result? [W24] Where do we perform pre-processing? On the sensor device itself, on a personal device that collects data from the body-area network, or in back-end servers? Or a combination? The choice impacts our confidence in data quality. [W25] How does the system recognize where and how data pre-processing has occurred? Do we trust the components that perform data pre-processing? [W26] How much trust does the system place in these data pre-processing services? How can the system assess confidence in derived data, depending on its trust in the pre-processing servers, without knowledge of all of the raw sensor readings? How can confidence assessments in the raw sensor readings be factored into confidence in the pre-processed data? How do we deal with the potential data loss?

5 Related Work

Living, in-patient monitoring, sleep apnea monitoring and continuous blood glucose monitoring. An analysis of the risks to data quality should begin with a deeper understanding of the needs of a specific usage scenario and their implications on potential deployments. In this section we introduce existing literature helpful in understanding the design space of pervasive health monitoring systems followed by a discussion of other frameworks that have been proposed to analyze threats to data quality in pervasive health monitoring.

5.1 The design space of pervasive healthcare systems

Muras et al. [21] present a novel taxonomy of pervasive health monitoring that helps understand the breadth of the problem space. The taxonomy is based on the international classification of functioning, disability, and health, and provides a framework for describing different categories of user requirements within the healthcare domain. The taxonomy identifies a set of properties to describe various types of pervasive healthcare systems and serves as a useful guide in understanding where the system fits in within the broad spectrum of healthcare applications and characteristics of its operating environment.

The US Department of Health and Human services has released a detailed use case for remote patient monitoring [24] that describes the requirements of the problem space, issues and stakeholders involved and identifies typical information flows. The scope of the use case includes remote collection and communication of physiological, diagnostic, device tracking information and "activities of daily living" information. In an effort to standardize care co-ordination among different organizations, the document identifies specific roles of different stakeholders. The document also outlines the issues and obstacles that have to be overcome for effective adaptation of the new healthcare paradigm by all stakeholders. Particularly valuable to our work are the descriptions of candidate information flows from monitoring device to patient's electronic health record. The discussion details the primary and contextual flows and identifies system capabilities that support the flow at each step. The document serves as an important first step in identifying fundamental vulnerabilities in remote monitoring infrastructure and addressing them suitably.

Varshney [34] identifies different flavours of health monitoring and classifies existing projects in that space. Geer [4] discusses non-invasive pervasive medical devices and opportunities for cost-effective improved healthcare. Kulkarni et al. [18] discuss the design space of pervasive healthcare in the context of body sensor networks of non-invasive, portable sensors. Halperin et al. [11] discuss the unique challenges presented by wireless implantable medical devices. Baker et al. [1] describe five different prototypes that converge to an effective healthcare paradigm design, including infant and firefighter vital-sign monitoring.

5.2 Data assurance in pervasive health monitoring

Several recent studies have analyzed different categories of risks in pervasive healthcare systems. These threats can be viewed from system security, patient privacy and data integrity standpoints. Our view of data quality is similar to the data-centric trust approach proposed for a vehicular sensor network [29], that is, factoring assessment of different categories of risks into confidence in the reported sensor data. Our data assurance framework provides a holistic view of the associated risks in a pervasive healthcare scenario so that suitable countermeasures can be employed. While there are useful overlaps with existing literature, to the best of our knowledge, our framework covers a broader spectrum of factors and relationships between the various factors can be explored.

As part of the on going work in the Trusted Software Systems and Services project, Presti et al. [26], [27], [28] have developed a framework for analyzing trust issues in a pervasive computing. Their view of trust is a human-centric, composite and evolving belief; hence, trust issues are considered from perspectives of the different stakeholders, including patients and caregivers. For them, "trust" comprises trust in system components, data components and subjective components. Their approach involves scenario analysis to highlight trust issues and categorize them into a proposed trust-analysis grid. The range of issues presented in the framework show significant overlap with our data assurance factors. These issues are, however, factored into human-centric trust rather than confidence in reported data. The proposed trust-analysis grid may be useful in the design of trustworthy systems, but it is not clear how trust could be quantified in an ongoing manner based on observations from an existing system.

Maglogiannis et al. [19] describe a Bayesian network modelling approach to performing a risk analysis of health information systems. The model concisely presents the causes of and interactions between undesirable events within the system to identify and prioritize risks based on probability of occurrence. They present a prototype patient monitoring system, namely the VITAL-Home System, developed and maintained for a private medical center (Medical Diagnosis and Treatment S.A.), and apply the proposed framework to identify and prioritize associated risks. The proposed model considers threats to the system assets and other vulnerabilities from a system architecture standpoint.

The Warfighter Physiological Status Monitoring (WPSM) [2] is part of the US Army's research effort towards reliable physiological monitoring for warfighters. A Bayesian network is used to assess the status of the soldier and report confidence in the diagnosis based on clinical uncertainty and system reliability diagnostics such as sensor failure.

The Advanced Instrumentation group at the University of Oxford is investigating the design of self validating sensors using online uncertainty metrics and developing prototype applications [13]. A self validating sensor performs a set of assessments regarding its internal state and consistency checks on measured values to report quality metrics, such as online uncertainty, along with its measurements. Although traditionally applied to sensors in mechanical control systems, Peter et al. [25] recently demonstrated the application of their sensor validation approach to a wearable system that measures physiological parameters for emotion sensing. Sensor data is validated against previously received data and stored information about the measured variable. Sensor device status is also validated using a self test. Each self-validating sensor reports sensor data together with uncertainty based on the two kinds of validation results.

Other related studies use quality-driven sensor data acquisition by exploiting relationships among sensor data to perform validation checks. Tatbul et al.[31]have proposed a data-confidence model-driven method for physiological sensor data acquisition, which reports data only if the confidence level is acceptable. The confidence is derived from other observations such as data from multiple sensors.

Several data-validation schemes to obtain high confidence data have also been proposed. The data fusion architecture proposed by Carvalho et al. [3] uses evidence from redundant and multimodal sensors to obtain high-confidence data. The proposed data-fusion architecture is applied to a prototype health monitoring application to obtain high-confidence heart rate measurements using pulse oximeter and ECG sensors. Donoghue et al. [22] propose a real-time sensor-data validation framework for a home health monitoring system by correlating data using known boundary values, values from other sensors and patient information. The data-validation reports are used to estimate sensor reliability and presented to the caregiver.

Depending on the nature of the physiological signal being sensed, knowledge about the dynamics of the sensed signal can be leveraged for validation. Several recent papers correlate ECG or heart-rate sensor data with accelerometer data to obtain reliable readings in the presence of interference due to activity [5], [35], [36], [10]. Another recent paper applies clinical assessment techniques to mathematically model the accuracy of continuous glucose sensor data [17]. The factors considered in modeling the accuracy of the data are quality of calibration, physiology of glucose dynamics and sensor engineering. The C-BICC and MIMIC projects [23], [9] are investigating probabilistic models and machine-learning techniques for representing and reasoning about physiological data from critical-care sensors using knowledge of human physiology and sensor dynamics. Other related papers employ additional information, such as context of sensing to obtain reliable data from the health-monitoring sensors [33], [7], [20].

6 Summary

High-quality data is critical for many pervasive health-monitoring applications. We recognize that no system can ensure perfect data quality, and we highlight the need to assess *confidence* in the sensor data. In this paper we outline the key challenges related to ensuring or assessing the quality of sensor data in such applications. We identify six factors related to confidence in the sensors (Sensor Design, Sensor Manufacture, Sensor Calibration, Sensor Application, Sensor Integrity, Sensor Data Correlation), two types of factors related to human interactions(Trust in patient, Trust in caregiver),and three system architecture factors (Networking, Device Platform, Data Pre-processing). In the context of each factor, we identify and discuss research challenges in ensuring and assessing data quality. The actual impact of each factor (and the associated challenges) on data-quality assurance depends on the needs of the situation. Hence only a subset of these factors may be relevant in any given scenario. We recognize that to walk the fine line between enforcement and assessment it is important to understand the sources of risks and threats to data quality in each specific situation. The model of risks and threats for an actual deployment must account for the special needs of each usage scenario, from the point of sensor-data capture to presentation to the data user. As researchers, then, we must seek general-purpose frameworks that can capture and evaluate potential solutions. Ultimately, by resolving such challenges, we can help to provide quality healthcare in an effective and timely manner.

References

[1]   Chris R. Baker, Kenneth Armijo, Simon Belka, Merwan Benhabib, Vikas Bhargava, Nathan Burkhart, Artin Der Minassians, Gunes Dervisoglu, Lilia Gutnik, M. Brent Haick, Christine Ho, Mike Koplow, Jennifer Mangold, Stefanie Robinson, Matt Rosa, Miclas Schwartz, Christo Sims, Hanns Stoffregen, Andrew Waterbury, Eli S. Leland, Trevor Pering, and Paul K. Wright. Wireless sensor networks for home health care. In *AINAW'07: Proceedings of the 21st International Conference on Advanced Information Networking and Applications Workshops*, pages 832–837. IEEE Computer Society, 2007.

[2]   Maurizio Borsotto, C.T. Savell, Jaques Reifman, Reed W. Hoyt, Gavin Nunns, and Christopher J. Crick. Life-signs determination model for warfighter physiological status monitoring. Technical report, U.S. Army and GCAS Inc., Sept 2004.

[3]   H.S. Carvalho, W.B. Heinzelman, A.L. Murphy, and C.J.N. Coelho. A general data fusion architecture. *Proceedings of the Sixth International Conference of Information Fusion*, 2:1465–1472, 2003.

[4]   D. Ceer. Pervasive medical devices: less invasive, more productive. *IEEE Pervasive Computing*, 5(2):85–87, April-June 2006.

[5]   Chung-Min Chen, Hira Agrawal, Munir Cochinwala, and David Rosenbluth. Stream query processing for healthcare bio-sensor applications. In *ICDE '04: Proceedings of the 20th International Conference on Data Engineering*, page 791. IEEE Computer Society, 2004.

[6]   Sriram Cherukuri, Krishna K. Venkatasubramanian, and Sandeep K. S. Gupta. BioSec: A biometric based approach for securing communication in wireless networks of biosensors implanted in the human body.

In *Proceedings of the 2003 International Conference on Parallel Processing Workshops*, page 432, Los Alamitos, CA, USA, 2003. IEEE Computer Society.

[7] Ahyoung Choi and Woontack Woo. Context based physiological signal analysis in a ubiquitous VR environment. In Dongpyo Hong and Seokhee Jeon, editors, *ISUVR*, volume 260 of *CEUR Workshop Proceedings*. CEUR-WS.org, 2007.

[8] FDA. FDA's human factors program. As viewed April 2008. http://www.fda.gov/cdrh/humanfactors.

[9] MIT Laboratory for Computational Physiology. Integrating Data, Models, and Reasoning in Critical Care project, A Bioengineering Research Partnership. Project web site, as viewed March 2008. http://mimic.mit.edu/index.html.

[10] Liliana Grajales and IonV. Nicolaescu. Wearable multisensor heart rate monitor. In *BSN '06:Proceedingsof the International Workshop on Wearable and Implantable Body Sensor Networks*, pages 154–157. IEEE Computer Society, April 2006.

[11] Daniel Halperin, Thomas S. Heydt-Benjamin, KevinFu, TadayoshiKohno, and William H. Maisel. Security and privacy for implantable medical devices. *IEEE Pervasive Computing*, 7(1):30–39, Jan.-March 2008.

[12] HIPAA. As viewed April 2008. http://www.hipaa.org.

[13] University of Oxford Invensys UTC, Department Engineering Science. Self Validating sensor project at University of Oxford. Project web site, as viewed March 2008. http://seva.eng.ox.ac.uk/self validation.html.

[14] Evangelos Bekiaris Ioannis G. Damousis, Dimitrios Tzovaras. Unobtrusive multimodal biometric authentication: The HUMABIO project concept. *EURASIPJournal on Advances in Signal Processing*, 2008.

[15] David Jea, Jason Liu, Thomas Schmid, and Mani B Srivastava. Hassle free fitness monitoring. In *Proceedings of the 2nd International Workshop on Systems and Networking Support for Healthcare and Assisted Living Environments (HealthNet)*, Jun. 2008.

[16] Andrew D. Jurik and Alfred C. Weaver. Remote medical monitoring. *Computer*, 41(4):96–99, 2008.

[17] Boris P. Kovatchev, Christopher King, Marc Breton, and Stacey Anderson. Clinical assessment and mathematical modeling of the accuracy of continuous glucose sensors (cgs). In *EMBS '06: Proceedings of the 28th Annual International Conference of the IEEE Engineering in Medicine and Biology Society*, volume 30, pages 71–74, Sep. 2006. *Communications Review*, 11(3):12–30, 2007.

[18] Prajakta Kulkarni and Yusuf Öztürk. Requirements and design spaces of mobile medical care. *SIGMOBILE Mobile Computing*

[19] I. Maglogiannis, E. Zafiropoulos, A. Platis, and C. Lambrinoudakis. Risk analysis of a patient monitoring system using bayesian network modeling. *J. of Biomedical Informatics*, 39(6):637–647, 2006.

[20] I. Mohomed, A. Misra, M. Ebling, and W. Jerome. Harmoni: Context-aware filtering of sensor data for continuous remote health monitoring. *PerCom 2008: Proceedings of the Sixth Annual IEEE International Conference on Pervasive Computing and Communications*, pages 248–251, March 2008.

[21] Joanna Alicja Muras, Vinny Cahill, and Emma Katherine Stokes. A taxonomy of pervasive healthcare systems. *Proceedings of the Pervasive Health Conference and Workshops*, pages 1–10, 2006.

[22] John O. Donoghue, John Herbert, and David Sammon. Patient sensors: A data quality perspective. In *Proceedings of the 6th International Conference on Smart Homes and Health Telematics*, pages 54–61, 2008.

[23] Department of Electrical Engineering and Berkeley Computer Science, University of California. Center for Biomedical Informatics in Critical Care (C-BICC) project at UC Berkeley. Project web site, as viewed March 2008. http://www.eecs.berkeley.edu/Research/ Projects/Data/102178.html.

[24] U.S. Department of Health and Office of the National Coordinator for Health Information Technology Human Services. Remote Monitoring, detailed use case. Detailed use case document published on March 21, 2008. www.hhs.gov/healthit/usecases/documents/ RMonDetailed.pdf.

[25] Christian Peter, Eric Ebert, and Helmut Beikirch. Awearable multi-sensor system for mobile acquisition of emotion-related physiological data. In *ACII '05: Proceedings of the 1st International Conference on Affective Computing and Intelligent Interaction*, Lecture Notes in Computer Science, pages 691–698. Springer, 2005.

[26] StephaneLo Presti, Michael Butler, Michael Leuschel, and Chris Booth. Atrust analysis methodology for pervasive computing systems. In *Proceedings of the 7th International Workshop on Trustin Agent Societies*, volume 3577 of *LNCS*, pages 129–143. Springer, 2004.

[27] StephaneLo Presti, Michael Butler, Michael Leuschel, Colin Snook, and PhillipTurner. Formal modelling and verification of trust in a pervasive application. Technical report, Trusted Software Agents and Services for Pervasive Information Environments, University of Southampton, June 2004. Available as project deliverable at url=http://eprints.ecs.soton.ac.uk/10183/1/TSAS -WP4-01 v1.pdf.

[28] Stephane Lo Presti, Mark Cusack, Chris Booth, David Allsopp, Mike Kirton, Nick Exon, and Patrick Beautement. Trust issues in pervasive environments. Technical report, Trusted Software Agents and Services for Pervasive Information Environments project, University of Southampton, Sept 2003. Available as Project deliverable at http://eprints.ecs.soton.ac.uk/10183/1/TSAS -WP2-01 v1. pdf.

[29] Maxime Raya, Panagiotis (Panos) Papadimitratos, Virgil Gligor, and Jean-Pierre Hubaux. On data-centric trust establishment in ephemeral ad hoc networks. In *INFOCOM '08: Proceedings of the 27th Conference on Computer Communications*, pages 1238– 1246. IEEE Computer Society, April 2008.

[30] Jatinder Singh, Jean Bacon, and Ken Moody. Dynamic trust domains for secure, private, technology-assisted living. In *ARES '07: Proceedings of the The Second International Conference on Availability, Reliability and Security*, pages 27–34. IEEE Computer Society, 2007.

[31] Nesime Tatbul, Mark Buller, Reed Hoyt, Steve Mullen, and Stan Zdonik. Confidence-based data management for personal area sensor networks. In *DMSN '04: Proceeedings of the 1st international workshop on Data management for sensor networks*, pages 24–31. ACM, 2004.

[32] Trusted Computing Group (TCG). Project web site, as viewed April 2008. https://www.trustedcomputing-group.org/home.

[33] Surapa Thiemjarus, Benny Lo, and Guang-ZhongYang. Context aware sensing -what's the significance? In *Perspective in Pervasive Computing*, pages 163–170, October 2005.

[34] Upkar Varshney. Pervasive healthcare and wireless health monitoring. *Mobile Networks and Applications*, 12(2–3):113–127, 2007.

Session 6:
Future of Trust: New Models for Network, Device and Infrastructure Security

Towards one PC for systems with different security levels

David N. Kleidermacher[1] · Joerg Zimmer[2]

[1] Green Hills Software, Inc.
30 West Sola Street
Santa Barbara, CA 93101
USA
davek@ghs.com

[2] Green Hills Software GmbH
Siemensstr. 38
53121 Bonn
Germany
jzimmer@ghs.com

Abstract

Companies and organisations caring about the protection of critical data or critical systems have long struggled with the burden of maintaining separate computers. Commercial grade operating systems and virtualization solutions such as Windows, Linux, and VMware are unsuitable for security assurance to the high levels required for this kind of application sharing on a single PC platform. Custom solutions have failed to gain acceptance as cost containment pressures favour commercial, off-the-shelf (COTS) platforms. In addition, common PC hardware has had serious security limitations that prevent even a high assurance software solution from achieving the required domain separation. The hope for a truly high assurance, multi-level secure PC is coming closer to reality by virtue of recent innovations, both in software and hardware.

1 Introduction

Two major classes of problems plague computing infrastructure used by companies or organisations caring about data or systems which need to be protected. First, user communities are hopelessly dependent upon legacy computer systems and software that were never designed for a high level of security assurance and hence are riddled with known and as yet undiscovered security vulnerabilities.

The second class of problems leads directly from the first: due to the lack of high assurance computing solutions, policy is compelled to rely upon a physical separation (air gap) between computer systems and networks that manage information at disparate security levels and/or that have disparate user trust levels. Thus, highly trusted users (with access to information from different security levels or control accesses of critical systems) are forced to struggle with multiple computer systems, connected to multiple networks.

D. Gawrock, H. Reimer, A.-R. Sadeghi, C. Vishik (Editors): Future of Trust in Computing, Vieweg+Teubner (2009), 145-151

1.1 What level of assurance is needed?

The operating system bears a tremendous burden in achieving security. Because the operating system controls the resources (e.g. memory, CPU, devices) of the computer, it has the power to prevent unauthorized access to these resources and information flowing through them. Conversely, if the operating system fails to prevent or limit the damage resulting from unauthorized access, disaster can result.

Operating system security is not a new field of research. Yet today there is only one operating system that has been certified at the highest levels of assurance – Evaluated Assurance Level (EAL) 6 or 7 – the highest security levels of the Common Criteria, an internationally conceived and accepted security evaluation standard. The high assurance levels are difficult to reach because they require an extremely rigorous development process, formal design and a formal proof that the security policies of the system are upheld. One of the reasons for the lack of secure operating systems is the historical approach taken in operating system architecture. Most operating systems attempt to provide a kitchen sink of services, all running in the computer's supervisor mode. A single flaw in the hundreds of thousands or even millions of lines of code running in the kernel can provide complete access to all computer resources. In addition, the weak access control and privilege paradigm employed by most operating systems allow simple flaws in application programs to open up the entire system to improper access.
The Common Criteria states that "EAL 4" (a relatively low level of assurance) "EAL4 is the highest level at which it is likely to be economically feasible to retrofit to an existing product line" [COMM07] Windows and Linux have been evaluated at assurance level 4. The reality of monolithic systems like Windows and Linux, in which the base of code that must be trusted amounts to millions of source lines, is that there is simply no practical way to achieve an acceptable level of security for critical information and infrastructure when such a software platform directly controls the computer hardware. For years, most operating system experts have been convinced that microkernel architectures enable superior system reliability (fig. 1).

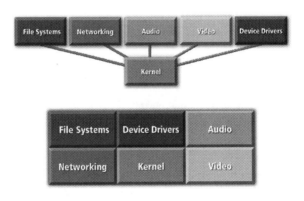

Figure 1: Microkernel vs. monolitic architecture

Green Hills Software's INTEGRITY – a microkernel-based real-time operating system - is the first operating system to be certified to EAL6+ [PROD07]. Designed to achieve EAL 7, the highest level, this certification at EAL 6+ represents what the United States National Security Agency (NSA) deems as the required level to ensure 'high robustness": protection of national secrets in the face of attack by highly determined and resourceful enemies [PROT07]. In addition to the formal methods mentioned earlier, part of a high robustness evaluation requires withstanding penetration testing by the NSA's own expert hackers who have complete access to the source code and months in which to carefully craft methods of attack. This same operating system is currently being used in communications devices that manage national secrets, avionics systems that control passenger and military jets, and a wide variety of other safety and security-critical systems. Other vendors are working towards this high robustness goal too.

2 Virtualization

While it has been proven that new operating systems can be designed to reach a high level of security, what can we do about our dependence upon legacy systems? One promising technology is computer system virtualization. At the start of the millennium, VMware proved the practicality of full system virtualization, hosting unmodified, general purpose, "guest" operating systems such as Windows, on commodity PC hardware.

In 2005, Intel (with AMD close behind) launched its Virtualization Technology (VT), which both simplified and accelerated virtualization. Consequently, a number of virtualization software solutions have emerged (alternatively called virtual machines or hypervisors), with varying characteristics and goals.

Computer virtualization is not new, IBM having pioneered the concept in its mainframes of the 60s and 70s. Computer scientists have long understood many of the applications of virtualization, including the ability to run distinct and legacy operating systems on a single hardware platform, sandboxing untrusted software, server provisioning and consolidation, and enhanced portability of legacy software.

3 Hypervisor architecture

Hypervisor architectures seen in commercial applications (such as VMware) typically employ a monolithic architecture (fig. 2). Similar to monolithic operating systems, the monolithic hypervisor requires a large body of operating software, including device drivers and middleware, to support the execution of one or more guest environments. In addition, the monolithic architecture often uses a single instance of the virtualization component (itself a complicated piece of software) to support multiple guest environments. Thus, a single flaw in the hypervisor may result in a compromise of the fundamental guest environment separation intended by virtualization in the first place.

A number of studies of virtualization security and successful subversions of hypervisors have been published, including [KING06] and [ORMA07]. Even so called "Type 1" hypervisors that run on bare metal without a full featured host operating environment actually contain large TCBs. In addition, these hypervisors usually employ a "console guest operating system" in which one of the guest domains is used by the other guest operating environments for I/O and other services. Thus, the amount of code that must be trusted in order to guarantee confidentiality between distinct guest environments is prohibitively large. The risk of an "escape" from the virtual machine layer, exposing all the guests is very real. In order to provide high robustness separation between multiple guest environments managing information at varying security levels, an improved hypervisor architecture is required. Figure 3 shows our proposed microkernel-based architecture.

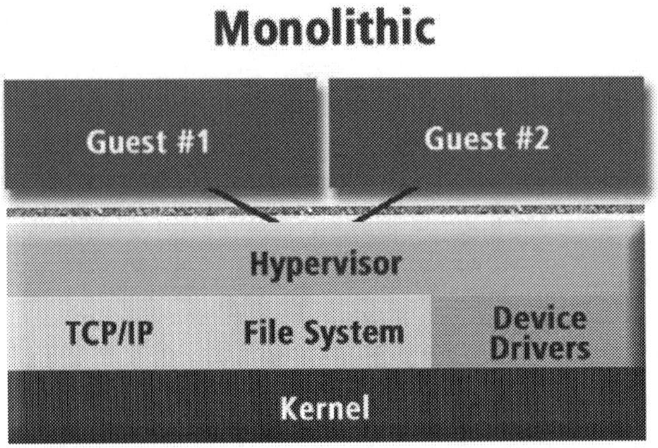

Monolithic

![Monolithic diagram]

Figure 2: Monolitic Hypervisor Architecture

Our architecture places all of the virtualization complexity into user-mode applications outside the trusted kernel. In addition, a separate instance of the hypervisor is used for each guest environment. Thus, the hypervisor need only meet the equivalent (and relatively low) robustness level of the guest itself. The kernel is a full-featured (but high robustness) operating system, enabling secure native applications, such as regraders and audit log reviewers, to be developed and then deployed alongside familiar PC operating environments. The combination of virtualized and native applications results in a powerful hybrid operating environment for the deployment of highly secure yet richly functional applications.

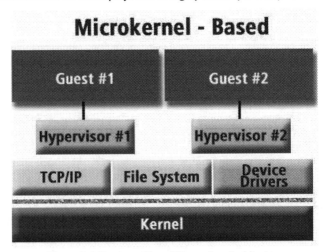

Figure 3: Microkernel based Hypervisor Architecture

4 Hardware trends

Intel and AMD have been adding important features to their chips and chipsets which aid in both virtualization performance and platform security. In August 2007, Intel announced its latest vPro™ chipsets which include Intel TXT and VT-d technologies which enable secure boot and attestation as well as protection against rogue peripherals. Inability to guarantee a secure initial state and protect against untrusted peripherals have been major roadblocks in meeting multi-level security requirements on commodity PC platforms.

Green Hills Software has used the aforementioned hypervisor architecture and Intel's hardware virtualization and security features as the foundation of a multi-level secure PC, called INTEGRITY PC. INTEGRITY PC adds a multi-level secure windowing environment to display and manage information at varying security levels.

Another key component of the Multi-Level Secure (MLS) PC is a cross-domain information transfer framework. Existing air gap infrastructure requires "sneaker net" – manual manipulation of files using media such as USB sticks - to move information between computers and networks at disparate security levels. In addition to being inconvenient, this method is error prone, leading to "spills" where sensitive information is improperly transferred or lost. By collapsing onto a single PC, the opportunity is provided for secure electronic transfer of text and files between security levels. Here again is where the ability to run secure, native applications outside of virtualized environments is critical. The cross domain transfer agent is a high robustness native application that sits between multiple virtualized environments and provides a certifiable "cut and paste" capability, following a configurable security policy.

Other MLS components of the INTEGRITY PC include shared keyboard and mouse drivers and a multi-factor authentication mechanism. Each of these components manages information at multiple security levels and hence must meet high assurance requirements.

4.1 Intel TXT and secure boot

One of the more promising hardware security features in modern commodity PC hardware is Intel's Trusted Execution Technology (TXT). TXT enables a computer user to gain a measure of trust in the platform upon which they are depending. Without TXT, there really is no way for a user to know with any degree of certainty that the platform – including the chipset option ROMs, BIOS, and security kernel – has not been replaced with malicious, impersonating versions. With TXT, known good versions of these platform components can be programmed into hardware by the manufacturer or OEM and verified at boot time, again by the hardware. With TXT, a chain of trust is established such that increasingly higher levels of software can be measured. For example, the security kernel can launch a measured virtualization environment so that even key application components can be attested.

There are two ways to establish trust at boot time. The first is the use of a "white list", which was just described: the PC itself verifies the hardware measurements (computed by a TPM – Trusted Platform Module – that is part of TXT) and simply terminates the boot sequence if a key component fails to match any known good value. The second method uses remote attestation. The PC's platform measurements are computed and stored in the TPM; but no action is immediately taken. Rather, a remote server is used to query the PC's measurements later, for example when the PC is used to access a secure network. Remote attestation uses security protocols defined by the Trusted Computer Group (TCG) specifications. Remote attestation enables policy centralization which may be desirable in some organizations.

4.2 Intel VT-d

Device drivers are notorious for causing security problems in general purpose operating systems. In monolithic operating systems such as Windows and Linux, device drivers run in the kernel domain. A single error in a driver can bring down the entire system or expose it to malware, viruses, and other attacks. In addition, external peripherals often act as bus masters, with unfettered access to system memory. A rogue peripheral can easily subvert the entire system.

Because of this device access risk, hypervisors have historically been required to interpose their own device drivers. When the guest attempts to manipulate a device, the hypervisor intercepts the device request, verifies the validity of the operation, and then performs its own security-critical manipulation of the device on behalf of the guest. In the microkernel-based architecture, this device software is called a "virtual device driver": device drivers execute as user-mode applications, enabling complex devices used exclusively by a single guest (such as a dedicated disk drive or Ethernet port) to be handled easily and securely by the microkernel platform software.

Although the microkernel-based hypervisor architecture provides a secure device approach that the monolithic approach cannot match, device driver interposition is still problematic, both due to the inevitable performance degradation as well as the necessity for virtual device drivers to be written for each device that may be needed in the PC ecosystem.

Intel's VT-d technology provides a compelling solution to this problem. With VT-d, the guest operating system can be provided direct access to the device, allowing DMA to be executed both by the guest device driver as well as by the peripheral itself. VT-d uses a dedicated hardware mapping table that confines all DMA accesses to the memory allocated to the guest environment by the hypervisor. A rogue driver or peripheral can no longer gain access to the kernel, another virtual machine environment, or any other component that lives outside of the assigned virtual machine. Thus, VT-d improves virtualization performance while enabling the hypervisor to take immediate advantage of the vast ecosystem of PC devices.

4.3 Multicore

Multicore microprocessors are now commonplace in PCs and servers. Multicore architectures improve the usability of hypervisors and the MLS PC. For example, on a dual-core system, native applications, such as the MLS window manager, can execute concurrently with a virtual machine, enabling a guaranteed quality of service for the guest and the critical application. Depending on their security levels, multiple guest environments may be permitted to execute concurrently on the multiple cores, improving overall system performance. Native real-time applications (such as a command and control system) can be assured optimal response by time by being bound to a core running independently of guest operating environments. The proliferation of multicore devices is likely to increase the proliferation of hypervisors: symbiotic growth for two disruptive technologies.

5 Conclusion

The multi-level secure PC can drastically improve security without sacrificing the utility of legacy software. The ability to consolidate computers and networks provides a compelling IT cost advantage for government computer users and administrators who manage high value information and cannot rely on commercial-grade virtualization solutions that are unable to meet high robustness security requirements.

The MLS PC, based on a high robustness, microkernel-based hypervisor architecture, has been deployed in a number of advanced government and intelligence organizations. Future work includes additional certifications, ports to new hardware platforms, and additional administration features.

INTEGRITY PC consolidates PCs by enabling multiple guest environments to execute on a single hardware platform. Each guest is provided exclusive access to the network matching its security level.

References

[COMM07] Common Criteria for Information Technology Security Evaluation Version 2.1; Part 3: Security assurance requirements; http://www.commoncriteriaportal.org/files/ccfiles/ccpart3v21.pdf

[PROD07] INTEGRITY-178B - NIAP products in evaluation, http://www.niap-ccevs.org/cc-scheme/in_evaluation/

[PROT07] "Protection Profiles Frequently Asked Questions", http://www.niap-ccevs.org/cc-scheme/faqs/pp-faqs.cfm#robustness

[KING06] Samuel King, et al., "SubVirt: Implementing malware with virtual machines", http://www.eecs.umich.edu/virtual/papers/king06.pdf, 2006

[ORMA07] Tavis Ormandy, "An Empirical Study into the Security Exposure to Hosts of Hostile Virtualized Environments", http://taviso.decsystem.org/virtsec.pdf, 2007

Trust Relationships in Networked Context Aware Systems

Veikko Punkka

Nokia Corp.
Devices R&D, Maemo SW
veikko.punkka@nokia.com

Abstract

This paper discusses challenges in building trust in networked context aware systems. It does not even trying to solve the challenges. Instead, it concentrates in discovering the requirements for trustworthy systems.

It introduces the concept of context in the context of context aware systems. It introduces trust relationships as a way to express requirements for trustworthiness. Trust relationships, as special kind of use cases, are useful as a starting point in software and system engineering.

This paper classifies networked context aware systems using the architecture as criteria. It further examines the trust relationships of various networked context aware systems.

1 Context Aware Systems

Dictionary [Dict08] defines context as "the set of circumstances or facts that surround a particular event, situation, etc." In this paper, context refers to the context of a user of a mobile device. This means the people and places that are significant to the user. The people include the user and those somehow associated with her. The association may be due to location, being physically close by. Associated people also include those with whom the user is communicating. They also include those met recently, those going to meet, those known personally, those heard of, those trying to avoid and so on. Historical associations as well as future associations are also part of the context. The places equally include the location of the user, the places close by, those visited recently, those going to, those heard of, those trying to avoid and so on.

Various attributes characterize the people and places within the context. In the context of mobile devices these attributes include things like name, age, gender, relationship to user, available methods of communication, times of last communications, number or frequency of communication, received content, sent content, recommended content and so on. Some of these attributes change more frequently than others do. The lifetime of these attributes and the impact of these lifetimes to the validity of the context is an interesting question, but beyond the scope of this paper.

The contexts of the people within the context and the people in the places within the context form a network of contexts. The whole network is an extension of the immediate context. The full extent of the extended context is never apparent to the user or the devices the user is using. Equally, a mobile device can only be aware of a subset of the context network. However, mobile devices are good in observing

D. Gawrock, H. Reimer, A.-R. Sadeghi, C. Vishik (Editors): Future of Trust in Computing, Vieweg+Teubner (2009), 152-156

and recording certain types of aspects of the user's context, such as the user's location and communication history.

We consider a system to be context aware if its behavior, either internal or external somehow depends on the context, as defined earlier. Typically, we also require that the change in the device behavior is somehow beneficial to the user. As a rule, the change should make the most common user actions easier or more efficient while keeping the less common ones possible.

A mobile device can modify its behavior in two different ways. It can change either the way it looks, feels, or sounds like, or the way it responds to the user action. Since it is much more difficult to maintain user interface consistency while doing the second one, the first one is much more common. In this study, we concentrate on the more common cases.

We can find a simple example of a mobile device modifying its behavior according to he user's context from most mobile phones. If the user presses the green "send" key while in the idle state, he sees a list of contacts most recently called. This simple application displays the typical pattern of a context sensitive application in a mobile device. Application reformats and displays information that is already available elsewhere in the device, in the phone book, according to the context of the user. The challenge in the interaction design is to integrate the functionality of the optimized application with the one providing the full content.

Context aware systems appear more user friendly than context unaware systems mainly because most users are predictable most of the time. This means that given the user's past history of choices, combined with the contexts in which the user made the choices, it is easy to build a model that predicts the user's choices within a given context. The accuracy of such models is surprisingly good.

User's context is inherently personal. In other words, it is frequently possible to identify the user based on the context. The context can be for example the people the user has recently contacted, or the places he has recently visited. At the same time, the user's context can be highly sensitive. In other words, revealing the context to others may cause the user embarrassment, nuisance, financial loss or other undesirable effect. Yet in another words, context can be highly private to the user and mere using a device that is aware of the user's context involves a lot of trust from the user.

2 Trust Relationships

Positive user experiences build trust slowly, but negative ones destroy it easily. In order to enable the building of trust, it is useful to express the requirements for the enablers of trust – the positive experiences that build trust. As usual with functional user requirements, use cases are useful in expressing them [Jaco92]. We call the use cases that involve two parties, one of which provides potentially sensitive or valuable information to another, trust relationships.

It is easy to find an example of trust relationships – buying something using a credit card. When the buyer provides the seller enough details of the credit card, the seller can continue with the transaction. The buyer obviously trusts some potentially valuable information to the seller. In this example, the trust relationship is in between the buyer and the seller. It is quite straightforward to see the implications of this trust relationship to the seller.

Like ordinary use cases, trust relationships have their life cycles. They begin at the point the information transmission and end at the point the information destruction. Alternatively, the trust relationship can end at the point of making the information anonymous. From the user perspective, there is no difference in between these two alternatives. In our credit card example, the trust relationship started at the time the buyer provided the card details to the seller. The trust relationship continues until the point, when the seller no longer holds enough information to charge the credit card.

Trust relationships are really use cases. The notion of use cases brings in a machinery to design, implement, and verify functionality specified by them. We can use the whole use case machinery with trust relationships. Describing the machinery beyond the fact that it exists be beyond the scope of this article.

With trusts relationships we reduce the dilemmas in building trust to systems to discovering the necessary trust relationships. Once we do that, the rest is software engineering.

3 Trust with Networked Context Aware Systems

Context aware systems are by definition aware of the context of the user and modify their behavior accordingly. Networked context aware systems provide the user access to resources that are outside the system itself i.e. networked resources. This in itself does not cause a trust dilemma with context aware systems. Even though the user's context may contain highly sensitive information, the fact that the system is aware of it is not a problem as long as it remains in the user's control and the knowledge of the user's context does not leak outside the system. The dilemma arises from the system's need to modify its own behavior according to the user's context with respect to the resources outside the system.

In order to optimize the presentation of networked resources to the user one needs to be able to describe the networked resources with related metadata. The metadata is useful for optimizing the systems behavior. One also needs to possess a model that maps the metadata attributes together with the context information to the optimized behavior.

It is useful to think of a simple example of a networked context aware system. One is an application that senses the user's location and automatically downloads the latest weather forecast for that location. The location may be determined using the network access point used to connect to the network, or some sensor such as a GPS receiver. Every time the application downloads the latest weather forecast, it reveals a part of the user's context to the server providing the weather forecasts.

Networked context aware systems can fundamentally have two different approaches to provide the user networked resources in a way that is somehow optimal to the user according to the user's context. The first one is to access the metadata related to the networked resources and then present the networked resources according to the user's context. In this approach, the model lies within the client and optimizes the client's behavior based on the metadata and context. The second one is to provide a subset of the user's context outside the device. This can be to the party providing the networked resources or a third party with access to the metadata related to the networked resources. That outside system then has the model and optimizes the presentation of the network resources based on the metadata and the subset of user's context. I call the first approach client side optimization and the second one server side optimization.

Examples of both approaches exist in the wild. A good representative of the first one is the recently introduced TomTom IQRoutes™ [Tomt08]. An equally good representative of the latter one is the Omniture Web 2.0 Optimizations tool [Omni08]. The author has no relationship to the former, but has worked as an architect in the early development phases of the latter.

Networked context aware systems also share all the trust dilemmas of non-networked context aware systems, but they are out of scope of this study.

4 Dilemmas with Client Side Optimization

The main dilemmas with client side optimization lie within the building the model. One can only base the model on the observed user behavior within the context. The building of the model consists of three separate phases. The first one is seeding the model with good enough initial data. The second one is personalizing with user dependent attributes. The third one is maintaining the model as the tastes of the user and the culture around evolve.

For seeding the model with good enough initial data, the data needs to be collected from real users. In many cases, companies even collect the data from users that do not benefit from the system at all. In these cases, the user has no incentive in actively contributing in the building of the model. In fact, the opposite since the collecting of the data may incur him additional costs. In here, the trust relationship is in between the creator of the networked context aware system and the user of the system that provides the initial use data. While technically this is a very simple case, the trust relationship is very problematic. The user of the system may not be aware of being in a trust relationship and discovering it post facto may be a very bad experience destroying trust.

Personalizing the model involves accessing the user data and modifying the model accordingly. Here the trust relationship is in between the user of the networked context aware system and the system itself. Superficially, this trust relationship resembles that of the non-networked context aware system. There is only one difference and that difference is essential. The user needs to be able to trust that the system does not leak the user data outside the system.

Maintaining the data involves periodic updates of the initial data set used when seeding the model. Here the trust relationship is in between the creator of the networked context aware system and the system itself. This relationship is simple in technical terms, but practical problems remain.

There is a trust relationship in between the provider of the networked resources and the user of the networked context aware system for the distribution of the metadata, but this is not essentially different from the trust relationship in between the provider of the networked resource

5 Dilemmas with Server Side Optimization

The main dilemma with server side optimization lies within the sharing of the context data. In various scenarios there is a number of trust relationships involved. In the following, we examine some of them.

The model can make use of several kinds of context data. The context data to be needs to be in the possession of the party holding the model. The device can gather the context data and transmit it to the model holder. Alternatively, the holder of the networked resources may gather the context data. In this case, the device transmits just the identity of the user to the gatherer of the context. The context then mainly contains user actions related to the provider of the networked resources.

In case the provider of the networked resources holds the model, there is an additional trust relationship in between the user of the networked context aware system and the supplier of the networked resources. This relationship is similar to the other trust relationship in between the same parties, the provider of the networked resources and the user of the networked resources, but reversed.

In case the model lies within a third party, there is a trust relationship in between the provider of the networked resources and the third party. There is also one in between the user of the networked context aware system and the third party. While this case looks more complicated than the one, where the model lies with the provider of the networked resources, it also has some advantages. A third party that is doing this kind of optimization professionally, may be able to have a better protection of the private data than the provider of the networked resources may. The provider of the networked resources is more likely to be concerned with the resources he provides. In addition, the third party may be able to optimize networked resources from more than one provider. This may or may not be a desirable thing based on your point of view.

The network provider may act as the third party holding the model. It can optimize the access of virtually all networked resources. The network provider also has knowledge of the user identity. However, the consequences of the network provider loosing trust of the end user are particularly serious.

6 Challenges in Building Trust

Building trust means providing the users of the system positive user experiences as well as shielding them from negative ones. For different networked context aware systems, the number of trust relationships involved and many of them are essentially different from each other. Hence, it is obvious that no single solution will be sufficient to build trust over all the needed trust relationships.

In case you are in the business with networked context aware systems, your best bet is to identify the trust relationships you need to be in and assess each of them individually. It is a good approach to treat them as requirements to your system and build the enablers of trust to your system. However, a solution that is appropriate for some system may not apply another.

While this study has mainly concentrated in identifying the trust relationships involved with networked context aware systems and we have left the actual methods of building trust outside the scope, they might well be an interesting topic of further study.

7 Conclusion

Trust relationships are a useful way to describe the requirements for systems that need to be trusted. Networked context aware systems involve a number of different trust relationships. Trust relationships are useful when building concrete systems. They realize into requirements that are useful as a starting point in system and software engineering, building trustworthy systems.

For networked context aware systems, trust relationships are also a way to describe the complexity of the systems. The more complex the system needs to be the less likely it is to be implementable.

References

[Dict08]   *Dictionary.com Unabridged (v 1.1)*. Random House, Inc. 14 Jul. 2008. <Dictionary.com http://dictionary.reference.com/browse/context>.

[Jaco92]   Ivar Jacobson, Magnus Christerson, Patrik Jonsson, Gunnar Overgaard *Object-Oriented Software Engineering: A Use Case Driven Approach (ACM Press)* Addison-Wesley, 1992, ISBN 0201544350.

[Tomt08]   http://www.tomtom.com/iq-routes

[Omni08] http://www.omniture.com/en/products/online_business_optimization/business_optimizations

Towards Trusted Network Access Control

Ingo Bente · Josef von Helden

University of Applied Sciences and Arts, Hanover
Faculty IV – Business and Computer Science
{ingo.bente | josef.vonhelden}@fh-hannover.de

Abstract

Network Access Control (NAC) solutions promise to significantly increase the security level of modern networks. In short, they allow to measure the integrity state of an endpoint that tries to get access to the network. Based upon the measurement results, which are compared to a defined NAC policy, access to the network can be allowed or denied. One problem of all currently available NAC solutions is referred to as the "lying endpoint" problem. Normally, special software components are responsible for gathering the relevant integrity information on the endpoint. If an attacker modifies those software components, an endpoint can lie about its current integrity state. Therefore, endpoints which are not compliant to the defined NAC policy can get access to the network. Those endpoints must be considered as potential threat. This paper summarizes a possible solution for the lying endpoint problem based upon the specifications of the Trusted Computing Group (TCG) and the results of the two research projects TNC@ FHH and Turaya. The goal is to develop an open source, TNC compatible NAC solution with full TPM support within a new research project: tNAC.

1 Motivation

Over the last years, the structure of networks has changed significantly, from static and homogeneous to more dynamic and heterogeneous ones. Nowadays, particularly mobile endpoints connect to and communicate with various networks. Employees are using their laptops in different, (un)protected environments and need to have remote access to their company's network. Furthermore, it is often required to allow guest devices to access some parts of the own network.

Due to the new structure of modern networks, the strategy of hackers has changed and therefore there are new threats to face. Instead of directly attacking well-secured servers, they are now focussing on compromising the devices of the users first, where the security-level is generally lower. As a consequence of that, it is not sufficient to secure its own network with well-known, well-proven and central security solutions like Firewalls and Intrusion Detection Systems (IDS), which are just not able to protect mobile endpoints which are used in different environments. Even worse: those potentially compromised endpoints are a threat to any network they are connecting to.

That's why Network Access Control (NAC) is becoming more and more important in securing today's networks. In addition to the mentioned, classical security tools, NAC systems allow to face some of the new threats that appeared in the past. One of the main benefits is that NAC allows to counter threats at the network's edge. Only healthy endpoints which are compliant to a defined NAC policy are allowed to access the network. The access decision is enforced at the point through which the respective device tries to get access to the network (e.g. a switch or a VPN gateway). One crucial aspect of the NAC proc-

D. Gawrock, H. Reimer, A.-R. Sadeghi, C. Vishik (Editors): Future of Trust in Computing, Vieweg+Teubner (2009), 157-167

ess is assessment. Assessment means gathering data about an endpoint (e.g. integrity data like installed OS, anti virus and firewall software) and the current user. Based on this data, a NAC system determines if the endpoint is healthy in respect to a specified NAC policy defined by the network administrator or not.

There are several ways to actually gather the assessment data. One of the most common one is an agent-based approach. A specific software component (called the agent) on the endpoint is responsible for gathering the necessary data and communicating it to the NAC server that protects the network. This way, the current status of the endpoint can be evaluated against the defined NAC policy.

Although this approach sounds quite reasonable, one aspect has to be considered: One has to trust the agent. What if it lies about the current status of the endpoint? The agent is just another software component on the endpoint and can therefore get compromised, too. That this threat is real has been demonstrated during the Black Hat conference 2007 ([RoTh07]). The agent of Cisco's NAC solution was modified in such a way that access to a protected network was granted although the endpoint was not compliant with the defined NAC policy. This issue is not restricted to Cisco's NAC solution. Any agent based NAC system is in general vulnerable to this kind of attacks.

Trusted Computing (TC) together with Trusted Network Connect (TNC) are promising approaches to counter this threat. TNC is an open NAC standard defined by the TCG. Basically, its architecture and the supported features are similar to proprietary approaches like Cisco's NAC ([CNAC]) or Microsoft's NAP ([MSNAP]). Especially, all of them are agent based approaches. However, in contrast to CNAC or MS NAP, the TNC approach includes support for the Trusted Computing technology. By using the Trusted Platform Module (TPM), the trustworthiness of the data gathered by the agent can be assured. An attack like the one described above which is based upon compromising aspects of the endpoint to successfully lie about its real status would fail because the modifications made to the agent (or other aspects of the endpoint) can be detected.

One further advantage of TNC compared to the proprietary NAC solutions is its openness. All of the specifications defining the TNC architecture are publicly available. This openness enables to achieve real interoperability between TNC compatible NAC solutions and thus prevents vendor lock-in. Unfortunately, there are currently no completely TNC compatible NAC solutions available.

2 Introduction to Trusted Network Connect

Trusted Network Connect (TNC) is an open architecture for Network Access Control (NAC). It is specified by the TNC working group of the TCG. The process of checking the integrity of an endpoint, evaluating the measurements against a given NAC policy and deciding to what extent access to the network is granted is referred to as TNC Platform Authentication. It is important to note that the term Platform Authentication in the context of TNC refers to both checking the identity of a platform (Platform Credential Authentication) and its integrity state (Integrity Check Handshake) in addition to an optional user authentication.

2.1 Basic Architecture

The TNC architecture ([TNCA08]) conceptually specifies the elements that must be available in an IT infrastructure for performing a TNC Platform Authentication. It basically is a client server model that consists of several entities, layers, components and interfaces. **Figure 1** depicts a simplified version of the TNC architecture that will be described in the following.

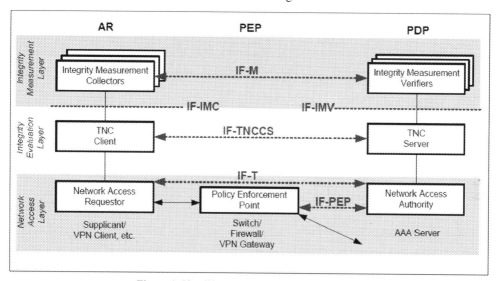

Figure 1: Simplified TNC architecture ([TNCA08])

2.1.1 Entities

Vertically, the TNC architecture is divided into three entities:

- The Access Requestor (AR) is the entity that tries to get access to a TNC protected network. Normally, this is an endpoint (e.g. a laptop) on which the appropriate TNC software is running.
- The Policy Decision Point (PDP) is responsible for deciding to what extent an enquiring endpoint gets access to the protected network. This decision is based upon the current integrity state of the AR which therefore must be measured and communicated to the PDP.
- The Policy Enforcement Point (PEP) is the entity in between the AR and the PDP. The PEP is responsible for enforcing the access decision made by the PDP. Normally, the PEP matches a switch, a firewall or a VPN gateway.

2.1.2 Layers

Horizontally, the TNC architecture is divided into three layers. Each layer combines those entities that fulfil a similar task within the TNC Platform Authentication.

- The bottom layer is referred to as Network Access Layer (NAL). It consists of all the components that are responsible for technically implementing the communication with the network. Each entity has one component in the NAL.
- The middle layer is referred to as Integrity Evaluation Layer (IEL). The components in this layer are responsible for communicating the integrity measurements taken by the components of the

top layer. Furthermore, they evaluate the overall integrity state of an endpoint and derive an access decision.

- The top layer is referred to as Integrity Measurement Layer (IML). As the name implies, those components are responsible for actually measuring and evaluating the integrity state of an endpoint.

2.1.3 Components

There are nine sorts of components in the TNC architecture which are described according to their appropriate layer.

2.1.3.1 Components of the IML

This layer normally consists of an arbitrary number of component pairs, each made up of an Integrity Measurement Collector on the AR and an Integrity Measurement Verifier (IMV) on the PDP. Each of those IMC/IMV pairs is responsible for measuring and evaluating certain properties of the AR. I.e., the measurements are taken by the IMC on the AR, communicated to the corresponding IMV on the PDP by using the components of the two other layers, which then evaluates the received measurements against a given policy. The IMV communicates the result to the TNCS in form of a recommendation that specifies to what extent access to the network should be granted.

2.1.3.2 Components of the IEL

The IEL consist of two components: the TNC client (TNCC) on the AR and the TNC server (TNCS) on the PDP. Their primary task is to enable the communication between IMCs and IMVs by forwarding the IMC/IMV messages to the NAL. Furthermore, the TNCS on the PDP is responsible for deriving an overall access decision based upon the single recommendations provided by the IMVs. This overall access decision is then communicated to the NAA.

2.1.3.3 Components of the NAL

The NAL consist of three components. Within the AR, the Network Access Requestor (NAR) realizes the technical access to the network. If TNC is used within a LAN environment, prominent examples for the NAR are 802.1X supplicants like Xsupplicant and wpa_supplicant. On the PDP, the Network Access Authority (NAA) performs a similar task. Furthermore, this component is responsible for actually deciding to what extent access to the network is granted. Normally, it takes the recommendation received by the TNCS without any modifications and instructs the third component, the Policy Enforcement Point (PEP) to enforce the decision.

2.1.4 Interfaces

The communication between the components mentioned above is mainly standardized by appropriate interfaces (depicted as dotted lines in **Figure 1**). Explaining the details of all the interfaces is out of the scope of this paper. Nevertheless, the purpose of the IF-M interface should be summarized in the following.

IF-M is the interface that enables the communication between an IMC and an IMV. This interface, though mentioned in the TNC architecture, is not standardized. Since IMC/IMV pairs are developed by different parties and each of those IMC/IMV pairs is responsible for measuring and evaluating different aspects of the endpoint, it is up to the developers to define an appropriate interface or protocol that fits their needs. I.e., an IMC from vendor A will normally not be able to talk to and IMV from vendor

B in a reasonable way. That means there are several IF-M interfaces – not just one. However, the TNC Subgroup expects to standardize certain, widely useful IF-M interfaces in the future.

2.2 The TNC Platform Authentication

The process that happens when an endpoint tries to get access to a TNC protected network is referred to as TNC Platform Authentication (see **Figure 2**). It consists of three phases:

1. Assessment
2. Isolation
3. Remediation

The assessment phase is the first one that takes place. Here, the integrity of the AR is measured and communicated to the PDP. On the PDP, the installed IMVs evaluate the measurement results. Then, each IMV gives a recommendation whether the endpoint is compliant to the defined NAC policy or not. The TNCS is responsible for gathering all the recommendations provided by the IMVs and form an overall recommendation regarding the policy compliance (and therefore the trustworthiness from the network administrator's point of view) of the AR. If the AR is compliant to the NAC policy, access to the network is allowed.

If the AR is generally allowed to access the network (e.g. it is a corporate laptop), but it currently does not comply with the NAC policy (e.g. if not all necessary patches for the OS are installed) the isolation phase starts. I.e. access is not completely denied. Instead, the endpoint is isolated in a special segment of the network. This network segment has to be isolated from the rest of the network which can be achieved by using Virtual LANs (VLANs) or Access Control Lists (ACLs). This way, an endpoint that is not compliant to the NAC policy is no threat to the productive network. Furthermore, special services can be provided within the isolated network segment that enable the endpoint to become compliant to the NAC policy (e.g. by providing a source for downloading necessary OS patches).

The process of fixing the integrity state of an endpoint and making it compliant to the NAC policy again is referred to as Remediation and makes up the third phase of the TNC Platform Authentication. After the Remediation phase, the endpoint can again try to get access to the network by performing another assessment phase. If the Remediation process was successful, the endpoint should be compliant to the NAC policy and access to the network is granted.

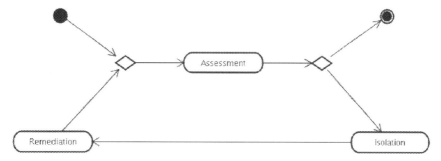

Figure 2: The three phases of the TNC Platform Authentication

2.3 TPM Support within TNC

In addition to its openness, one further advantage of the TNC architecture is the optional support for using the functions of a TPM within the TNC Platform Authentication. This could be a promising approach for solving the lying endpoint problem. The goal is to ensure the integrity of the TNC subsystem located on the AR.

The basic idea is to use TPM capabilities within the TNC Platform Authentication by creating so called integrity reports. Those integrity reports reflect the current integrity state of the AR. For countering software based attacks, PCR values signed by the TPM are included in those reports. If integrity reports that reflect the integrity of the TNC subsystem are communicated from the AR to the PDP, the AR can not lie successfully about its current integrity state anymore.

2.3.1 Additional Components for TPM Support

Additional components are required that enable the use of TPM functions within the TNC Platform Authentication. Three of them are well known in the context of Trusted Platforms:

- The Trusted Platform Module (TPM)
- The Trusted Software Stack (TSS)
- The Integrity Measurement Log (IML)

Furthermore, there is a fourth component mentioned in the TNC specifications: the Platform Trust Services (PTS). This is a system service located on the AR that exposes the Trusted Platform capabilities to the TNC components through the IF-PTS interface ([IFPTS06]). The PTS especially features the following:

- It enables TNC components to create TPM signed integrity reports, making them available within the TNC Platform Authentication. Furthermore, the PTS ensures that those integrity reports are rendered in an interoperable format as specified by the TCG schemas.
- The PTS itself measures the integrity of the TNC subsystem on the AR and appends those measurements to the IML. Therefore, the integrity of the TNC subsystem can be evaluated within the TNC Platform Authentication.

The additional components are depicted in **Figure 3**.

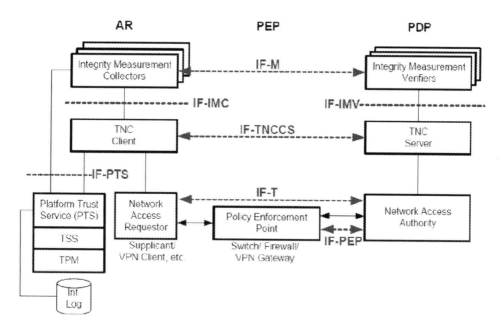

Figure 3: TNC architecture with TPM support ([TNCA08])

2.3.2 PTS and the Chain of Trust

Now that the additional components have been introduced, the question that arises is: Why should one trust the PTS? It is just another software component on the AR and can therefore get compromised as any other component, too.

The answer lies in the concept referred to as Chain of Trust or Transitive Trust Chain. This is a fundamental concept in the area of Trusted Computing as it is specified by the TCG. In short, the Chain of Trust deals with the fact that the integrity of a component has to be measured before that component is executed. Otherwise, if the component is compromised and the measurement is done after the component is executed, the measurement itself could be compromised by this component.

If the PTS itself now is a part of the Chain of Trust, one could securely recognize if it has been compromised or not. As already mentioned, for becoming part of the Chain of Trust, the integrity of the PTS must be measured before it is executed. The OS is expected to do that. Since normal OS do not have the necessary functions for adding components to the Chain of Trust, a so called Trusted OS is needed.

Once the PTS is part of the Chain of Trust, it can be executed. Then, the PTS is responsible for further integrity measurements of the TNC subsystem located on the AR. This way, it is possible to build up a Chain of Trust starting from the Root of Trust including (among other things) the BIOS, the OS loader, the OS image, the PTS and the TNC components on the AR. An integrity report that captures all those components can be used within the TNC Platform Authentication to correctly reflect the integrity of the TNC subsystem on the AR. This way, lying endpoints can be securely recognized.

2.3.3 PTS-IMC/IMV

The next question that arises is: How does the communication of integrity reports between the AR and the PDP work? The answer is: one special IMC/IMV pair called PTS-IMC/IMV is responsible for communicating the appropriate integrity reports. I.e. the PTS-IMC interfaces with the PTS to obtain the integrity reports and communicates them to the PTS-IMV during the TNC Platform Authentication . The PTS-IMV evaluates the received reports against a given policy.

Unfortunately, the TNC specifications do not mention how this communication should take place. This is a consequence of the IF-M interface, which is normally vendor specific and therefore opaque to the rest of the TNC framework. However, the TCG has stated that certain, widely useful IF-M interfaces should be standardized in the future. The IF-M interface between PTS-IMC/IMV certainly is widely useful and essential for using TPM functions within TNC. There is currently no schedule available when the IF-M-PTS interface will be published.

2.4 Establishing TNC Subsystem Integrity

To sum things up, the following steps are necessary for establishing the integrity of the TNC subsystem:
- Pre-OS Boot: Measure integrity starting from RTM over BIOS, OS Loader and OS Image
- Pre-PTS Start: OS must measure PTS (including the TSS).
- PTS Operation: Measures TNC components (NAR, TNCC, PTS-IMC, further IMCs) and renders them in interoperable format.
- PTS-IMC Collection: Obtains integrity report(s) containing Chain of Trust measurements up to TNC components from PTS.

After that, the integrity report(s) can be communicated between PTS-IMC and PTS-IMV via IF-M-PTS. The PTS-IMV evaluates the integrity reports against a given policy and provides an access recommendation, along with all other IMVs.

3 tNAC – Trusted Network Access Control

tNAC is a research project started on July, 1st 2008. It is scheduled for three years. The project team is a consortium consisting of three universities and three companies:
- University of Applied Sciences and Arts Hanover
- University of Applied Sciences Gelsenkirchen
- University Bochum
- Datus AG
- Sirrix AG
- Steria Mummert Consulting AG

The project is sponsored by the Federal Ministry of Education and Research in Germany. The overall goal is to develop an open source, TNC compatible NAC solution with full TPM support (referred to as tNAC) as described in this paper.

One important issue is the strong involvement of the companies mentioned above. They will especially participate in the definition of requirements based upon real world scenarios and the fact, that tNAC must still be manageable in a convenient way despite its complex functionality. Last but not but not least, it is expected that the project members will contribute to the specification process of the TNC Subgroup, especially concerning the IF-M-PTS interface between PTS-IMC/IMV.

3.1 tNAC = Turaya + TNC@FHH

tNAC will not be developed from scratch. Instead, the results of two former research projects will be used as fundament for tNAC.

3.1.1 Turaya

Turaya is an open source based Trusted Computing platform that was developed within the EMSCB project ([EMSCB]). Basically, Turaya is a L4 micro-kernel based, secure operating system. By the concept of virtualisation, it allows the user to run arbitrary software in isolated compartments. Furthermore, these compartments can be secured by using a TPM. This way, Turaya enables the user to run normal operating systems and highly secured applications in parallel by defining appropriate compartments. Since TPM usage is supported, the integrity of such a compartment can be measured by the TPM and evaluated before it is allowed to be executed. Even if a compartment gets compromised, the system can still continue to work since the other (still secure) compartments are completely isolated from the compromised one.

3.1.2 TNC@FHH

TNC@FHH ([TNCFHH]) is an open source implementation from the University of Applied Sciences and Arts in Hanover, Germany (FHH). It was started to gain experience with TNC, particularly concerning functionality, interoperability and feasibility of the TNC approach.

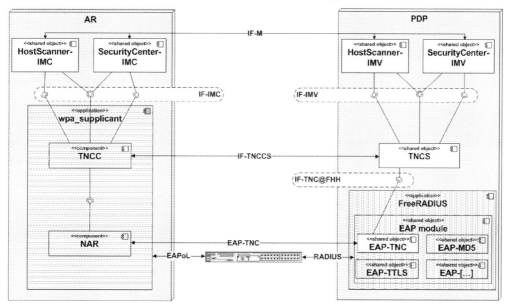

Figure 4: Architecture of TNC@FHH

Today the main components of the TNC entities and the interfaces between them are implemented. **Figure 4** shows the architecture of TNC@FHH. White boxes indicate components which were developed within the TNC@FHH project, forming also the vertical interfaces depicted as ovals. Vertically lined boxes indicate open source software components that are used by TNC@FHH.

In more detail, at the Network Access Layer EAPoL and RADIUS are used as protocols for transporting the packets over the network. The TNC messages (i.e. TNCCS and IMC/IMV messages) are encapsulated by using the EAP-TNC method. The Network Access Authority (NAA) is implemented via extending the FreeRADIUS ([FREERA]) server with an EAP-TNC module. The Network Access Requestor (NAR) and the TNC Client (TNCC), both depicted as horizontally lined boxes, had originally been implemented from the scratch within the TNC@FHH project, assembling EAP-TNC packets and communicating them via 802.1X and EAPoL to and from the switch. Since 2008, the TNC@FHH implementations of those components have been replaced by other open source software. I.e., the wpa_ supplicant and the Xsupplicant are now used, since both of them support TNC, in addition to numerous other authentication methods.

The TNCS which is attached to the FreeRADIUS server by the EAP-TNC module, exemplarily Integrity Measurement Collectors (IMCs) and Integrity Measurement Verifiers (IMVs), as well as the horizontal and vertical interfaces between them were all implemented from the scratch.

The PDP is running under Linux while on the AR side Linux and Windows are supported.

3.1.3 Integration

It is expected to combine Turaya and TNC@FHH in such a way that lying endpoints can be securely detected during the TNC Platform Authentication. The question is how this integration can be done in a reasonable way.

The simplest way could be to set up a compartment which includes all the TNC components of the AR, including the PTS and the TSS. Turaya would be responsible for measuring all the components starting from the RTM at boot time up to the TNC compartment. The PTS would be responsible for obtaining the measurements done by Turaya and rendering them in an interoperable format. Then, those integrity reports can be used during the TNC Platform Authentication.

4 Conclusion

In this paper, we described the status quo of Network Access Control as a new mechanism for increasing the security level of modern networks. All of the currently available NAC solutions share the same problems:

- Normally no interoperability of proprietary NAC solutions.
- No mechanisms available to detect lying endpoints.
- The TNC architecture defined by the TCG promises to solve both of the mentioned problems (1) by being open and (2) by supporting the TPM functionalities within the TNC handshake. Unfortunately, at present there are no solutions available which are both completely TNC compatible and make use of the necessary TPM functions in a secure manner. It is the overall goal of the tNAC project to develop a NAC solution based upon the security platform Turaya and the TNC implementation TNC@FHH which solves the problems mentioned above by (1) being open, (2) being TNC compatible, (3) supporting the full set of TPM functions and (4) being manageable.

References

[CNAC]   Home of Cisco Network Admission Control http://www.cisco.com/en/US/netsol/ns466/networking_solutions_package.html

[EMSCB]   Home of EMSCB project: http://www.emscb.com/

[FREERA] Home of FreeRADIUS: http://freeradius.org/

[IFIMC07] TCG Trusted Network Connect, TNC IF-IMC. In: https://www.trustedcomputinggroup.org/specs/TNC/. Specification Version 1.2, Revision 8, 05 February 2007, Published

[IFIMV07] TCG Trusted Network Connect, TNC IF-IMV. In: https://www.trustedcomputinggroup.org/specs/TNC/. Specification Version 1.2, Revision 8, 05 February 2007, Published

[IFMAP08]TCG Trusted Network Connect, TNC IF-MAP binding for SOAP. In: https://www.trustedcomputinggroup.org/specs/TNC/. Specification Version 1.0, Revision 25, 28 April 2008, Published

[IFPEP07] TCG Trusted Network Connect, TNC IF-PEP: Protocol Bindings for RADIUS. In: https://www.trustedcomputinggroup.org/specs/TNC/. Specification Version 1.1, Revision 0.7, 05 February 2007, Published

[IFPTS06] TCG Infrastructure Working Group, Platform Trust Services Interface Specification (IF-PTS). In: https://www.trustedcomputinggroup.org/specs/IWG/. Specification Version 1.0, Revision 1.0, 17 November 2006, FINAL

[IFSOH07] TCG Trusted Network Connect, TNC IF-TNCCS: Protocol Bindings for SoH. In: https://www.trustedcomputinggroup.org/specs/TNC/. Specification Version 1.0, Revision 0.08, 21 May 2007, Published

[IFT07]   TCG Trusted Network Connect, TNC IF-T: Protocol Bindings for Tunneled EAP Methods. In: https://www.trustedcomputinggroup.org/specs/TNC/. Specification Version 1.1, Revision 10, 21 May 2007, Published

[IFTNCCS07]   TCG Trusted Network Connect, TNC IF-TNCCS. In: https://www.trustedcomputinggroup.org/specs/TNC/. Specification Version 1.1, Revision 1.00, 05 February 2007, Published

[LIBTNC] Home of Project libtnc: http://sourceforge.net/projects/libtnc

[MSNAP] Home of Microsoft Network Access Protection http://technet.microsoft.com/en-us/network/bb545879.aspx

[RoTh07] Roecher Dror-John, Thumann Michael, NACATTACK. In: Black Hat Europe 2007, http://www.blackhat.com/html/bh-europe-07/bh-eu-07-speakers.html

[TNCA08] TCG Trusted Network Connect, TNC Architecture for Interoperability. In: https://www.trustedcomputinggroup.org/specs/TNC/. Specification Version 1.3, Revision 6, 28 April 2008, Published

[TNCFHH]Homepage of TNC@FHH: http://tnc.inform.fh-hannover.de

[WPASUP]Homepage of wpa_supplicant: http://hostap.epitest.fi/wpa_supplicant/

[XSUPPL] Homepage of Xsupplicant: http://open1x.sourceforge.net/

Session 7: Usability

User-Friendly and Secure TPM-based Hard Disk Key Management

Ulrich Kühn · Christian Stüble

Sirrix AG security technologies
Germany
{u.kuehn | c.stueble}@sirrix.com

Abstract

Today, computing platforms contain sensitive data of enterprises and private users. However, simple hard disk encryption solutions are not sufficient: swap areas and hibernation features still allow data leakage; the usage of authentication mechanisms based on passphrases, USB sticks, or other security tokens is cumbersome and of limited security benefit; finally, the encrypted data needs to be bound to the computing platform and/or the system software to prevent data leakage due to reboots and software manipulations.

We describe work-in-progress towards using Trusted-Computing technology for hard disk encryption and secure hibernation, allowing to detect integrity breaches of system software. The design of the TPM-based key management scheme considers requirements of both business scenarios and private users to guarantee availability of the encrypted data.

The main advantage of our solution is that it protects data at rest while providing a very high degree of user-friendliness: In one setting the system does not require any more user interaction than a completely unprotected system.

1 Problem Description

Today, the use of notebooks containing sensitive information is prevailing in business environments and also by private users. However, a breach of confidentiality of sensitive data can have a severe impact on private users as well as businesses. Thus, securing a platform, especially a mobile platform, against such a form of compromise is an important step towards more information security. However, as explained below, simple hard disk encryption solutions are not sufficient:

1.1 Data at Rest

A number of standard solutions for protecting confidentiality and integrity of transmitted data are available and routinely applied, e.g., Virtual Private Networks (VPN). However, we are concerned here with the security of *data at rest*, e.g. data stored on the hard drive of a (mobile) PC.

On a typical PC or laptop several GBytes of data are stored on internal hard drives. A part of this data is typically sensitive, e.g., on a personal laptop this might be personal emails, photos, personal notes, banking data, whereas on a business laptop it could be, e.g., business plans, address lists, credentials for a corporate network, and customer data.

D. Gawrock, H. Reimer, A.-R. Sadeghi, C. Vishik (Editors): Future of Trust in Computing, Vieweg+Teubner (2009), 171-177

While typically only a small part of the stored data is of this sensitive nature, exposure of confidential data can have a severe impact, e.g., embarrassment, bad reputation, lost business opportunities, or legal penalties.

1.2 Swap and Hibernation

A typical feature of today's operating system is swap space, i.e., the use of the hard disk to temporarily swap out parts of the RAM which is currently unused. This virtually extends the RAM size available to the operating system and user programs. Thus, sensitive data might also be swapped out and written to the swap space on the disk.

Another common-place feature, especially used for laptops, is *hibernation*[1]. Using this feature, the system can be fully shut off, saving battery, and later be reactivated such that the user can continue from a state just before the hibernation was activated. Technically, during hibernation the system's RAM contents as well as the processor and device states are written out to mass storage. At resume-time, the state is recovered from mass storage, and execution continues.[2]

While the hibernation feature is very convenient, it comes with a considerable security risk: as the full state of the machine ends up on the hard disk, all sensitive data, including cryptographic keys, that is in RAM ends up there, too. If the hard disk is not encrypted – unencrypted hibernation is usually the default – there is a serious risk of compromise of the sensitive data.

Even worse, sensitive data will rest in the hibernation file as long as it is not explicitly overwritten. Further, even memory that is officially free might contain old sensitive data. This might be written to disk, too, depending on the actual implementation and circumstances.

Thus, hibernation takes the security issues of swap space to the extreme.

2 Solutions

Below we describe our proposal to solve the problems identified above. We have implemented the system as a proof-of-concept demonstrator that has already undergone extensive day-to-day testing.

2.1 Requirements

Here we describe two classes of requirements for our solution, one regarding security, the other regarding usability.

From a security point of view, the solution must address the risks identified above. Regarding data at rest, the confidentiality shall be protected. In fact, it should be at least as well protected as if the machine were left running, e.g., during lunch-time. Further, if essential system software were manipulated, this should be detected, or the data should not be readable. The confidentiality of hibernation images must be preserved.

Further, for the swap and hibernation images we want to achieve *forward security*. This means, that old swap and hibernation images shall not leak information about which data has been processed.

---

1 Also called *suspend to disk*.
2 Contrast this to suspend-to-ram, which keeps the RAM powered in order to preserve its contents; this uses some amount of energy, running down the batteries of a laptop after a couple of days.

From a usability point of view, the solution should require as little user interaction as possible, during normal booting, hibernation, and resuming. The solution should be as transparent as possible to the user. Further, the solution should allow easy administration. System updates, for example, must not violate availability requirements.

2.2 Key Management Layer

The key management layer allows to have a lot of flexibility for different methods to obtain the key. Such possibilities include using the TPM and its sealing/unsealing feature, encryption, and, as future possibilities, using smart cards or other security tokens. Currently our implementation supports using a TPM, and keys asymmetrically encrypted using GnuPG, such that the private key used for decryption might either reside on the system or be stored externally on a USB-stick.

Using asymmetric encryption instead of symmetric is a design decision in order to allow the encryption being done without the user or administrator having to input a passphrase. Further, for normal operation, we decided against using passphrases for TPM-controlled keys used for sealing or for the sealed key blobs themselves, as this would also require input of the passphrase during the seal operation.

Using the TPM for sealing/unsealing without user interaction results in the most user-friendly solution. However, there is one security issue here. While the unsealing of keys for encrypted partitions shall be possible during boot time without user interaction, the same operation must be prevented during normal operation. This can be done be having a selected PCR on which sealed keys depend – in addition to the PCR that the measurements for the system are placed in – and which is extended by some preselected value after the boot process is complete, such that unsealing will be blocked from this point on until the next reboot.

To still allow key and seal management the keys are encrypted under an administrator's key. An alternative is to have the keys sealed, however without depending on the mentioned PCR but requiring a passphrase.

2.3 Protecting Data at Rest: Hard Disk Encryption

The solution we describe here is based on *Linux Unified Key Setup* (LUKS) provided by the `crypt-setup` user-space tool. It provides a key management scheme that is based on a master or partition key K_m used for the encryption of the data blocks of the respective device. Further, there are a number of *key slots*, typically there is space for 8 slots. Each key slot can be either empty or filled with an encrypted version of the partition key, encrypted under a key K_p derived from passphrase that is usually provided by the user: $C_i = E_{K_p}(K_m)$. At least one key slot is always occupied, e.g. by the passphrase that was initially used to set up the encrypted partition. In our solution this initial passphrase is employed in a second role, i.e. as a recovery passphrase that can be used to provide emergency access to the encrypted partition.

For our key management layer we use one additional key slot with a passphrase that is a randomly generated key, denoted here by K_s. We apply the `TPM_Seal` operation to K_s, with the current configuration c, using the *Storage Root Key SRK* : $S_c \leftarrow \text{TPM\_Seal}_{SRK,c}(K_s)$, and store S_c, indexed by the configuration c, so that several different configurations can be supported by providing a different expected configuration $\tilde{c}$ instead of c.

During the boot process the `dm-crypt` based cryptographic mapping has to be set up, i.e. supplied with a valid passphrase for a key slot. To do so, a user-space helper obtains the current configuration c running on the machine, retrieves S_c (if available) and unseals it $K_s \leftarrow \text{TPM\_Unseal}_{SRK}(S_c)$. If successful, K_s is passed to `cryptsetup` for setting up the encryption/decryption for the partition.

Note that this method can be used to make selected data available only under certain system configurations, and block access under others. For example, the keys for a company's VPN connection can be stored inside an encrypted container, and the key sealed for the company-provided software configuration, while at the same time allowing a multi-boot environment with other operating systems or options.

2.4 Swap and Hibernation

Securing the confidentiality of the swap space against compromise is rather straight-forward by using an encrypted partition or container file. In order to achieve forward security, a new random key K_s is used to re-initialise the swap area. In fact, this is a typical standard security measure for Linux and is supported by various distributions, although usually not enabled by default. This method results in any old contents of the swap space being irrevocably unavailable after the old key is removed or forgotten after power-down of the RAM.

However, for securing the hibernation feature, more efforts are needed. The solution is to provide the key to the kernel at the next system start before it tries to read back the hibernated state. This allows to set up the encrypted swap space such that the the hibernation image stored there can be read. For the Linux kernel this is possible by using the *early userspace* mechanism, i.e. using an *initial ram disk*, which is a popular method to have user-space tools running even before the root partition is accessible. As suspend-to-disk implementation we use TuxOnIce [TuxOnIce] which allows using encrypted swap space and triggering the resume process from the initial ram disk.[3]

Our key management works as follows: the key K_S for the encrypted swap area is stored in sealed form, i.e. $S_{swap} \leftarrow \text{TPM\_Seal}_{SRK,c}(K_S)$, with the currently running software configuration c, determined by the BIOS, the TCG-enabled boot-loader, the kernel, its parameters, and the initial ram disk image, as the configuration expected for unsealing. The code in the initial ram disk tries to access the sealed data object S_{swap} on the hard disk and unseal it. If successful, the kernel can be supplied with the right key to make the encrypted swap space readable again, along with a possibly existing hibernation image. Then the resume process is triggered. Otherwise the normal boot process continues.

To enable the described method for resuming, the key for the encrypted swap space needs to be sealed, which is done during the normal boot process using a helper program that seals this key to be released by the TPM under the currently running system configuration. The sealed key is stored on the hard disk where is can potentially be accessed next time during the early boot process, as described above.

2.5 Managing and Sealing Keys

After setting up an encrypted partition with a key/passphrase that is sealed for release under a predetermined boot configuration, there is the problem of software updates, e.g. kernel, initial ram disk image, or even the kernel command line, which is also measured by the TCG-enabled TrustedGRUB boot loader.

---

3 Note, however, that this scheme does provide forward security when a normal boot happens without resuming from a hibernation image. While after resuming the swap space could potentially be re-initialised using a newly-generated key, we decided not to do so, as this might fail due to the swap space still being used, so that the re-initialisation would overwrite system state.

The basic idea here is that during installation of the new components, while still running the "old" configuration, the future configuration is pre-computed. Then selected or all of the sealed keys/passphrases are unsealed/decrypted and resealed for future release under the new configuration. While this issue has been addressed in [Kühn05], to our knowledge we are the first to describe a running prototype of a seal manager that solves the issue.

We have implemented two administrative user-space tools, a key manager and a seal manager. The key manager allows to set a new key/passphrase for an encrypted partition and seal it. It uses the recovery passphrase for the encrypted partition to set a new one and to seal it for the currently running software configuration. Likewise it allows to encrypt the key/passphrase also asymmetrically under GnuPG public keys, e.g. belonging to an administrator. Additional user public keys are also possible, allowing key management without the TPM.

The seal manager allows to handle sealed keys/passphrases for other than the currently running software configuration. It maintains pre-computed PCR values for all possible configurations available from the TrustedGRUB boot menu. These PCR values will be present after the respective boot entry has been booted. The pre-computation is done using the SHA-1 hashes of the e.g. kernel, initial ram disk image, kernel parameters.

Based on these pre-computed PCR values it can seal those keys/passphrases for the respective future configuration. However, due to the necessary blocking of unsealing after boot-time (see Section 2.4) direct unsealing of the sealed keys for encrypted partitions is not possible. Instead, the keys can be decrypted using the administrator's private key. Finally, the newly sealed keys/passphrases are stored where they can be found during the boot process.

An alternative is to use keys encrypted under a user's public key, such that during boot the user needs to supply, e.g., a USB-stick with a private key and a passphrase for decrypting the key to access an encrypted partition. Future developments aim at including smart cards or combinations of such means.

3 Protecting System Integrity

During the system boot the trusted boot process maintains a chain of trust by first measuring software and storing the result in the TPM by extending a PCR before executing the software. When using TrustedGRUB as boot loader, this chain does include the Linux kernel, its boot parameters and (possibly) the initial ram disk.

The inclusion of the initial ram disk in the measurements opens the possibility to check the integrity of further components of the system against known-good values. Such integrity checks are necessary, both in the case of an unencrypted system partition, and also in the case of an encrypted system partition, as encryption ensures confidentiality, but usually does *not* provide integrity protection (see, e.g., remark 7.16 in [MOV96]). With integrity protection missing an adversary could manipulate essential system components not present in the initial ram disk, e.g. to obtain encryption keys or sensitive data.

We have implemented a mechanism that includes both hash-based as well as signature-based integrity checking for inclusion in the initial ram disk. The hash-based mechanism includes a list of files and their respective hash values in the initial ram disk at its creation, so that this list is also included in the boot loader's integrity measurement. However, when updating or deliberately changing a file in the list, the initial ram disk needs to be recreated and the seal manager be run. To cope with files that can change more often, and not only during system updates, we implemented the possibility to have another list of files for which we can perform a signature verification against a public key that is also included in the initial ram disk.

At boot time, when the root partition get mounted, but before anything is loaded from that partition, we run the checks against the known-good list in the initial ram disk. Further, any files scheduled for signature verification are checked. The result of these integrity checks are stored in the TPM by extending a PCR for future use, i.e. by having sealed keys for encrypted partitions depend on this PCR's value.

A typical set of files to check would be the all kernel modules, components of the security solutions described here, along with essential system binaries and libraries, and essential configuration files. The files for user management, e.g. the passwd, group, and shadow password files are candidates for the signature-based integrity check, as they can change, e.g., when a user changes his/her password. Then only a new signature is necessary instead of rebuilding the initial ram disk and updating all sealed keys for encrypted partitions.

The performance of this combined mechanism is very good, it takes only a few seconds during boot time to check several hundred files.

4 Discussion

Regarding the security of our solution it should be noted that the system can start up without user interaction, i.e., without a passphrase etc. Thus, the system is essentially as secure as it would be while being left unattended but running on the desk. A further improvement in security can be configured – at the expense of user-friendliness – by requiring a token with a private key and input of a passphrase before the keys for encrypted partitions are decrypted. With both options any data residing in the encrypted partition is protected, as well as any data being swapped out or placed in the swap partition during hibernation. This is a significant improvement over unencrypted swap and data partitions.

We note that the functionality of our encryption solution has a certain similarity to Bitlocker [Micro05] found in the Enterprise and Ultimate versions of Windows Vista. One option that is of particular interest here is the possibility to also include a TPM into Bitlocker's key management.

Our solution runs basically on every Linux system and can potentially be adapted to other operating systems. Further, there are severe differences when it comes to managing system updates, for which we have the seal manager. The seal manager is an important improvement over the respective functionality of Bitlocker: Windows Vista's Bitlocker handles the issue of intended system updates by switching off the TPM sealing, and temporarily storing the key, encrypted with a passphrase, on the hard disk.

We argue that our solution with pre-computing the configuration that will be present after the next reboot into the new components is the much cleaner approach. Furthermore, our solution provides forward security for the swap and hibernation area. This is also an improvement over what Bitlocker offers, where the hibernation image is always encrypted with the (fixed) volume key.

One additional feature is that our solution provides for the possibility of integrity checks of important system software and configuration files. Certainly it would be convenient to have *secure boot* (see [AFS97]). However, *trusted boot* (which can be analysed *after the fact*) as implemented by the trusted computing approach does not offer the guarantee that the system reaches one of a number of predefined states during boot. Nevertheless, our solution for integrity verification of important system files does provide an indication to the user that the system has not been tampered with. Furthermore, compared with integrity checking by the boot loader, as implemented in the TrustedGRUB boot loader, our solution can also run checks on encrypted system partitions.

5 Conclusion

We have presented a user-friendly solution for having encrypted data partitions under Linux. Further our solution solves the hibernation problem, i.e. that the system state is stored unencrypted on the hard disk. The use of a TPM makes this solution both secure and user-friendly. Additionally, the measured boot process allows to implement an integrity check of important system software and configuration files.

Further, the inclusion of asymmetric encryption allows easy administration, and the possibility to require user authentication before allowing access to encrypted partitions.

In summary, we argue that the TPM-based solution should be seen as baseline security. As it does not ask more of the user than an unencrypted system would, we propose our solution as a standard security measure.

References

[AFS97]   Arbaugh, William A.; Farber, David J.; Smith, Jonathan M.: A Secure and Reliable Bootstrap Architecture. Proc. IEEE Symposium on Security and Privacy, 1997, pages 65—71.

[Kühn05]   Kühn, Ulrich; Kursawe, Klaus; Lucks, Stefan; Sadeghi, Ahmad-Reza; Stüble, Christian: Secure Data Management in Trusted Computing. In: J. R. Rao, B. Sunar (eds.): Cryptographic Hardware and Embedded Systems – CHES 2005. Volume 3659 of Lecture Notes in Computer Science, Springer-Verlag, 2005, pp. 324—338.

[Micro05]   Microsoft Corporation. Secure startup – full volume encryption: Technical overview. Technical Report, April 2005.

[MOV96]   Menezes, Alfred J.; van Oorschot, Paul C.; Vanstone, Scott A: Handbook of Applied Cryptography. CRC Press, 1996.

[TuxOnIce]Tux On Ice. http://www.tuxonice.net

Requirements and Design Guidelines for a Trusted Hypervisor Interface

Dirk Weber[1] · Arnd Weber[1] · Stéphane Lo Presti[2]

[1]Forschungszentrum Karlsruhe
Institute for Technology Assessment and Systems Analysis
{dirk.weber | arnd.weber}@itas.fzk.de

[2]Department of Computing
City University
Stephane.Lo-Presti.1@city.ac.uk

Abstract

Hypervisor technology in combination with tamper-resistant hardware such as Trusted Platform Modules has the potential of providing a significant new level of security for computers. These new systems will be able to protect legacy applications from applications such as malware, and they will enable the creation of new secure applications. This paper analyses the requirements for the graphical user interface (GUI) of such a system. First, application scenarios are presented to illustrate how extended Trusted Computing (TC) systems might be used in the future. Requirements for a trusted GUI are then derived from the analysis of articles on TC found in the media and from a survey of experts in information technology. These requirements are compared to existing proposals, showing how some of them are either inconvenient or insecure in the hands of end users. Based on this analysis, proposals are derived for the design of a trusted GUI suitable for laypersons and administrators, which uses familiar patterns, and yet protects against visual mimicry attacks. These proposals pave the way for hypervisors' security-enhanced GUI.

1 Introduction

In the recent years, there has been a growing trend in the use of hypervisors in the whole of computing, not only for servers but also for PCs and even recently for mobile devices. Intel proposed the Trusted Execution Technology (TXT) [Hiremane07] to secure computers running legacy operating systems (OSs) by compartmenting them in a tightly-controlled memory space and providing the means to enforce a white list that defines the only programs allowed to execute. AMD also proposed a similar architecture, codenamed AMD-V, which facilitates the secure start of a hypervisor. Next-generation processor architectures will provide better isolation of applications through the use of hypervisors, whose success is exemplified by the number of companies that are pushing this technology into their systems or also by the popular Linux module KVM.

Another recent trend is the increased deployment of Trusted Platform Modules (TPMs) to enable Trusted Computing (TC). Combined together, these technologies can be used to design a hypervisor-based system which is protected by TC functionalities, forming a robust Trusted Computing Base (TCB). For instance, the TC "sealing" functionality can be used to ensure that part of the TCB can access secret data only if the TCB is in a in a trustworthy state, i.e., if it corresponds to the TCB value specified at sealing time and if it has not been manipulated.

D. Gawrock, H. Reimer, A.-R. Sadeghi, C. Vishik (Editors): Future of Trust in Computing, Vieweg+Teubner (2009), 178-189

The objective of the Open Trusted Computing project, partially funded by the European Union, is to design such a TC-enabled hypervisor, whose architecture is presented in Figure 1. A more detailed description of the Open Trusted Computing system can be found in [Kuhlmann06a]. The issue of how to design the graphical user interface (GUI) of such a system naturally arose during development discussions. The handling and management of such a system is not straightforward to anyone without specialist knowledge, be it an administrator or an end user. The additional functionalities increase the complexity of the system and the management of these functionalities makes the problem of usability important. The design of the GUI requires choosing which features can be omitted, which features should be displayed in selected part of the display, or which ones should be handled outside of the computing system, with new hardware keys or on different displays such as mobile devices.

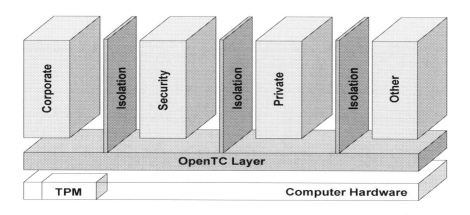

Figure 1: Open Trusted Computing architecture overview.

The OpenTC layer isolates the various compartments above it using the underlying security hardware, thus providing the means to identify various levels of trust depending on the application.

During the past few years, security has seen the emergence of attacks where the GUI is used to fool users into believing that a given graphical element is trustworthy, while in reality it is hiding the exploit. This includes phishing attacks, where the various tabs of a web browser can be used to ask the user to input his credentials which are then handled by a malicious application in a different tab. It is thus natural to ask how users can be protected against attacks using such visual mimicry, and also how they can be protected against erroneously trusting certain visual elements.

2 Usage Scenarios

When designing the user interface of the Open Trusted Computing system, several usage scenarios were discussed to find the most realistic and interesting ones. The two following scenarios were specified [Kuhlmann06b]:

- *Corporate computing at home:* In this scenario, the user has an OS that is controlled by its corporate organisation running in parallel to the one used for personal non-business tasks. Both OSs execute in isolated compartments, and run at the same time and on the same physical computer. The corporation is guaranteed that its OS will run in a well-known and attested operating environment, and it controls how its OS is used, while the user is free to use the other OS in whatever way. For example, the user may run arbitrary applications and surf on arbitrary websites in the personal compartment, but not in the corporate one. Therefore, the user needs to know which compartment she is currently using.

- *Private Electronic Transactions (PET):* This scenario aims to improve the trustworthiness of interactions with remote servers. Transactions are simply performed by accessing a web server through a standard web browser running in a dedicated, isolated compartment. In the PET scenario, the server is assumed to host web pages belonging to a bank; however, the setup also applies to other e-commerce services. The trusted compartment protects the user against malware, such as Trojan horses, or phishing attacks, a common threat in home banking. The compartment only provides applications for a specific kind of transaction and is locked down to a well-known configuration that can be attested, possibly locally via an unsealing operation. When this compartment runs next to other compartments, it has to be identifiable so that the user does not manipulate sensitive data in the wrong compartment.

The actual implementation of the first scenario will probably have more compartments. For example, the anti-virus software may be put into a compartment of its own outside the host OS to ensure that it cannot be tampered with. Similarly, encryption and digital signature applications may require isolated compartments, so that there is no eavesdropping on cryptographic keys in memory or information gathered from the application's usage. Future users may use a variety of compartments as sandboxes or for the transition from one OS to another. Furthermore, administrators may have to handle dozens of compartments on client or on server machines. Future scenarios envisaged for the TC-enabled hypervisors seem to demonstrate extended use of compartments for sensitive and dynamic systems. These systems are likely to benefit from isolation in order to ensure the privacy and confidentiality of various applications and data, thus delivering multi-level, multi-party security to all kinds of customers. This scenario differs greatly from merely securing the entry of credentials.

3 Requirements Analysis

In the two scenarios envisaged for the Open Trusted Computing system, the case of *corporate computing at home* is the more difficult one. In this scenario, the end user is given a well-designed TCB with strong isolation between compartments on an existing PC. Two problems may easily arise. First, the user may configure the system incorrectly or suboptimally, or even modify the TCB in such a way that it is no longer trustworthy. The second problem is that a malware might be installed in the user compartment which fools the user into modifying the corporate OS or even into using a seemingly secured application which in reality spies on the corporate compartment. The question then remains of how the TCB should communicate its state to the user as well as which actions are safe in that state. Providing full support for managing the TCB could result in a complex user interface that is likely to be confusing to the end user. In order to design the TCB user interface, we gathered information and ideas from two main sources. First, we reviewed the existing media feedback on TC, in order to learn about concerns and preoccupations of interested people. Secondly, we conducted a small survey among experts in information technology.

3.1 Media Review

On the internet, in discussion fora and in articles, many opinions on TC have been critical of the technology. Some people believe that TC is to be used for tracking citizens' activities, locking computers into proprietary configurations, enforcing unfair business models for content or software provision, and even automatically deleting emails and documents without the user's approval. We reviewed and evaluated these criticisms for designing sensible applications [Kuhlmann06b]. In the context of the design of the user interface, our research on media articles about TC arrived at two conclusions of relevance in our context:

- It would be good to confine the impact of TC-based enforcement mechanisms to certain components. This would allow the user to run unmodified code in other parts, i.e., legacy OSs, Linux code or other applications that could be executed on top of the virtualisation layer.

- The discussion on TC and the Sony rootkit shows that it would be desirable to be able to delete TC applications. As long as this deletion does not restrict the integrity verification of the hypervisor, the user should be in control of the computer (at least as the legal owner of that machine) and that means that being able to delete a compartment to get rid of undesired code.

The following requirement regarding the user interface can be derived from these conclusions:

1. The user interface should provide the means to create a new compartment and delete a running one.

In the situation where a corporation supplies computers equipped with TC-enabled hypervisors to its employees, if the hypervisor is designed so that an instance of the corporate OS could be deleted by the employee, the requirement would be fulfilled. Normally, a corporate employee would not do that, as this would possibly violate the company's policy regarding usage of computing equipment. But an employee could well, for example, install and execute a second instance of the corporate OS for testing a new piece of untrustworthy code, and later delete that compartment.

3.2 Expert Survey

Given the complexity of a computing system using TC in combination with a hypervisor and running several, possibly different OS, corporations may not support such a system because of too steep a learning curve or benefits that are too low to offset the cost of the technology. In this case, how can such a system be improved to be more easily manageable? This is the kind of question we asked of eight experts in the field, administrators and security specialists from various German corporations, in a survey made at the end of 2006. The questions were based on the paper by Kuhlmann et al. [Kuhlmann06a] describing the Open TC architecture, which the respondents read ahead of the interviews. Among the questions were the following:

- A user interface is required for administrating such a system. What should this interface do and what should it look like?

- The user wishes to see which compartment is currently active and whether it is secure. How would you show the user that the PC/OS is in a trustworthy state? Do you have any suggestions for this?

The suggestions made by the eight experts can be summarised as follows:

- The hypervisor must be manageable, e.g., for setting up new compartments or deleting them, for allocating resources and for managing communication between compartments, e.g. via the use of a clipboard.

- Managing rights and policies for compartments should be possible, although most rights should be handled automatically. Respondents understand that a compartment may be running under somebody else's policies.

- The hypervisor should have a simple GUI, e.g., with buttons using left and right mouse clicks. Neither administrators nor users want to spend time learning how to use new user interfaces and command line tools.

- In the future, the user may wish not to have to distinguish between a compartment and an application.

- Switching between compartments or applications should be as simple as today, e.g., using something similar to the Alt-Tab key combination or a mouse click.

- The status of a compartment should be displayed in particular when it is started or when the user switches to it. There should be a visible display of information showing whether the compartment is trusted (successfully unsealed and isolated) or not. The status should, for example, be displayed in red or green, or like a traffic light.

- No special display should be used apart from the usual screen, as the user might not find it convenient to look at two displays. A secure display on the keyboard, the mouse, or an attached mobile device may not be looked at in frequent, daily operations. Having a separate, secure display forces the user to refocus on it, which might incur such unnecessary stress that the user stops looking at it.

- A virus scanner should be manageable from the hypervisor GUI.

- The trustworthiness of a connection to a remote computer should be displayed.

At a high level of abstraction, these expert opinions can be summarised in the following user interface requirements:

1. A *graphical* user interface should be available for managing compartments, not only function keys.

2. Information about the TCB should be provided on the main screen, not on a separate display, and should be easily manageable, as via a mouse click.

3. If information on the status of a certain compartment or other component is to be provided to the user, this should be done with easy-to-grasp graphical artefacts.

These requirements follow concepts familiar to today's administrators and users.

4 Related Work

Though the issue of trusted interfaces is not recent, it is one that has seen few mainstream developments in the recent years, while systems like the L4 microGUI and nitpicker are slowly emerging, and the focus seems to be on heavy interfaces that are visually appealing rather than trustworthy, e.g. Linux's Beryl 3D interface. The issue has sometimes been studied from the point of view of conceptual perception [Gajek07] rather than visual perception. Here we review important works on trusted GUIs.

Gasser [Gasser88] proposes implementing a trusted path consisting of special lights on the terminal controlled by the kernel, or a special area of the screen reserved for kernel communication. As our expert interviews showed, special displays might be ignored by the end user, and it does not seem appropriate to create a trusted path between the system and the user, even if the use of a connected mobile device might appear convenient. Nevertheless, the use of special displays as a kind of "periscope", where the user carefully inspects part of the executing environment, would provide a much needed communication path for securely displaying confidential information or a text to be given a digital signature [Pfitzmann01]. But what is needed for the TC-enabled hypervisor usage scenarios is an interface for performing many different operations, and the use of the main display for this is not only convenient, but also more flexible.

Several ideas can be found in the literature on how users could be guided by information displayed on the main screen. Pfitzmann et al. [Pfitzmann01] suggest that the host should specifically manage a reserved section of the screen to indicate whether an OS or application is secure or not. Dhamija and Tygar [Dhamija05] explore the solution of augmenting applications, including password-inputting windows, with "security skins" where a background is bound to a user-defined picture or a "visual hash" of a website address that can then be easily checked by the user by familiarity.

A similar approach was taken by Gajek et al. [Gajek07]. However, these two approaches do not allow the user to distinguish between a correct TCB and one that has been attacked or modified. They also assume that users switch between OSs using hotkeys, the operation of which had to be learned by the users in the first place.

Assuming users have several compartment windows that can be displayed on screen, it is obviously important to know which compartment the TCB is displaying at any one time. Several works suggested that lines between the TCB and a compartment should clearly illustrate the difference [Yee02] and that special window borders might be used [Gajek07]. Users might be able to select the line colours, but this could perhaps be guessed by an attacker, in particular if a limited number of colours (e.g., 16) are used. It also requires dedicating some screen space to this feature. Alternatively, windows not in the foreground can also be dimmed to indicate the active status of the foreground window.

Although these approaches appear to be pretty neat, it is still not quite clear to the user whether display of an untrusted status means the TCB was modified by mistake or following an attack. When a hardware module which the attacker cannot attack easily, such as the TPM, is used and thus the TCB management procedures cannot be mixed up accidentally by the user, there remains a need to display to the user that the trustworthy path is still correctly in place. A proposal was recently made and patented by Cihula et al. [Cihula05]. The authors suggest that a trustworthy background picture is only displayed if the TCB is intact. The TC-enabled hypervisor can then for example seal the background picture to the platform configuration where the corresponding compartment is executing.

The requirements for a trusted user interface gathered from the literature, and in particular [Yee02], can be summarised as:

- Things do not become unsafe all by themselves. (Explicit Authorization)
- I can know whether things are safe. (Visibility)
- I do not choose to make things unsafe. (Path of Least Resistance)
- I know what I can do within the system. (Expected Ability)
- I can distinguish the things that matter to me. (Appropriate Boundaries)
- I can tell the system what I want. (Expressiveness)
- I know what I am telling the system to do. (Clarity)
- The system protects me from being fooled. (Identifiability, Trusted Path)

To the best of our knowledge, these principles have never been applied to the design of a TC-enabled hypervisor that executes mainstream OSs, such as Windows or Linux, and is administered by end users.

5 Design Conclusions

On the basis of requirements from the media and expert surveys (Section 3), and from the literature (Section 4), we can now try to exemplify these user requirements into concrete ideas for the user interface design of the TC-enabled hypervisor system that we will use to implement the usage scenarios specified in Section 2.

As stated by the experts we questioned, all information should ideally be displayed on the main screen. For ease of use and convenience, the user interface should be graphical rather than text-based. For protection against visual mimicry attacks, the TCB should reserve a small part of the screen for providing information on the content of the remainder of the screen. This would allow the user to trust what is displayed and to distinguish between a successfully unsealed compartment that can be trusted and a compartment that may have been modified maliciously. As opposed to the solution of only using function keys, there are some benefits to the solution of always reserving part of the screen to inform the user which compartment is active. For example, the user may be reminded that a private or untrusted compartment is being used so that this is not forgotten after a while and sensitive actions performed in an inappropriate context. On the other hand, reserving a small part of the screen for this feature may have three disadvantages:

- One is that the screen space used to display the compartment where the user works is slightly reduced, so working can become slightly less convenient, and may additionally cause some resolution scaling problems.

The reservation of part of the main screen must be enforced inflexibly by the controlling hypervisor by simply limiting the access to the screen that guest OSs have. The design of how OSs access the display may be impacted by this enforcement, depending on how much space should optimally be reserved.

- Secondly, certain applications use special functions of graphic cards which require direct access to the memory to run efficiently (DMA) and so the graphics card controls what is displayed without knowledge from the controlling hypervisor.

This issue can be fixed with next-generation trusted hardware platform such as Intel Trusted Execution Technology (TXT) [Grawrock06] where a NoDMA memory table is provided to the hypervisor for specifying which programs are allowed to use the DMA feature. This technology could be coupled with Intel's VT-d [Kuhlmann06a] Virtualization Technology for Directed I/O designed to backup TXT outside of the graphics card. This form of DMA policy enforced by hardware can also be augmented by proposals in next-generation graphics cards to support virtualisation technology, so that such applications can access specific parts of the memory.

- Thirdly, users may be fooled into believing that some graphic element corresponds to a trustworthy part of the screen, while in reality it is produced by malicious software, for example a compartment that copies the appearance of another, as is done in phishing attacks where websites are copied in every detail.

Protection against this latter attack would be to have the trusted part display confidential information known only to the user, such as a picture chosen by the user, and the TCB should ensure that malware cannot access this information, for example by sealing it to the configuration of the TCB. We propose use of an image, as it is more difficult to guess than a password, needs less space than a pass-phrase, and integrates smoothly into the hypervisor GUI.

We can now refine the requirements identified above and the existing proposals into a number of concrete design guidelines:

- The GUI should have similarities to existing GUIs of common OSs, in terms of being easily understandable and fast to learn for the end user, but it should also display certain differences so as to be identifiable, in particular with regard to the new TCB layer and its trusted status.

- Switching between OSs should be similar to switching between applications, but also be different from today. Therefore, an additional taskbar unlike the ones currently used should be provided and be accessible via the mouse, but also via keyboard shortcuts comparable to the standard Alt+Tab.

- A sealed image should be displayed in the new taskbar. This would indicate a proper state of the TCB to the user, as it could only be unsealed and displayed by the TCB in this proper state. If this picture is not shown, the user would see that there is a problem and act accordingly. The background of the TCB display could then turn red to indicate an error in the TCB, while in the case of an attack against the TCB, there would be no such warning, and the confidential information would simply not be displayed.

- Control of the TCB is similar to the control of a normal OS, with the provision of a desktop and context menus. From the "hypervisor" menu in the TCB display, the user can create and delete compartments by right-clicking on the desktop and selecting the corresponding command in a context menu.

- The task bar could provide information on the trustworthiness of compartments, whether they have been attested remotely, and on the isolation between them. It also provides information on which compartment is active.

Figure 2: OpenTC taskbar (cropped).

It shows an unsealed image (personalised with a facial image by the authors) as a protection against visual mimicry attacks, and a pressed button (indicating the compartment currently being displayed on the remainder of the screen).

Figure 3: OpenTC taskbar (cropped) with a red button indicating that the TCB is not in a known state and that unsealing the image has not been possible.

Figure 2 shows a proposal for the implementation of these GUI design guidelines. The GUI reflects:

- Protection against a manipulated hypervisor, with an image that is only shown if the TCB has successfully unsealed the picture.

- Which compartment is active by highlighting the corresponding button and thus enhancing its visibility for ease of recognition by the user (in this case the corporate compartment).

- The task bar uses a bar design and buttons similar but different to existing ones on common OSs, e.g., a black look&feel indicating isolation.

- The "Hypervisor" button provides access to the management interfaces of the hypervisor and the TCB.

In this way, the GUI reflects concepts familiar to the user, such as taskbars and right-clicks, for moving between compartments, while still being different enough to reflect the fact that there are several compartments.

Figures 2 and 3 show the preliminary taskbar of the OpenTC system, in the two cases where the image has been unsealed successfully (Fig. 2) and unsuccessfully (Fig. 3). It takes some of the findings of this paper into account and shows a corporate Windows compartment, a Linux-based secure compartment to be used for online banking, and a button to access the hypervisor[ ]. Future user tests should be used to verify the usability of the concept and to address open issues, such as whether the image is properly placed, the size it should have, when it should be conveniently and securely inputted in the system, whether a selection of pre-installed images could be used, etc. The image could also become smaller or darkened, or become larger and lightened, or even move when clicked. The issue of whether the new, or all, status bars could be placed to the left or to the right of widescreen displays should also be investigated.

Some of the design proposals are shown in Figures 4 and 5 where a first prototypical implementation of such a TCB taskbar is displayed. The GUI allows users to manage the usage scenarios presented in Section 2. The user sees in a trustworthy manner whether the TCB is correct and whether the corporate compartment or another one is being used. Another proposal is to securely auto-hide the bar when it is not in use, and display it again if a key is typed on the keyboard or the mouse is clicked. Another important issue is to determine the best way to move the mouse from one compartment to the other. In our first implementation, the mouse can freely move into the task bar area. Similarly, user interfaces for managing any channels between compartments need to be defined, such as for clipboards.

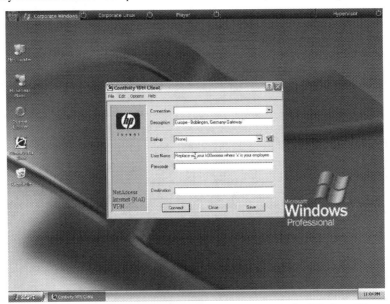

Figure 4: OpenTC with its status bar and a compartment running Windows XP.

We have now shown proposals of what is needed for a user to trust the taskbar and the buttons corresponding to the active compartment. However, a user may be fooled into installing a malicious compartment on her platform, or alternatively a Trojan horse as an application that looks like a legitimate compartment. This is similar to the current situation where the user surfs the Web and gets a pop-up window which displays a picture of a dialog box, except that corporate compartments or applications are faked here instead. Dimming such a compartment designed by malware programmers, as done by Feske and Helmuth [Feske05], would not help, as it is either lit as a proper one or is simply an application of a foreground compartment.

It would, therefore, be beneficial if the user were reminded during normal operation of what type of compartment she is currently using. A good way of providing this feature would be to use another sealed picture. The compartment button and the background of the compartment should display the same picture. Users could be advised to use a "family" of pictures of relatives, animals or other topics easily identifiable to them. This may require some additional space in the compartment windows, but would also increase the trust that the end user has in the system. Alternatively, the TCB could add a picture in the foreground at a place convenient to the user, since it has control of the whole display.

Figure 5: OpenTC with its status bar and a compartment running OpenSUSE Linux.

One topic that could be investigated is the suitability of a GUI in which the sealed picture is not displayed if a compartment uses the whole portion of the screen available to it; however, this might lead to inconsistencies as the image is sometimes shown and sometimes not. The use of such a chain of pictures could be simplified if a global infrastructure existed which certified compartments. Users could be advised to install these certified compartments and trust them "out of the box", or they could be pre-installed automatically. In the real world there will, however, be compartments which are not certified. Therefore, any administrator, including the end user in the system we consider here, needs to have the means to make the display of compartments trustworthy by sealing information to it. Unfortunately, this opens the possibility of malware leading users to install a malicious compartment as trustworthy. Therefore, the procedure required to seal compartments should be designed in such a way so that users cannot express their trust without having been warned by the system via clear messages that are acknowledged. In other words, if a user gets a bank compartment from an untrustworthy source and installs it as trustworthy, this cannot be entirely prevented but only discouraged. Hopefully, as users are educated to understand what to trust and distrust, they will not be as easily fooled as they were a few years ago. At the same time, our approach would have the benefit of allowing users to surf insecure websites securely and isolated from sensible applications and data, install unknown code, etc. while being in a position to entirely delete any infected compartments.

6 Outlook

The scope of our empirical research was limited, and the current status of knowledge of the problem tackled in this paper is also limited. It actually makes sense to test different implementations with various degrees of simplification and different types of users, e.g., administrators, employees, end users, and younger gamers. Tests could also address the usability of these ideas for server-based systems, as well as for mobile systems where UIs may be designed in different ways (e.g., the iPhone). It would be necessary to demonstrate that administrators can handle components well that will be used by other parties (employees, business partners, etc.). Only concrete use in a large and realistic demonstrator would show whether the TC-enabled hypervisor approach is manageable in terms of costs and benefits. Ideally, a consistent GUI toolbox should be created to ease the provision of usable interfaces on any hardware platform.

Our entire proposal is fragile to a certain degree. If attacks or errors occur, users may lose their newly created trust very quickly, and it would be much more difficult to regain that trust. For instance, if the TCB were to be attacked in such a way that it became corrupted, but the trusted image were still displayed, this could transform the approach into such a way as to fool users and exploit their willingness to trust the system. Therefore, such a system should only be rolled out on a large scale if the whole TCB is sufficiently robust and evaluated, for example to a common criteria standard. Alternatively, the trust-related messages which are displayed should perhaps be less bold. In any case, the appropriate visualisation of compartments, applications and the channels between them will remain a challenge.

Despite these desiderata, the findings and conclusions presented in this paper provide a first empirically founded starting point for a usable interface of a TC-secured hypervisor.

References

[Cihula05] Cihula, Joseph; Brickell, Ernie; Yu, Chiung-Chen: Displaying a Trusted User Interface Using Background Images. US Patent Application Publication, 2005. http://www.freepatentsonline.com/20050275661.pdf

[Dhamija05] Dhamija, Rachna and Tygar, J.D. The Battle Against Phishing: Dynamic Security Skins. In: Proceedings of the 2005 Symposium on Usable Privacy and Security (Pittsburgh, Pennsylvania, July 06 - 08, 2005). SOUPS '05, vol. 93. ACM, New York, NY, 77-88.

[Feske05] Feske, Norman; Helmuth, Christian: A Nitpicker's guide to a minimal-complexity secure GUI. In: Proceedings of the 21st Annual Computer Security Applications Conference, pp.85-94, December 05-09, 2005.

[Gajek07] Gajek, Sebastian et al.: Compartmented Security for Browsers – Or How to Thwart a Phisher with Trusted Computing. IEEE International Conference on Availability, Reliability and Security (ARES'07), Vienna (Austria), 2007.

[Gasser88] Gasser, Morrie: Building a Secure Computer System. Van Nostrand Reinhold Co., New York 1988.

[Grawrock06] Grawrock, David: The Intel Safer Computing Initiative. Building Blocks for Trusted Computing. Intel Press 2006.

[Hiremane07] Hiremane, Radhakrishna: Intel Virtualization Technology for Directed I/O. http://www.intel.com/technology/magazine/45nm/vtd0507.htm?iid=techmag_0507+rhc_vtd

[Kuhlmann06a] Kuhlmann, Dirk; Landfermann, Rainer; Ramasamy, Harigovind; Schunter, Matthias; Ramunno, Gianluca; Vernizzi, Davide: An Open Trusted Computing Architecture – Secure virtual machines enabling user-defined policy enforcement. 2006. http://www.opentc.net/images/otc_architecture_high_level_overview.pdf

[Kuhlmann06b] Kuhlmann, Dirk; Weber, Arnd (eds.): Requirements Definition and Specification. OpenTC Project Deliverable D02.2. 2006. http://www.opentc.net

[Pfitzmann96] Pfitzmann, Andreas; Pfitzmann, Birgit; Schunter, Matthias; Waidner, Michael: Mobile User Devices and Security Modules: Design for Trustworthiness. IBM Research Report RZ 2784, 1996

[Pfitzmann01] Pfitzmann, Birgit; Riordan, James; Stüble, Chris; Waidner, Michael: Weber, Arnd: The PERSEUS System Architecture; IBM Research Report RZ 3335, 2001.

[Yee02]   Yee, Ka-Ping: User Interaction Design for Secure Systems. In: R. H. Deng, S. Qing, F. Bao, and J. Zhou (eds.): Proceedings of the 4th International Conference on Information and Communications Security. Lecture Notes In Computer Science, vol. 2513. Springer-Verlag, London, 2002, 278-290.

Acknowledgments

Support for the research has been provided by the European Union-funded project Open Trusted Computing (project IST-027635). More information about the project can be found at http://www.opentc.net/. The authors would also like to thank the members of the OpenTC consortium who participated in the preparation of the media analysis, the expert survey and the interpretation of the findings, in particular Dirk Kuhlmann, Matthias Schunter and Wolfgang Weidner. Thank you to Alison Hepper for her help with proofreading. Last but not least, we express our thanks to the interviewed experts.

Session 8:
TCG Technology: Issues and Applications

Offline dictionary attack on TCG TPM weak authorisation data, and solution

Liqun Chen[1] · Mark Ryan[2]

[1]HP Labs, UK
liqun.chen@hp.com

[2]University of Birmingham
M.D.Ryan@cs.bham.ac.uk

Abstract

The Trusted Platform Module (TPM) is a hardware chip designed to enable PCs achieve greater security. Proof of possession of values known as authData is required by user processes in order to use TPM keys. We show that in certain circumstances dictionary attacks can be performed offline on authdata. In this way, an attacker can circumvent some crucial operations of the TPM, and impersonate the TPM owner to the TPM, or the TPM to its owner. For example, he can unbind data or migrate keys without possessing the required authorisation data, or fake the creation of TPM keys. This means that any application that relies on the TPM may be vulnerable to attack.

We propose a new solution and some modifications to the TPM specification to prevent the offline attacks, and we also provide the way to integrate these modifications into the TPM command architecture with minimal change. With our solution, the user can use a password-type of weak secret as their authData, and the TPM system will be still safe.

1 Introduction

The Trusted Platform Module (TPM) is a hardware chip specified by the Trusted Computing Group (TCG) industry consortium, with the aim to enable computers to achieve greater levels of security than was previously possible. There are 100 million TPMs currently in existence, mostly in high-end laptops. The TPM stores cryptographic keys and other sensitive data in its shielded non-volatile memory. Application software such as Microsoft's BitLocker and HP's HP ProtectTools use the TPM in order to guarantee security properties.

The Trusted Platform Module (TPM) stores cryptographic keys and other sensitive information in shielded locations. Processes running on the host laptop or on other computers can use those keys in controlled ways. To do so, such processes have to prove knowledge of the relevant authorisation data, called authData. The authData is chosen by the user process, and sent encrypted to the TPM. The TPM stores the authData along with the relevant keys or other sensitive information. In any communication between the user and TPM which requires owner authorisation, the authData is used as a HMAC key.

Although authData is 160 bits and is therefore capable of being a high-entropy value, it may be that actual authData is derived from human-memorable passwords, and is therefore low-entropy. The TPM specification [5] has no restrictions about the entropy expected in authData. If low-entropy data is used, an attacker could try successively to guess all the possible values of the authData, and verify each guess

D. Gawrock, H. Reimer, A.-R. Sadeghi, C. Vishik (Editors): Future of Trust in Computing, Vieweg+Teubner (2009), 193-196

in turn. Such attacks are called dictionary attacks. The TPM specification stipulates that TPM manufacturers should implement resistance to dictionary attacks on authorisation data, for example, by permitting only a small number of incorrect guesses per minute.

We show that guesses of low-entropy data can be verified offline, so that the resistance offered by the
TPM is ineffective. We propose a new solution and modifications to the TPM specification to prevent
the offline dictionary attacks, and we also provide the way to integrate these modifications into the TPM
command architecture with minimal change. With our solution, the user can use a password-type weak
secret as their authData, and the TPM system will be still safe.

2 The offline dictionary attack

We show that an attacker that can observe some dataflow between the TPM and the user processes can
perform an offline dictionary attack. Specifically, if the attacker can observe:

- A command containing proof of possession of authData (typically during an Object-Independent
  Authorization Protocol (OIAP) session), and the TPM response;
- Or, a command containing proof of possession of the shared secret associated with such auth-
  Data (typically during an Object-Specific Authorization Protocol (OSAP) session), and the TPM
  response;

then the attacker can conduct an offline dictionary attack to discover the authData. This is possible because the attacker can confirm its guess of authData by reconstructing the authorisation HMACs based
on the guessed authData, and comparing with the observed HMAC. If they are equal, that confirms the
guess. The TCG specification assumes that the required traffic observations by the attacker are possible,
and was intended to protect against them.

Moreover, the TPM specification uses shared secrets derived from authData to protect new authData
supplied by the user for newly created keys. Once a single piece of authData is compromised, any new
authData protected by it is also compromised. Therefore the technology specified in the current TPM
specification version 1.2 can only work safely with the condition that users always choose a strong
secret as their authData and never disclose their authData to any mistrusted entities. Obviously this
condition restricts the TPM applications.

We propose a new solution and modifications to the TPM specification to prevent the offline dictionary
attacks, and we also provide the way to integrate these modifications into the TPM command architecture with minimal change. With our solution, the user can use a password-type weak secret as their
authData, and the TPM system will be still safe.

3 Password-based key agreement

Password-based authenticated key agreement is a cryptographic primitive that addresses this kind of
problem. It is specified in IEEE P1363.2 [1] and ISO/IEC 11770-4 [2]. There are a large number of such
key agreement protocols. The most attractive one for the current purpose is SPEKE (Simple Password
Exponential Key Exchange) by Jablon [3, 4]. It enables a pair of entities A and B to establish a strong
shared secret s based on a weak secret w that they already share.

To do this, they run a Diffie-Hellman key exchange protocol, in which they use the shared weak password to compute a group generator. Let G be a finite field group of prime order q and prime modulus

p, where q is at least 160 bits, and p is at least 1024 bits, such that $q \mid p-1$. Let H be a secure hash function $H : \{0,1\}^* \to G$. We assume that the values q, p and the function H are known to A and B (they are not secrets), and also that the weak shared secret w is known to A and B. The exchange proceeds as follows.

- A creates a new random $x \in Z_q^*$ and sends $H(w)^x \mod p$ to B. For simplicity, we omit "mod p" in $H(a)^b \mod p$ for any values a and b in the remaining part of the paper.
- A responds by creating a new random $y \in Z_q^*$ and sends $H(w)^y$ to B.
- Now, A and B can each compute the strong shared secret as $s = H(w)^{xy}$.

4 Solving the offline authData attack

Our proposed new method of TPM resistance to offline dictionary attack on weak authorisation data has been developed based on the SPEKE protocol. We assume that the user process can introduce new authData to the TPM in a reliable way (e.g., by encrypting it with an already established TPM key). It remains to demonstrate how the user process can later prove its knowledge of the authData when it wants to execute an authorised command.

In our basic solution, we directly make use of the SPEKE scheme between the TPM and user process to derive a strong secret based on the weak authData. SPEKE applied to this situation would look as follows. Every time a user process executes a command requiring authorisation with authData d, the user process and the TPM engage in the SPEKE protocol using d as the weak shared secret w. The user process chooses a random x and sends $H(d)^x$ to the TPM; the TPM chooses a random y and sends $H(d)^y$ to the user. Then they each compute the strong secret $s = H(d)^{xy}$ as explained above. After that, the value w is replaced by the value s as a HMAC key.

We have a number alternatives of the above basic solution, each of which achieve a unique requirement, which might be needed by different applications. We will give the details in the full paper.

Alternative 1: Password-based key retrieval. The aim of this version is to reduce the TPM's computation task in the basic solution. Instead of choosing a fresh y each time, the TPM has a long-term secret key y, called the "authData key", which is used to process multiple authData values. At the time the user process sends the encrypted newly chosen authData d, the TPM stores d and returns the value $H(d,t)^y$ where t is some object-specific text (such as the name or the digest of public key of the object). Every time a user process executes a command requiring authorisation, it creates a new random x and sends $H(d,t)^x$ to the TPM, together with the command requiring authorisation using $H(d,t)^{xy}$ as the HMAC key.

The object-specific text t is required to avoid an online attack. Without t, an attacker could use the TPM as an oracle to confirm his guess d' of some authData d by introducing a new object with authData d', and comparing $H(d)^y$ with $H(d')^y$. The TPM should not resist such an attack.

Alternative 2. Password-based proof of knowledge. The aim of this solution is to avoid the TPM's long-term authData key being directly used by multiple users in multiple sessions, in order to enhance safety of the key. Again, the TPM has a long-term secret key y. At the time the user process sends the encrypted newly chosen authData d, the TPM stores the value $k = H_0(d, y, t)$ where H_0 is a secure hash-function $H_0 : \{0,1\}^* \to Z_q$ and t is the object-specific text; then the TPM replies with the message $H(d)^k$, and discards d. To demonstrate authorisation for a command, the user process chooses a random x and sends $H(d)^x$, and uses the value $H(d)^{kx}$ as the HMAC key for the command requiring authorisation. The user process may use the same x across several authorisations, or it may pick a new x each time.

Alternative 3. Password-based proof of knowledge without long term key. The aim of this solution is to further reduce the TPM's computation and storage task in the previous solutions. At the time the user process sends the encrypted newly chosen authData d, the TPM chooses a random value $k \in Z_q^*$ and stores it. The TPM replies with the message $H(d)^k \in G$, and discards d. To demonstrate authorisation for a command, the user process chooses a random x and sends $H(d)^x \in G$, and uses the value $H(d)^{kx} \in G$ as the HMAC key for the command requiring authorisation. The user process may use the same x across several authorisations, or it may pick a new x each time.

5 Integration with TPM command architecture

We show how to integrate our solutions into the TPM command architecture, requiring minimal changes to the existing command set. We illustrate that for "Alternative 3". The changes listed are described from the point of view of the TPM:

1. Commands that introduce newly created authData require to be changed. The incoming and outgoing operands and their sizes do not need to be changed, but the TPM should not store the authData d. In the place of d it stores the new random k that it created, and it discards d.

2. Commands that require proof of possession of authData also require to be changed. The value $H(d)^x$ computed by the user process should be supplied as an additional incoming operand. The TPM then retrieves the value k that it stored in place of the authData, and it uses $H(d)^{kx}$ in the HMAC key in order to reconstruct and verify the incoming HMAC.

6 Conclusion

We have proposed a new solution for TCG TPM resistance to offline dictionary attack on weak authrisation data. The new solution offers the following advantages over the existing solutions: (1) The new solution protects the weak authorisation data from offline dictionary attacks. (2) The new solution can be integrated into the TPM command architecture, requiring minimal changes to the existing command set.

Acknowledgments. Many thanks to Carsten Rudolph for pointing out the necessity of the object-specific text t in alternatives 1 and 2.

References

[1]   IEEE P1363.2/D26 Draft Standard for Speci_cations for Password-based Public Key Cryptographic Techniques. grouper.ieee.org/groups/1363/passwdPK/index.html

[2]   ISO/IEC 11770-4:2006. Information technology { Security techniques { Key management { Part 4: Mechanisms based on weak secrets.

[3]   David Jablon. Strong password-only authenticated key exchange. Computer Communication Review 26(5):5{26. ACM SIGCOMM. October 1996.

[4]   David Jablon. Extended password key exchange protocols immune to dictionary attack. In Proceedings of the Sixth Workshops on Enabling Technologies: Infrastructure for Collaborative Enterprises (WET-ICE'97), pages 248{255. IEEE Computer Society, 1997.

[5]   Trusted Computing Group. www.trustedcomputinggroup.org

Trusted Virtual Disk Images

Carlo Gebhardt · Allan Tomlinson

Royal Holloway,
University of London
{c.gebhardt | allan.tomlinson}@rhul.ac.uk

Abstract

Many solutions have been proposed to raise the security level of virtualisation. However, most overlook the security of virtual disk images. With our paper we present a secure, flexible and transparent security architecture for virtual disk images. Virtual machines running on our architecture transparently benefit from confidentiality and integrity assurance. We achieve this by incorporating the concepts of Trusted Computing and in particular the Trusted Platform Module (TPM). This enables us to provide a secure and flexible trusted virtual disk infrastructure to a broad number of platforms. Furthermore, the unique concept of Trusted Virtual Disk Images (TVDI) allows an image owner to stay in control over the disk image throughout its complete life-cycle.

1 Introduction

Virtualisation is not a new technology, basic concepts and ideas have already emerged as early as 1959 [11]. It was not until the early 90's, when virtualisation became a growing field of interest among commercial and academic researchers. Combined with the continuously falling costs and constant increasing performance of modern computers, virtualisation is extensively used in today's data centres. Due to the many advantages virtualisation offers in management processes, server utilisation as well as flexibility, virtualisation is also widely used in the context of grid computing [6, 7].

However, with the many benefits offered by virtualisation, new security challenges and concerns also emerge [4, 5]. Addressing those security concerns requires a sophisticated architecture based on solid security principles as well as ongoing research. Security for virtual disk image is only one example of this research. As already outlined in [4, 5] a particular threat for virtual disk image is the fact, that it can be copied without the legitimate user's knowledge. If the image is copied or stolen, private data or security credentials might be exposed. More severe, the image can be deliberately manipulated to foist malicious code on the image consumer.

The security challenges posed by virtualisation also change in the context of trusted computing. For instance, it is rather difficult to assure an user that their visible virtual application corresponds with what they expect to see. Further, from a technical point of view, it is a complicated to trust the complex software around a virtual machine monitor. Virtualisation and trusted computing will influence and comprehend each other rather than be competing for the best solution. We have seen an adoption of trusting concepts in virtualisation [2] and in a similar way the convergence of virtualisation and trust [13]. Future virtualisation technologies would be expected to honour the unique requirements of a trusted system.

D. Gawrock, H. Reimer, A.-R. Sadeghi, C. Vishik (Editors): Future of Trust in Computing, Vieweg+Teubner (2009), 197-207

2 Related Work

The work carried out by Garfinkel et al. [3] provides a high assurance virtual machine monitor by partitioning a general-purpose platform and combining this with the concepts of trusted computing. However, we distinguish our work in two ways; first, by aggregating write operations and thus enhancing performance; and second, by utilising a metafile as a container for necessary data integrity measurements. Moreover, we provide the possibility of a snapshot capability in our vision of trusted virtual disk images.

OS circular was proposed by Suzaki et al. [14] in 2007 as a framework for internet based virtual disk images. This framework targets the distribution of one single read-only virtual disk image to a large set of clients. Image consumers are therefore able to perform integrity checks by using a stackable virtual disk driver, based on the implementation of a trusted HTTP-FUSE CLOOP driver [14].

Many disk encryption software solutions are available as of today such as dm-crypt, TrueCrypt, File-Vault and Bitlocker, but they lack support for integrity protection or support for legacy operating systems. Hardware based disk encryption on the other hand such as Intel's Danbury are tightly bound to a specific physical platform. Most disk encryption solutions target a specific application, operating system or use-case and therefore are tightly tailored to the targeted system. Hence most system lack the flexibility required in modern data centres.

By providing features such as live migration and resource aggregation, virtualisation has transformed the requirements for flexibility and security of data centres in the past. Unfortunately, none of the existing technologies address the unique requirements of securing virtual disk images in computing environments.

3 Background

3.1 Motivation

Virtual disk images are mostly represented by a single or a set of large files, which are then exported by the hosting environment to the guest system and represented as a physical hard-drive. The handling of a virtual disk image is similar to handling any type of file [4, 5]. Hence it can be copied, moved and altered. Without appropriate protecting mechanisms this can be done without the knowledge of the legitimate owner. As a result, an image could be manipulated or replaced completely. Thus sensitive data could be modified or malicious code injected and executed without the user's awareness.

Moreover, as the image can be copied partly, or as a whole, sensitive information might be leaked. Some usage scenarios may require the transmission of sensitive information to a third party to be processed. For instance, cloud computing, such as Amazons EC2, offer cheap processing capabilities, but do not ensure confidentiality or integrity. Moreover, distributed environment such as this are not able to provide the fine-grained access control mechanisms costumers might want. Consequently it is difficult to provide confidentiality and integrity while maintaining flexibility and interoperability at the same time.

3.2 Assumptions

As outlined in section 3.4, to protect the virtual disk image we propose to use the concepts of Trusted Computing and, in particular, the Trusted Platform Module (TPM). Hence we require a TPM to be present on the platform which hosts a virtual machine instance. Virtualised guests therefore do not have to be aware of the presence of a TPM.

Additionally, we utilise the TPM to measure and attest to the integrity of the virtual machine monitor and a set of userspace applications. This is necessary to ensure that the hosting system is trustworthy and only executes unmodified code. Work on a reduced trusted code base carried out by McCune et al. [8] demonstrates how a system can be trusted with only a minimum amount of code, whilst providing hardware-supported isolation of security-sensitive code. Further work conducted by Seshadri et al. [12] demonstrates how to ensure code integrity for commodity operating systems. Additionally, we assume that hardware virtualisation features are available on the host system to provide protected page tables as described in [12]. We use this in order to secure a shared address space in the existing XEN disk driver model, as well as reducing the trusted code base.

3.3 Design Principles

We aim to provide data integrity and confidentiality for virtual disk images, while at the same time maintaining flexibility and backward compatibility. Our goal is to ensure integrity and confidentiality on an end-to-end basis and thus enable the image owner to stay in control over the image content throughout the disk's image life-cycle. Those services shall protect the disk image transparently to the guest system as well to the user.

Our current trusted virtual disk image approach is based on the existing virtual disk image driver implemented in XEN [19]. XEN implements a set of "Domains", which have different functions and privileges: The management Domain 0, is created during the boot process of the system, and controls the user domains (Domain U). Administrative tasks like creating, suspending, destroying and access to the physical hardware are only possible from within the privileged Domain 0. Hence, the user domains represent lower privileged virtual machines.

XEN implements different techniques to access resources from unprivileged domains, however, in the following we focus on the so-called paravirtualised driver model, which we build our trusted virtual disk image design on. The para-virtulised driver model implements a simplified front-end driver available to the Domain U, which forwards requests to the sophisticated back-end driver in Domain 0. In the case of disk I/O, we base our model on the existing blktap driver [19].

Our design targets security, but we also intend to keep the implementation and performance overhead to a minimum.

3.4 Trusted Computing

We make use of the principles of Trusted Computing (TC) as the protection mechanism for virtual disk images. In particular we utilise the functions supplied by the Trusted Platform Module (TPM) as described by the Trusted Computing Group.

The TPM specifications [15–17], describe a tamper-resistant device with cryptographic coprocessor capabilities. This device provides the platform, in our case the host machine, with a number of services. These services include: special purpose registers for recording platform state; a means of reporting this state to remote entities; asymmetric key generation, encryption and digital signature capabilities. For the purposes of this paper we make use of three TC related concepts: integrity measuring, sealing and public key operations.

Integrity measuring: An integrity measurement is the cryptographic digest or hash of a platform component (i.e. a piece of software executing on the platform). For example, the integrity measurement of a program can be calculated by computing a cryptographic digest of a program's instruction sequence, its initial state and its input. Integrity measurements are stored in special purpose registers within the TPM called Platform Configuration Registers (PCRs).

Sealing: This is the process by which data is encrypted and associated with a set of integrity metrics representing a particular platform configuration. The protected data can only be decrypted and released for use by a TPM when the current state of the platform matches the integrity metrics to which the data was sealed.

Asymmetric keys: A TPM can generate an unlimited number of asymmetric key-pairs. For each of these pairs, private key use and mobility can be constrained, where usage is contingent upon the presence of predefined platform state (as reflected in the host platform's TPM PCRs). Additionally, a private key can be either migratable, non-migratable, or certifiable migratable. A non-migratable key is inextricably bound to a single TPM instance, and is known only to the TPM that created it.

A certificate for a non-migratable key and its security properties may be created by the TPM on which it was generated. A certifiable migratable key (CMK) can be migrated but also retains properties which the TPM, on which the CMK was generated, can certify. When a CMK is created, control of its migration is delegated to a migration (selection) authority. In this way, controlled migration of the key is possible, whereby an entity other than the TPM owner makes some contribution to the decision as to where the CMK can be migrated to. This ensures that the certified security properties of the key are retained.

3.5 Driver model

As mentioned in section 3.3, we base our implementation on the existing blktap driver model. The blktap driver is a modular userspace implementation of a virtual block device. This allows us to use existing userspace tools and libraries, which minimises implementation overhead while at the same time remains compatibility.

4 Trusted Vitual Disk Images

4.1 Integrity Protection

Typical disk images are large files, which makes generating and checking integrity metrics a challenging task. With writeable images, for instance, a single changed bit requires to recalculate integrity metrics over the complete image. Readonly images, on the other hand, can be deployed with pre-calculated integrity metrics, but also require calculation of the image's integrity to be able to compare it to the expected value. Hence it is difficult to measure integrity in a timely and practical manner. Our proposal is to split a virtual disk image up into chunks or containers of a fixed size. Thus only the integrity of those containers which have been updated has to be recreated and additionally we are able to perform operations in parallel.

Rather then trading calculation time at the systems start-up for calculation time during runtime by applying a Merkle hash tree [10] over the image, we decided to divide the image into independent containers. As a consequence, chunks can be treated separately. This allows us to reduce the number of hash operations necessary, and additionally enables us to implement an efficient snapshot functionality as described in section 5.4.

The following steps describe how we intend to provide integrity protection to the virtual disk image.

4.1.1 Generating integrity metrics

We propose to use a metafile as outlined in section 4.4 to store integrity metrics of each individual chunk of an image. The metafile itself is protected by the TPM's sealing capabilities and bound to a distinct platform in a specific configuration.

Creating an integrity value for a chunk is triggered by a write operation of a Domain U to its virtual block device. The I/O request is forwarded by the Domain U front-end to the back-end driver in Domain 0. Here the correspondent chunk is updated and before being written to disk, its integrity value is generated and updated in the metafile. Figure 1 outlines the detailed trusted virtual disk implementation.

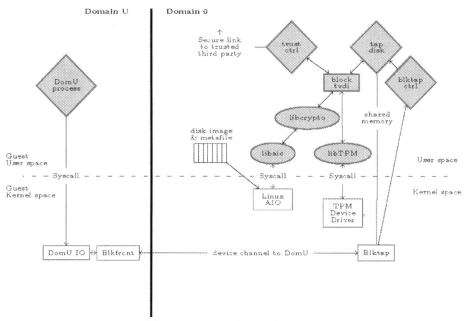

Figure 1: TVDI implementation in Xen

4.2 Checking Integrity

In detail this takes place as described in the following: An I/O request is forwarded by a special character control device (blktap ctrl) to the backend driver of Domain 0. The drivers communicate via an event channel and shared memory. The userspace and kernelspace part of the back-end driver communicate via named pipes and shared memory [19]. First and foremost, the metafile is loaded by the block tvdi application, which invokes libTPM to unseal and check the metafile. After being unsealed the metafile is maintained in the host's memory until the guest system is finally paused or halted. Once the metafile is unsealed, the block tvdi application will then invoke libcrypto to create integrity metrics for the chunks which have been altered and update the corresponding entries in the metafile. Finally an I/O library such as libaio is used to write out the data.

This allows transparent and concurrent operation for multiple virtual guests. Implementation overhead will be minimal and limited to block tvdi and trust ctrl as described in section 4.5. Existing libraries such as libaio, libcrypto and libTPM are commonly available.

4.2.1 Checking integrity before operation

Integrity checks are either performed all at once, before the guest is able to access the image, or during operation as outlined in the subsequent section 4.2.2. Hence, before starting, resuming or migrating, the integrity of all chunks is checked against their pre-stored values from the metafile. Hashes of individual chunks are independent. This allows the operations to be performed in parallel. In comparison to a traditional approach to hash a single large file, our approach benefits from the speed up gained by paral-lelisation. Moreover, as outlined in the following it is not always necessary to check an image before operation, but possible to measure it during operation or even recover from integrity failures.

4.2.2 Checking integrity during operation

If a virtualised guest is powered up, migrated or resumed, the first I/O request is forwarded to the Do-main 0 as outlined in section 4.1.1. The initial request triggers the userspace control program to invoke libTPM to unseal, load and check the metafile for further processing. A first read request causes the back-end driver to load the appropriate chunk of the image and measure its integrity, which is then compared to its pre-stored value in the metafile. In more detail, the request is forwarded from the guest's front-end driver to the Domain 0 back-end driver via the blktap ctrl control device. Crypto operations are consequently carried out by libcrypto.

4.2.3 Policy model

Different policies to handle integrity failures are possible:

- Enforcing policy -If an integrity check fails, the back-end implementation will deny further ac-cess to the virtual disk image. The trust control program in Domain 0, for instance can pause the effected machine and report the incident.
- Reporting only policy -The guest will be allowed further access to the virtual disk image, yet the incident will be reported. If the guest system itself needs to be notified, modifications to the front-end driver are required.

4.2.4 Recovery from integrity failure

If an integrity check fails to validate, correct operation can not be guaranteed, for instance arbitrary changes to program code may render the virtual machine un-operational. To mitigate this issue a virtual guest may be set up to automatically recover from an integrity failure. This can be accomplished by returning to an earlier, trusted snapshot. A similar procedure to recover from integrity failures during bootstrapping has been proposed by Arbaugh et al. [1]. However, we do not require a trusted repository as security is provided by the disk image itself. Any repository holding copies of the last functional snapshot is sufficient. A snapshot repository has to be set up in advance and the control program has to be provided with its location. In the case of an integrity failure the control program could then move the faulty chunks and obtain the working chunks from the repository. To prevent flooding or denial of service attacks effecting other virtual machines on the same host, defective chunks are moved to a quarantine directory and additionally the number of recovery attempts are limited to a defined amount per time span. Afterwards the control program may proceed with one of the policies described in the previous section.

4.3 Confidentiality

Confidentiality in our scheme is provided by encrypting each chunk with a suitable encryption algorithm. The encryption key itself is expected to be held in the metafile. However, an alternative would be to derive the key from an interactive pass-phrase asked upon powering up or migrating the virtual disk image. Solutions to implement encrypted disk image for XEN such as [9] are already available, however, for flexibility and simplicity we propose to utilise the external libcrypto library.

The metafile which contains the encryption key is sealed to a TPM on a specific platform in a specific state. Hence only this particular platform in its distinctive state may reveal the encryption key provided in the metafile.

In practice, this allows the chunks and the metafile to reside on untrusted storage and trespass unsecured networks. Therefore both integrity and confidentiality can be provided transparently while existing, potentially, insecure legacy storage and communication structures may be used.

4.4 Metafile

The metafile is central to our trusted virtual disk image design: It holds the encryption key and integrity metrics for each chunk, thus it needs special protection mechanisms. Consequently, we require the metafile to be confidential and tamper-evident. The file itself is protected by the TPM's sealing mechanism. This allows the metafile to be only revealed if the particular host is in a defined state, including a distinct software configuration e.g. Hypervisor, userspace control programs, libraries, etc. Hence the metafile handling should be managed by the userspace control program in Domain 0.

Upon the first I/O request to a virtual disk image, the userspace control program will call libTPM to unseal the metafile in order to get access to the encryption credential and integrity metrics. Once the metafile is loaded and checked, it is held in a secure part of memory and receives updates throughout the guest system's lifetime. If the guest system is powered off, suspended or migrated the metafile will be updated and sealed.

We decided against the obvious approach of mapping block addresses to chunk file names, in order to implement a snapshot capability. We propose to implement a unique and random identifier (NextFreeChunk) as an addition to the basename (e.g. cunk[i]). By doing so, no information about a chunk's source or allocation is revealed. As a result, the metafile reflects the block address mapping via the BlockAddress directive in the according section. A sample metafile is shown in listing 4.4.

We refer to the chunk size via the ChunkSize directive in the header section of the metafile. A small chunk size would result in a constant, but unnecessary re-hash if information within the chunk had changed. A large chunk size on the other hand would result in an increased execution time, as the complete chunk needs to be hashed during runtime. To reduce additional read/write overhead and the amount of hash operations, we suggest using a fixed chunk size equal to the cache size of the underlying hard-drive or file system. By choosing chunk sizes of 8 to 16 Megabytes the performance impact of multiple chunk read/write operations, for instance caused by fragmentation, can be further reduced.

```
<sampleImage>
<header>
...
        <SHA256>894f435gd ... fas32dag</SHA256>
        <EncryptionKey>3b23894f ... fce3bc95</EncryptionKey>
        <EncryptionAlgorithm>AES</EncryptionAlgorithm>
        <ChunkSize>16777216</ChunkSize>
        <ImageSize>536870912000</ImageSize>
        <NextFreeChunk>123</NextFreeChunk>
        <SnapshotVersion>2</SnapshotVersion>
</header>
...
<chunk.122>
        <SnapshotVersion>2</SnapshotVersion>
        <BlockAddress>00040000</BlockAddress>
        <ChunkPath>/sampleImage/chunk.122</ChunkPath>
        <SHA256>dc460da4ad72c ... 6899d54ef98b5</SHA256>
        ...
</chunk.122>
</sampleImage>
```

Listing 1: Sample metafile

4.5 Trust Control

A trust control process is required to take charge of reporting and assuring a third party instance that the trusted virtual disk image implementation is correct and trustworthy. It will do so by measuring each component's integrity before launching the trusted virtual disk image system. The integrity values are stored in the platform's PCR registers and attestation of their values can be made to a remote entity on request. Furthermore, it delegates the metafile, by migrating it to a different host in case a virtual machine is being moved.

5 Life cycle

5.1 Initialisation

Constructing a new trusted virtual disk image requires the initialisation of one metafile per disk image instance. Chunks themselves grow dynamically during their lifetime due to their sparse capability. The sparse format allows the image to utilise disk space more efficiently by only saving allocated disk space and storing empty disk space in an abbreviated way. This allows data to be stored more efficiently and at the same time it allows the image to dynamically grow during operation. However, it is still necessary to specify the disk image's maximum capacity during initialisation, as it is treated by the guest operating system as a hard-drive with fixed physical layout. Parameters such as encryption and hash algorithm, may be specified during initialisation or be set automatically to a default value. The encryption key itself will be generated and placed in the header of the metafile. Depending on the usage scenario the initialisation procedure can be carried out on the host, or by a trusted third party, for instance the content provider. Finally, the metafile is sealed to its target host by using the trusted computing sealing mechanism. Hence, only the target machine can unseal the metafile and reveal the encryption key for the disk image. New chunks will be created dynamically by the block tvdi driver up to the maximum specified capacity of the image.

5.2 Backup

A metafile is bound to a specific platform in a distinct configuration. This renders recovering from a hardware fault quite difficult. Consequently, we may allow the image creator to keep a copy of the metafile or even the encryption key of the chunks themselves. The metafile, however, must never be stored in the clear, hence we require the backup to be protected in a suitable manner, for instance by sealing it to a TPM on the backup platform. Recovering from a backup source, however, may fail integrity checks as integrity metrics may be outdated.

5.3 Migration

Currently, our design of a trusted virtual disk image only allows offine migration. Hence, the virtual guest has to be powered off or suspended and the image subsequently released. In section 3.2 we assume a TPM is present on the hosting platform. This must also be the case for the platform the image is migrated to. Once the virtual guest is powered off, we utilise the trust control processes on both hosting machines to establish mutual trust and a secure link. During this phase the remote machine attests its state to the source machine, which will then decide weather the remote state is trustworthy and safe to migrate to. This is followed by invoking libTPM and calling "TPM MigrateKey" [17] to migrate the key protecting the metafile to its new destination. After the metafile and chunks are made available to the targeted machine, the trust control process can unseal the metafile and proceed with normal operation. In a suspended state, the memory content which will be written to disk will be encrypted. Therefore the encryption key is placed into the header section of the metafile.

5.4 Snapshots

We believe that providing a snapshot feature is a very valuable and desirable property in the context of virtualisation. Consequently, we want to apply this functionality to our trusted virtual disk image design.

A snapshot is created by increasing the SnapshotVersion directive in the header section of the metafile. This causes the back-end driver to handle each chunk as readonly from this point on. Following write operations will create new chunks, new integrity metrics and a new unique chunk identifiers. This is reflected in the metafile by a SnapshotVersion entry in the according chunk section. To ensure a crash consistent state, all unsaved chunks and the metafile will be saved at this stage. After this point, if a chunk is modified, the existing chunk is copied in a copy-on-write mechanism. This allows a snapshot to be taken during normal operation, thus while a virtualised guest is running. Chunks that do not hold a snapshot version are therefore valid for all snapshot states.

We consider snapshotting as a valuable feature and decided to provide this component, even though it results in more fragmentation. By using a fixed chunk size a snapshot will create fragments and waste a certain amount of storage space.

5.5 Deletion

Our main design goals are to maintain confidentiality and integrity throughout the disk image's life-cycle. Consequently, those characteristics should still be intact once the disk image reaches the end of its lifetime. Moreover, the weakest attribute for confidentiality is the encryption key and its backups. The metafile is the digital equivalent to a key and thus it needs to be kept secure throughout the disk image life-cycle. Thus if the metafile and the encryption key are securely deleted then this effectively deletes the image. This requires careful control over the distribution of the metafile and encryption key.

Ensuring that the metafile can only be unsealed on a particular platform, gives some degree of control on the file's distribution.

6 Conclusion

With our solution we address the lack of integrity and confidentiality assurance of existing virtual disk images. The solution presented in this paper is capable of delivering those attributes with a great amount of flexibility and transparently to virtual disk images. Therefore, we base our scheme on the well known trusted computing concepts to enhance security while at the same applying those security properties transparently to the user. This enables trusted virtual disk images to be stored independent from storage location or transport mechanism without compromising security. For example, a virtual disk image could be hosted over the internet.

Moreover, confidentiality and integrity is applied to all data within an image, which allows protection of applications, data, logs etc., altogether. Trusted virtual disk images also allow the provision of integrity and confidentiality to legacy or commodity operating systems which do not support any of those attributes at all.

7 Future Work

Future work will be a proof-of-concept implementation which will deliver performance results as well uncover open issues. Furthermore, trusted live migration, thus migrating in a trusted manner without suspending the migratee, posses a serious design challenge. The Open Virtual Machine Format (OVF) proposed by VMware and XenSource in [18], targets an open and neutral standard for virtual appliances. Incorporating our trusted virtual disk images into the OVF could deliver confidentiality and integrity assurance to a broad range of applications. A general and vendor neutral secure disk image standard could be beneficial for a vast range of future trusted virtual applications.

References

[1]   [1] William A. Arbaugh, Angelos D. Keromytis, David J. Farber, and Jonathan M. Smith, Automated recovery in a secure bootstrap process, Proceedings of Network and Distributed System Security Symposium, Internet Society, 1998, pp. 155–167.

[2]   Stefan Berger, Ramán Cáceres, Kenneth A. Goldman, Ronald Perez, Reiner Sailer, and Leendert van Doorn, vtpm: virtualizing the trusted platform module, USENIX-SS'06: Proceedings of the 15th conference on USENIX Security Symposium (Berkeley, CA, USA), USENIX Association, 2006, pp. 21–21.

[3]   Haibo Chen, Jieyun Chen, Wenbo Mao, and Fei Yan, Daonity - grid security from two levels of virtualization, Inf. Secur. Tech. Rep. 12 (2007), no. 3, 123–138.

[4]   Tal Garfinkel, Ben Pfaff, Jim Chow, Mendel Rosenblum, and Dan Boneh, Terra: a virtual machine-based platform for trusted computing, SOSP '03: Proceedings of the nineteenth ACM symposium on Operating systems principles (New York, NY, USA), ACM, 2003, pp. 193–206.

[5]   Tal Garfinkel and Mendel Rosenblum, When virtual is harder than real: security challenges in virtual machine based computing environments, HOTOS'05: Proceedings of the 10th conference on Hot Topics in Operating Systems (Berkeley, CA, USA), USENIX Association, 2005, pp. 20–20.

[6]   Carl Gebhardt and Allan Tomlinson, Security considerations for virtualization, Tech. report, Department of Mathematics, Royal Holloway, University of London, 2008.

[7]   Hans Lohr, HariGovind V. Ramasamy, Ahmad-Reza Sadeghi, Stefan Schulz, Matthias Schunter, and Christian Stuble, Enhancing grid security using trusted virtualization. , ATC (Bin Xiao, Laurence Tianruo Yang,

Jianhua Ma, Christian Muller-Schloer, and Yu Hua, eds.), Lecture Notes in Computer Science, vol. 4610, Springer, 2007, pp. 372–384.

[8]   Jonathan M. McCune, Bryan J. Parno, Adrian Perrig, Michael K. Reiter, and Hiroshi Isozaki, Flicker: an execution infrastructure for tcb minimization , SIGOPS Oper. Syst. Rev. 42 (2008), no. 4, 315–328.

[9]   Mark McLoughlin, The qcow image format, http://www.gnome.org/~markmc/qcow-image-format.html.

[10] Ralph C. Merkle, Protocols for public key cryptosystems , Security and Privacy 00 (1980), 122–134.

[11] Arvind Seshadri, Mark Luk, Ning Qu, and Adrian Perrig, Secvisor: a tiny hypervisor to provide lifetime kernel code integrity for commodity oses, SOSP '07: Proceedings of twenty-first ACM SIGOPS symposium on Operating systems principles (New York, NY, USA), ACM, 2007, pp. 335–350.

[12] C. Strachey, Time sharing in large fast computers , vol. paper B. 2. 1, Proceedings of the International Conference on Information Processing, June 1959, pp. 336–341.

[13] Frederic Stumpf, Michael Benz, Martin Hermanowski, and Claudia Eckert, An approach to a trustworthy system architecture using virtualization, Proceedings of the 4th International Conference on Autonomic and Trusted Computing (ATC-2007) (Hong Kong, China), Lecture Notes in Computer Science, vol. 4158, Springer-Verlag, July 2007, pp. 191–202.

[14] Kuniyasu Suzaki, Toshiki Yagi, Kengo Iijima, and Nguyen Anh Quynh, Os circular: internet client for reference , LISA'07: Proceedings of the 21st conference on 21st Large Installation System Administration Conference (Berkeley, CA, USA), USENIX Association, 2007, pp. 1–12.

[15] TCG, TPM Main, Part 1 Design Principles , TCG Specification Version 1.2 Revision 103, The Trusted Computing Group, Portland, OR, USA, July 2007.

[16] _____, TPM Main, Part 2 TPM Data Structures , TCG Specification Version 1.2 Revision 103, The Trusted Computing Group, Portland, OR, USA, July 2007.

[17] _____, TPM Main, Part 3 Commands , TCG Specification Version 1.2 Revision 103, The Trusted Computing Group, Portland, OR, USA, July 2007.

[18] VMware and XenSource, The open virtual machine format whitepaper for ovf specification , Tech. report, VMware and XenSource, 2007. [19] Andrew Warfield and Julian Chesterfield, Blktap userspace tools + library , http://lxr.xensource.com/lxr/source/tools/blktap/README, June 2006.

Shall we trust WDDL?

Sylvain Guilley · Sumanta Chaudhuri · Laurent Sauvage
Tarik Graba · Jean-Luc Danger · Philippe Hoogvorst
Vinh-Nga Vong · Maxime Nassar · Florent Flament

Institut TELECOM, TELECOM ParisTech CNRS LTCI (UMR 5141)
Département COMELEC, 46 rue Barrault 75 634 PARIS Cedex 13, FRANCE
<firstname.lastname>@TELECOM-ParisTech.fr

Abstract

Security is not only a matter of cryptographic algorithms robustness but becomes also a question of securing their implementation. P. Kocher's differential power analysis (DPA) is one of the many side-channel attacks that are more and more studied by the security community. Indeed, side-channel attacks (SCA) have proved to be very powerful on cryptographic algorithms such as DES and AES, customarily implemented in a wide variety of devices, ranging from smart-cards or ASICs to FPGAs. Among the proposed countermeasures, the "dual-rail with precharge logic" (DPL) aims at hiding information leaked by the circuit by making the power consumption independent of the calculation. However DPL logic could be subject to second order attacks exploiting timing difference between dual nets. In this article, we characterize by simulation, the vulnerability due to timing unbalance in the eight DES substitution boxes implemented in DPL WDDL style. The characterization results in a classification of the nodes according to their timing unbalance. Our results show that the timing unbalance is a major weakness of the WDDL logic, and that it could be used to retrieve the key using a DPA attack. This vulnerability has been experimentally observed on a full DES implementation using WDDL style for Altera Stratix EP1S25 FPGA.

1 Introduction

The principle of "dual-rail with precharge logic" (DPL) is to protect the implementation against side-channel attacks such as the Differential Power Analysis (DPA) [4]. The DPL is a two-phase protocol composed of a precharge phase and an evaluation phase. Each signal is represented in dual-rail logic by its "true" and "false" parts, which are complementary. During the precharge phase, all signals are put in an initial state (assumed to be 00 in the sequel) to ensure that during the evaluation phase, the number of computations is fully predictable and constant whatever the inputs are. In this article, we focus on the the "wave dynamic differential logic" (WDDL), a DPL based on standard cell flow, proposed by K. Tiri [6].

However as described by D. Suzuki [5], DPL logic can still leak information because "true" and "false" parts can evaluate at different time according to the inputs. The root of this problem is the early evaluation. As a matter of fact, such difference in delay time will appear when early evaluation is combined with other unbalance factors, such as: difference of logical paths or unbalance of dual nets. Fig. 1b illustrates the principle of early evaluation for a 2-input AND gate and its dual 2-input OR gate, as represented on the Fig. 1a.

D. Gawrock, H. Reimer, A.-R. Sadeghi, C. Vishik (Editors): Future of Trust in Computing, Vieweg+Teubner (2009), 208-215

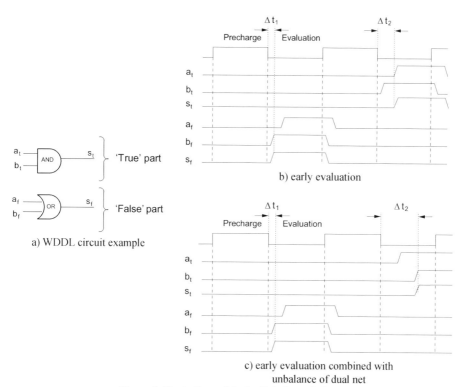

a) WDDL circuit example

b) early evaluation

c) early evaluation combined with
unbalance of dual net

Figure 1: Illustrations of dual-rail timing unbalance.

We observe that, depending on the inputs value, the switching delay time differs because of the early evaluation in AND and OR gates. In this example, it is clear that the OR gate evaluates as soon as one of its inputs is set to '1', on an other hand, the AND gate must wait until each of its entries are set to '1', in order to switch its output. Of course, the opposite behavior would take place if the first available input would have been set to '0' (the AND gate would have evaluated immediately and the OR gate would have waited for every inputs to be cleared).

Early evaluation is then linked to the equations defining the circuit and exhibits the timing difference between the signal a and b. In addition, for dual-rail logic, the difference of delay time could also be strengthened by two main factors:

1. The unbalance between the "true" and "false" nets, due to placement and routing differences, produces a timing difference between the true and the false net of a dual rail signal. In fact, if b_t is slower than b_f, the delay time Δt_2 could increase as shown on Fig. 1c.

2. The unbalance of logical paths between inputs of a given logical gate, due to the fact that some inputs have to pass through more logical layers than others, leads to a timing difference between these input signals on each half path. In the same way, if a_t is slower than a_f, Δt_2 could also increase significantly.

To summarize, the switching time of output $s(s_t, s_f)$ depends on the inputs $a(a_t, a_f)$ and $b(b_t, b_f)$ as well as the switching time difference between s_t and s_f depends on the inputs. As a consequence, if for one signal, Δt defined as $\Delta t \doteq \Delta t_1 - \Delta t_2$, can be detected by an measurement instrument (device), the activity of the node could be monitored and this can lead to the secret key. In order to estimate if this vulnerability could be exploited on a real design, we have simulated the eight DES substitution boxes (S-Boxes) implemented in WDDL on an Altera Stratix FPGA and analyzed the switching timing delay for every node of the S-boxes.

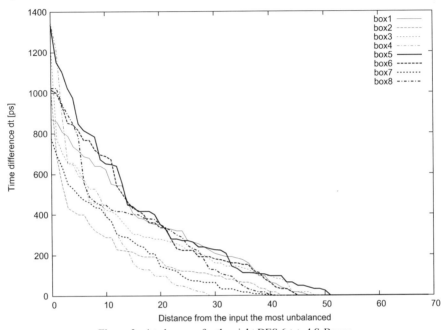

Figure 2: Δt decrease for the eight DES $6 \mapsto 4$ S-Boxes

So far, difference in timing delay has only been studied on elementary designs, consisting of a single gate. Our objective is to assess whether or not this observation scales up to a full-fledged hardware encryption accelerator (in our case triple-DES on FPGA). To reach our goal, we first evaluate the vulnerability by simulation, and then effectively attack the physical implementation. The remainder of the paper is structured as follows: Sec. 2 presents the methods used to analyze the timing unbalance in dual-rail logic, Sec. 3 presents how WDDL could be successfully attacked based on a criterion defined in Sec. 2. Finally, the Sect. 4 concludes this article. The appendix A provides with some precisions about the simulation realized in Sec. 2.

2 Timing Analysis of Differential Logic

We simulate the post-placed and routed compact S-Boxes designed specifically for FPGA as described in [1]. Each DES S-Box has a 6-bit input and a 4-bit output. The simulation environment provides the precharge and evaluation phases for all possible inputs. The main information extracted from the Value Change Dump (VCD) output file is the switching delay of each net during the precharge and evaluation phases. The switching delay is defined as the delay for one net to switch after the inputs are set. In our evaluations, we calculate for each node the absolute difference between the mean switching delay of the true net, and the mean switching delay of the false net. We call this difference Δt. The nodes of the S-Box are then sorted in descending order. The results are plotted for the eight S-Boxes in Figure 2.

According to Figure 2, the most vulnerable S-Box seems to be box 5 for two main reasons: ITS Δt is the highest and decreases the slowest

The analysis yields a classification of the nodes according to their vulnerability, namely the value Δt. In order to exploit this information for real attack, the following methodology is applied:

1. First selection: find nodes where Δt is higher than 1 ns (for experimental reasons: the timing difference should be visible with a sampling rate of 20 Gs/s and a bandwidth of 5 GHz).

2. Second selection: Among the nodes in the first selection, find the nodes where the dispersion of the switching delay do not overlap.

3. Third selection: Among the nodes in the second selection, select the ones having the smallest dispersion.

Figure. 3 presents the node selected for the eight S-Boxes of DES. It displays the repartition in time of the switching delay for the "true" and "false" nets. The node in box5 with nets *wire_e_true* and *wire_1_false* is chosen as the most vulnerable and will be used for a DPA attack on the DES implementation on our Altera Stratix FPGA (model EP1S25, in 130 nm technology). The separation between "true" and "false" evaluation dates is especially eloquent for S-Boxes 3, 4, 5 & 8.

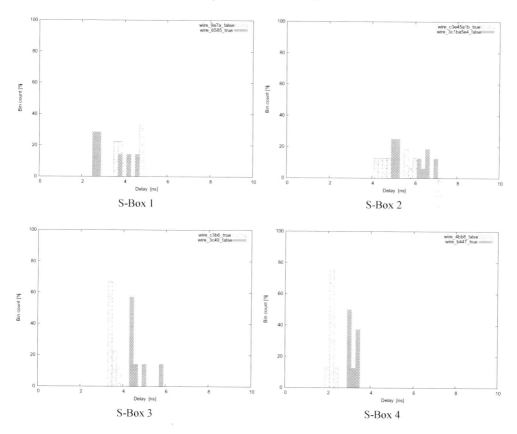

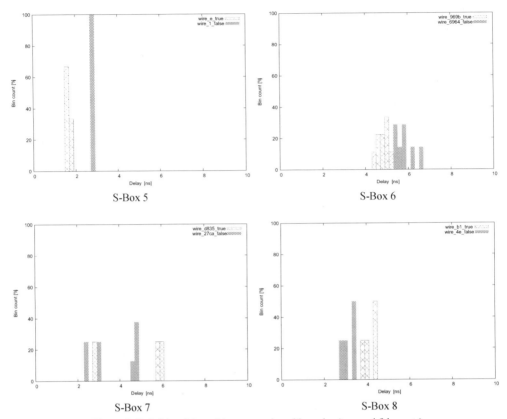

S-Box 5   S-Box 6

S-Box 7   S-Box 8

Figure 3: Switching delay of the most vulnerable nodes (true and false nets)

Moreover, the simulation on the $2^6 = 64$ possible inputs for the S-Boxes is also an easy way to extract information on the activity of each node. In fact, to apply a DPA on power traces collected on a real implementation, one should be able to define the selection function which depends on the node under attack. Based on the simulation, we can extract for each net, the list of inputs that make it switch, and therefore the selection function for the DPA.

3 Practical Test on DES WDDL Implemented in an Altera Stratix EP1S25 FPGA

In order to validate the results obtained by simulation, we have performed a DPA attack on the node identified as the more vulnerable. We mention that attacks based on correlations with one single bit do work in practice on unprotected implementations. A differential trace obtained with a single-bit correlation can be seen in Figure 2 of [3] or in Figure 4.

As our objective here is only to validate that the timing difference for dual nets is visible, we make the correct assumption for the key and perform the DPA with the correct selection function. Figure 5 shows the results of the DPA. We observe that the results match the expectation, e.g. that the DPA shows a spike that betrays the incriminated correlation.

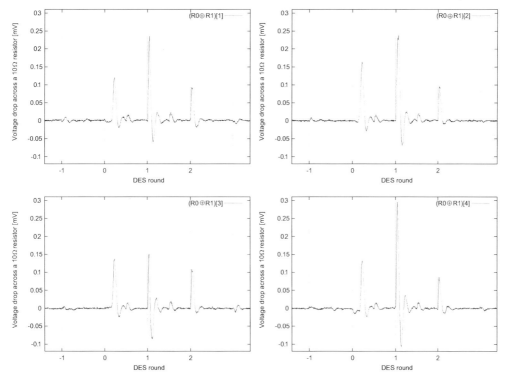

Figure 4: Example of four mono-bit differential trace on SecMatV1 DES (see §2.1 in [2])

4 Conclusion

Dual-rail with precharge logic is a technique that ensures that upon execution, a circuit always toggles the same number of nodes during each clock cycle. This technique reduces significantly the information leakage on the power side channel (see left part of Figure 5). With this technology, the attack based on the correlation between the key and the number of nodes toggled at a given clock cycle, is not possible anymore.

However some DPL technologies, such as WDDL, still leak information over the power side channel (see right part of Figure 5). The switching timing difference between dual nets of some internal nodes is correlated to the data being computed. The power consumption profile of such chip is therefore exploitable to lead a side-channel attack.

We conclude that this correlation can be exploited for some nodes where the timing difference is significant enough. In addition, the analysis of the simulation leads to a classification of the nodes according to their vulnerability. For the first time, it has been proved that such correlation could be exploited on experimental traces. Finally, this article leads to the conclusion that the timing unbalance of dual nets should allow power consumption attacks.

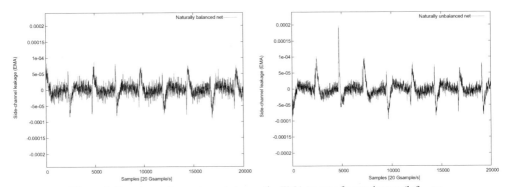

Figure 5: Experimental covariance between the EMA traces of a regular net (left – no leakage) & the most critical net value (right – very leaky, see peak around sample 5,000)

A Appendix: Details on Simulation and Timing Analysis

Table 1: Example of the VCD file for a given gate

```
$scope module i_dut_1 $end
$var wire 1 ! wire_a1_false $end
$var wire 1 " wire_5e_true $end
#0
$dumpvars
x"
x!
$end
#1761
0!
#2605
0"
#51915
1!
#101348
0!
#151915
1!
#201348
0!
#252274
1"
#301464
0"
```

The code snippet of Tab. 1 gives an example the VCD syntax. Tab. 2 presents an extract of the nodes classification for the S-Box 5.

Table 2: Extract of nodes classiffcation for S-Box 5

delta_t	wire/port name	activity	mean delay(ps)	std dev
1336	wire_9a95_false	32	5224.00	738.12
	wire_656a_true	32	3888.00	318.50
1152	wire_e_true	48	1696.00	116.12
	wire_1_false	16	2848.00	7.00
1104	wire_9569_true	32	5096.00	469.32
	wire_6a96_false	32	3992.00	250.02
1024	wire_3a5c_false	32	4416.00	269.61
	wire_c5a3_true	32	3392.00	222.74
976	wire_69_false	32	4656.00	199.41
	wire_96_true	32	3680.00	197.14
848	wire_9a_false	32	4064.00	812.79
	wire_65_true	32	3216.00	322.51

...

References

[1]   S. Guilley, S. Chaudhuri, L. Sauvage, T. Graba, J.-L. Danger, Ph. Hoogvorst, V.-N. Vong, and M. Nassar. Place-and-Route Impact on the Security of DPL Designs in FPGAs. In HOST, IEEE, pages 29–35, 2008. June 9, Anaheim, USA. ISBN = 978-1-4244-2401-6.

[2]   Sylvain Guilley, Laurent Sauvage, Jean-Luc Danger, Nidhal Selmane, and Renaud Pacalet. Silicon-level solutions to counteract passive and active attacks. In FDTC, 5th workshop on Fault Detection and Tolerance in Cryptography, IEEE-CS, Washington DC, USA, aug 2008.

[3]   Thanh-Ha Le, Cécile Canovas, and Jessy Clédiére. An overview of side channel analysis attacks. In ASI-ACCS, pages 33–43, 2008.

[4]   P. Kocher and J. Jaffe and B. Jun. Differential Power Analysis. In Proceedings of CRYPTO'99, volume 1666 of LNCS, pages 388–397. Springer-Verlag, 1999. (PDF).

[5]   Daisuke Suzuki and Minoru Saeki. Security Evaluation of DPA Countermeasures Using Dual-Rail Pre-charge Logic Style. In CHES, volume 4249 of LNCS, pages 255–269. Springer, 2006. http://dx.doi.org/10.1007/11894063_21.

[6]   K. Tiri and I. Verbauwhede. A Logic Level Design Methodology for a Secure DPA Resistant ASIC or FPGA Implementation. In DATE'04, pages 246–251, February 2004. Paris, France.

Trusted Computing Management Server Making Trusted Computing User Friendly

Sönke Sothmann · Hans Brandl

Infineon Technologies AG
{Soenke.Sothmann | Hans.Brandl}@infineon.com

Abstract

Personal Computers (PC) with build in Trusted Computing (TC) technology are already well known and widely distributed. Nearly every new business notebook contains now a Trusted Platform Module (TPM) and could be used with increased trust and security features in daily application and use scenarios. However in real life the number of notebooks and PCs where the TPM is really activated and used is still very small.

Main reasons for this low acceptance is mostly the complexity of the system and also handling problems by the ITC departments as well as the required amount of resources and work which is associated with daily management and operation, Additionally most users don't have the technical understanding of operating TPM features by themselves, they just expect that the enterprise PC (with built in TPM) works and all features are available as they know it from other software standard installations.

A similar situation was known about 15 years ago when PCs where very new and the little trained users also in large organisations where left alone with this new technology. The situation changed when networking and centralized ITC management came up and critical, inconvenient and demanding operations like data storage, backup procedures as well as installing new software was done using network centric management tools. Since that time the user can handle a PC as a simple tool and they are not required to learn in depth ITC technology. The typical enterprise PC user knows that the support for critical issues is just at the other end of the network.

We think that the current low use rates of trusted computing functions are based on similar experiences and expectations. Therefore the industry has now developed new TPM and TC management server capabilities, where the trusted platform functions of a PC can easily be handled by the centralized ITC department together with the already established network management functionality of the networks domain server.

1 Motivation

The Trusted Computing Groups (TCG) current TC standard was developed with the requirements of high level security and strong privacy in mind. As a consequence a large number of additional care and protection features where implemented into the standard, which need some additional user attendance. Already at the activation and installation of the TPM a lot of operations and handling has to be done by a user, which is usually not associated with a thorough understanding of security and trust. The associated amount of resources and personal costs associated by such a "barefoot management" however is currently higher than 10 or 100 times the investment costs of the TPM and associated application software itself. In large organisations however typically a centralized IT department (ITC) is ready to manage and activate all new IT equipment and infrastructure to handle such tasks efficient and free standard users

D. Gawrock, H. Reimer, A.-R. Sadeghi, C. Vishik (Editors): Future of Trust in Computing, Vieweg+Teubner (2009), 216-221

from such complex activities. It was necessary to find a method to run all these activities remotely by the ITC department.

Similar as with the PC learning experience we need also for TC the transition from users manually security management to centralized, automatic industrial and optimized processes. On the other hand such a large organisation, which plans to use TC technology, needs secure tools which manage, backup and control large TPM-PC fleets. It should be possible to run these operations from the seat of the ITC administrator automatically or at least semi automatically. Loading easily new TC software and functionality to the user machine is an absolute requirement in the same way as it is done for conventional PC software today with the help of the networks domain server.

If we look in detail into the TCG standard we find out that nearly all useful functions for secure and trusted remote management and the associated network services are already available in the standard and part of the TPMs function set. As shown in Figure 1 the trusted computing platform of the user can establish a trusted channel to a central management facility just by using the already present authentication, key management and trusted link establishment capabilities from the existing TCG standard. It's only a matter of standardisation and developing the necessary management framework by using these basic function set, and integrating them into the existing enterprise network management structures to use these functions and make them available for easy operating and handling of trusted computing platforms out in the field.

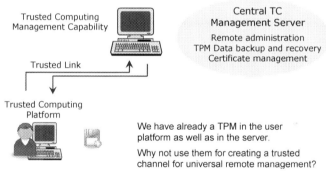

Figure 1: Using Trusted Computing secure and trusted link capabilities for establishing a trusted management channel

2 Managing and operation tasks for TC platforms

TPM activation and Take ownership:
For privacy reasons and due to some critical public statements in the beginning of trusted computing standardisation a TPM needs two separate activities for switching it on at the user site during system installation:

Activation (making it accessible to the system) of the TPM, which is usually done by a BIOS setting at first switch on (the deeper reason is that out of privacy issues no owner of a new PC should be required to have a running TPM in his machine independent of its needs)

Take ownership creates individual key and certificate material for the new owner of the computer, to earmark this TPM as its very own.

Already these both functions are too complicated for some users. Newly developed systems contain now special BIOS which sends the required commands for both functions to the TPM and make activation very easy by just entering one keystroke. However there is also the need to create some backup capability, keep passwords in mind and similar and allow an orderly system management. Traditional methods need still (costly) installation people at the PCs location and keeping the system data in normal database is also not the most advanced method. As standard PC installation is scripted with so called "silent installation", a similar procedure for TPMs would really be advantageous. It is the task of this Trusted Computing Management Server (TCMS) to run all these management functions under the control of the central administrations service through secure and trusted links, offered by TPM functions.

2.1 Key backup and recovery

Also PCs motherboard can get defective and even TPMs die from time to time. As in the rest of the ITC world, also for TC data backup and recovery is the most important activity. As in principle such procedures could also be done manually and may be planned cold blooded, the situation changes dramatically in the real situation. The blood pressure of the poor user (when he looses all the access to its data) will go high and the probability of getting the data back under stress will go down with the same speed. Also here we learn from experience that negative surprised humans may not be the optimal rescue for endangered data. What is here also needed is some automatic system, which performs data and key backup often, regularly and on system changes and supports also the recovery without showing human stress symptoms.

Data encryption and access to authentication tools
One of the most typical applications of TPMs is the management of keys and certificates for data or mail encryption. The TPM will take care about these valuable goods deep inside in his silicon organism and give it back only to its rightful owners. But watch the situation in a large organisation: Employees can get ill or much worse, change organisation or just loose their passwords. The benefit of an absolutely secure piece of silicon, like a TPM, could easily be reversed if the organisations data are not accessible any more e.g. by the companies rightful owners. The support of adequate emergency operations is really necessary. Also for these needs the possibility to control all the critical functions and data through a secure link via a central backup and management server is absolutely necessary for smooth daily operations.

2.2 Silent installation

Already today some TPM vendors have software installation packages and scripts available (free of charge) which allows an ITC department to install TPM at the user machine by the usual remote software installation procedures without manual and local interaction. Such a "silent installation" procedure is a first step, but does not yet deliver full control by the administrator. TCMS is a much more powerful extension as also most follow on functions are also supported.

3 The Solution: Centralized and integrated Trusted Computing and TPM management by a server.

The new Trusted Computing Management Server (TCMS) from Infineon solves most of these handling problems: It enables enterprise deployment of trusted computing clients by providing centralized management of client TC platforms. Using the available network connections and technology together with the secure and trust features of the TPM and the TSS stack itself it provides automated and centralized management of an infrastructure of trusted platform systems. TCMS allows an administrator located at a trusted domain to access any TPM-equipped PC in a domain and perform all required administration remotely.

The TCMS architecture is readily integrated into existing management frameworks and client solutions, providing flexibility for solution integrators and end user organizations. Utilizing Microsoft's standard domain management architecture with active directory allows an easy interface with the existing administration systems. Furthermore all user and machine policies can be enforced via Microsoft Windows Policy Management.

TCMS enables **remote administration** of TCG-compliant TPM hardware in a Trusted Domain by using the individual certificates of the TPM together with the verification features of the TPM inside the TCMS platform. Using well known cryptographic procedures, the TCMS server can identify its TPM out there in the network by using strong authentication and e.g. secure messaging protocols as we know already from smartcard installations.

The full TPM Platform initialization procedure can be controlled and initiated by the TCMS in an automatic process initiated by the administrator in a remote procedure via the network:

- Take Ownership while setting the Owner Secret
- Create and install key pair for key backup
- Save key pair for key backup to removable media
- Configure key backup archive location
- User related administration tasks
- Make sure that user credential backups are up-to-date
- Restore user credentials during platform replacement
- Support migration of user credentials to other platforms
- Provide support in case of forgotten password
- Provide support for Dictionary Attack Detection Reset

Platform and User Enrolment/Removal
Automatic enrolment for platforms and users belonging to an enrolment group (with Endorsement Key trustworthiness verification), Secure audit capability

Password Reset
Management GUI allows Trust Domain Administrator to prepare user password reset based on Trust Domain password reset key together with secure audit capability

Dictionary Attack Defence Level Reset
Entering wrong passwords is usually honoured by the TPM with blocking the user from access for an exponential growing time. Such a blocking of a system is positive in the sense of security but hinders operation in a large organisation. Resetting the defence level under control of the security administrator together with preparation and automatic reset will ease operation for real user.

Platform Restore
Backup/restore feature prevents data loss in event of failure of TPM or storage media by saving critical data of the TPM in an encrypted form on the secure backup area of the TCMS. Restores key and certificate data, platform security features such as TPM-enhanced Windows Encrypted

File System configuration, Personal Secure Drive (Encrypted Virtual Drive) configuration or for other security applications.

Strong Authentication of Platform and Users, distribution of certificates and data for networking:

- Installing WLAN or VPN with automatic and trusted key distribution via TPM and TCMS services.
- Network access protection
- Integrity measurement and policy enforcement

Full User Roaming

One of the most interesting new features which are possible with the help of the TCMS for trusted PC platforms is the full user roaming:

As every integrated TPM user of a network is well known to the TCMS management server and its keys are anyway securely stored in the server, it is possible to make all its key and critical data available to a user wherever he is currently located and on whichever trusted computer he logs in.

It is only necessary that such a user has the capability for an initial strong authentication with the help of the local TPM. The trusted client then calls its available TCMS server and loads all the key and data material securely down in its currently used TPM.

Additionally the design of the server system was planned with some well known easy to use applications support in mind:

BitLocker Key Management:

As Microsoft's Vista BitLocker application is today one of the most widely used and known standard applications, the integration of BitLocker into the TCMS functionality was a hard requirement from the market. BitLocker keys and certificate as well as the configuration can now be easily managed also from the centralized IT together with the standard parameters of a computer platform. Especially key backup and management can now be handled more easily and on a higher security level. The easy understandable need for authenticated boot mechanisms as well as volume encryption is now accepted more easily and without special training (esp. for data emergency situations) by the non security trained user.

3.1 An integrated server solution allows also easy management and effort saving by the ITC administrator

An easy to use trusted platform management solution for the system and network administrator needs not only the functionality for handling the users data via a trusted link but much more an administrator friendly and easy to handle man-machine-system interface. As it is shown in Figure 2 we will need for saving of costs and efforts:

1. Operator group management location for performing daily operational tasks for the server as well as the users trusted platforms.
2. The administration interface with the well proven separation of tasks and access rights between a trusted domain security officer and the administrator itself.
3. Integrated helpdesk working place which has access to all the related user and server data for an efficient user support
4. A direct connection to the system and networks management interface (e.g. the active directory from Windows) is essential for the necessary exchange of critical network and system data.

The controlled data exchange between the host network via the trusted computing management server to e.g. the certificate store of the users trusted platform is the backbone of all the targeted system functionality.

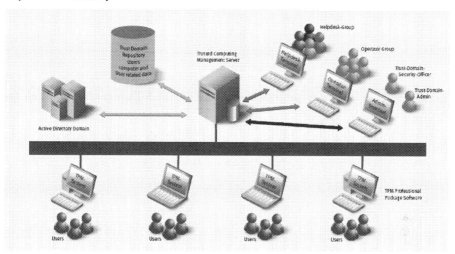

Figure 2: Full Trusted Computing enterprise system configuration

4 Conclusion

Adoption of Trusted Computing technology for using it as a security platform which supports standard security applications needs the same comfort and easy to use management interface as any other PC application scenario. Especially enterprise users are expected to use their computer for their work and not trying to management the computer by themselves. Specialized ITC departments have usually all the required tools for managing such ITC infrastructures. It is absolutely necessary for the deployment and efficient use of trusted computing applications to have similar tools and easy to handle procedures available. The concept of the TCMS together with the existent security interfaces and communication links allows an easy management from the exiting administrators working place. Flexible, comfortable and secure remote management tools will give the user a much broader adoption level of this technology and on the other hand a high level of trust for the network owner, that its system is safe and protected against any attackers.

References

[TCMS]   www.infineon.com/TPM ; Detailed information Trusted Computing Management Server

Index

A

B

C

D

E

L

Linux	23, 27, 31, 33, 59, 63, 64, 72, 127, 145, 146, 150, 166, 173–178, 181–183, 186, 187

M

malicious code	10, 53, 54, 123, 124, 197, 198
malware	3, 4, 6, 7, 9–11, 13, 14, 38, 42, 49, 50, 53, 54, 150, 151, 178, 180, 184, 186, 187
medical information	17, 18, 20, 121, 122

N

network access control	157, 158, 161, 164, 166

O

operating system	4, 8–10, 13, 17, 18, 21, 23, 27, 39, 41–43, 45, 56, 61–64, 72, 76–78, 125, 128, 146–148, 150, 165, 172, 198, 204

P

patient privacy	122, 138
pervasive healthcare	138, 141
PKI	39, 93–95
platform trust services	162, 167
privacy	4, 18, 24, 27, 29, 53, 68, 74, 79, 83–93, 96, 98–108, 111–114, 119–124, 126, 128, 137, 138, 141, 177, 180, 188, 207, 216, 217

R

remote entrusting	38–42
requirement	22, 25, 30, 31, 36, 56, 57, 77, 100, 106, 181, 195, 217, 220
risk	3, 4, 7–13, 45, 68, 96, 104–106, 114, 115, 118–120, 130, 135, 136, 139, 141, 147, 150, 172

V

W

Understanding IT

Eberhard Sturm
The New PL/I
... for PC, Workstation and Mainframe
2009. X, 304 pp. with 80 Fig. and Online Service Softc. EUR 59,90
ISBN 978-3-8348-0726-7

Klaus D. Niemann
From Enterprise Architecture to IT Governance
Elements of Effective IT Management
2006. xii, 232 pp. with 89 figs. and Online-Service. Softc. EUR 56,90
ISBN 978-3-8348-0198-2

Diffenderfer, Paul M.; El-Assal, Samir
Microsoft Dynamics NAV
Jump Start to Optimization
2., rev. Ed. 2008. XII, 304 pp. with 209 fig.
softc. EUR 49,90
ISBN 978-3-8348-0516-4

Karsten Berns | Ewald von Puttkamer
Autonomous Land Vehicles
Steps towards Service Robots
2009. approx. 250 pp. with 100 Fig. softc. approx. EUR 34,90
ISBN 978-3-8348-0421-1

VIEWEG+ TEUBNER

Abraham-Lincoln-Straße 46
65189 Wiesbaden
Fax 0611.7878-400
www.viewegteubner.de

Stand Januar 2009.
Änderungen vorbehalten.
Erhältlich im Buchhandel oder im Verlag.

IT–Sicherheit und Datenschutz

Heinrich Kersten | Gerhard Klett
Der IT Security Manager
Expertenwissen für jeden IT Security Manager - Von namhaften Autoren
praxisnah vermittelt
2., akt. und erw. Aufl. 2008. XII, 252 S. mit 21 Abb. (Edition <kes>)
Br. EUR 49,90   ISBN 978-3-8348-0429-7

Klaus-Rainer Müller
IT-Sicherheit mit System
Sicherheitspyramide - Sicherheits-, Kontinuitäts- und Risikomanagement -
Normen und Practices - SOA und Softwareentwicklung
3., erw. u. akt. Aufl. 2008. XXVI, 506 S. mit 38 Abb. mit Online-Service
Geb. EUR 74,90   ISBN 978-3-8348-00368-9

Norbert Pohlmann | Helmut Reimer (Hrsg.)
Trusted Computing
Ein Weg zu neuen IT-Sicherheitsarchitekturen
2008. VIII, 252 S. mit 49 Abb. Br. EUR 34,90   ISBN 978-3-8348-0309-2

Horst Speichert
Praxis des IT-Rechts
Praktische Rechtsfragen der IT-Sicherheit und Internetnutzung
2., akt. und erw. Aufl. 2007. XVIII, 368 S., mit 12 Abb. mit Online-Service
(Edition <kes>) Br. EUR 49,90   ISBN 978-3-8348-0112-8

VIEWEG+ TEUBNER

Abraham-Lincoln-Straße 46
65189 Wiesbaden
Fax 0611.7878-400
www.viewegteubner.de

Stand Januar 2009.
Änderungen vorbehalten.
Erhältlich im Buchhandel oder im Verlag.

IT-Management und -Anwendungen

Ralf Buchsein | Frank Victor | Holger Günther | Volker Machmeier
IT-Management mit ITIL® V3
Strategien, Kennzahlen, Umsetzung
2., akt. und erw. Aufl. 2008. XII, 371 S. mit 93 Abb. und Online-Service Br.
(Edition CIO) EUR 39,90   ISBN 978-3-8348-0526-3

Gernot Dern
Management von IT-Architekturen
Leitlinien für die Ausrichtung, Planung und Gestaltung von Informationssystemen
3., durchges. Aufl. 2009. XVI, 343 S. mit 151 Abb. Br. ca. EUR 49,90
                                                           ISBN 978-3-8348-0718-2

Knut Hildebrand | Marcus Gebauer | Holger Hinrichs | Michael Mielke (Hrsg.)
Daten- und Informationsqualität
Auf dem Weg zur Information Excellence
2008. X, 415 S. mit 108 Abb.
Br. EUR 39,90   ISBN 978-3-8348-0321-4

Helmut Schiefer | Erik Schitterer
Prozesse optimieren mit ITIL®
Abläufe mittels Prozesslandkarte gestalten - Compliance erreichen und Best
Practices nutzen mit ISO 20000, BS 15000 & ISO 9000
2., überarb. Aufl. 2008. VIII, 283 S. mit 80 Abb. und Online-Service
Br. EUR 49,90   ISBN 978-3-8348-0503-4

**VIEWEG+
TEUBNER**
Abraham-Lincoln-Straße 46
65189 Wiesbaden
Fax 0611.7878-400
www.viewegteubner.de

Stand Januar 2009.
Änderungen vorbehalten.
Erhältlich im Buchhandel oder im Verlag.